Ancient Ruins
and
Rock Art
of the
Southwest

T0308668

Ancient Ruins

and

Rock Art

of the

Southwest

An Archaeological Guide

FOURTH EDITION

David Grant Noble

TAYLOR TRADE PUBLISHING
Lanham • Boulder • New York • London

Published by Taylor Trade Publishing
An imprint of The Rowman & Littlefield Publishing Group, Inc.
4501 Forbes Boulevard, Suite 200, Lanham, Maryland 20706
www.rowman.com

Unit A, Whitacre Mews, 26-34 Stannary Street, London SE11 4AB, United Kingdom

Distributed by NATIONAL BOOK NETWORK

Copyright © 2015 by David Grant Noble

**All photographs, unless noted otherwise, are by David Grant Noble;
www.davidgrantnoble.com.**

Frontispiece: Petroglyph at the Three Rivers site.

All rights reserved. No part of this book may be reproduced in any form or by any
electronic or mechanical means, including information storage and retrieval systems,
without written permission from the publisher, except by a reviewer who may quote
passages in a review.

British Library Cataloguing in Publication Information Available

Library of Congress Cataloging-in-Publication Data
Noble, David Grant.
   [Ancient ruins of the Southwest]
   Ancient ruins and rock art of the Southwest : an archaeological guide / David Grant
Noble. — Fourth edition.
        pages cm
   Earlier editions have title: Ancient ruins of the Southwest.
   Includes bibliographical references and index.
   ISBN 978-1-58979-937-0 (pbk. : alk. paper) — ISBN 978-1-58979-938-7 (electronic)
   1. Indians of North America—Southwest, New—Antiquities—Guidebooks.   2. Southwest,
New—Antiquities—Guidebooks.   I. Title.
   E78.S7N63 2015
   979'.01—dc23   2015009155

∞™ The paper used in this publication meets the minimum requirements of American
National Standard for Information Sciences—Permanence of Paper for Printed Library
Materials, ANSI/NISO Z39.48-1992.

Printed in the United States of America

To Ruth Meria Noble, my partner and companion
as we memorably traveled throughout the Southwest
to explore, research, and photograph the
archaeological sites in this book

Contents

David Grant Noble. Courtesy of Colleen Spencer.

Preface

No part of our country has more archaeological sites open to the public than the Southwest. Its dry climate and desert environment have combined to preserve thousands of signs of the presence of past peoples and cultures on the landscape. The Southwest is a veritable outdoor museum. Over time, more and more sites are being found, studied, interpreted, written about, and opened to the public. This new edition of *Ancient Ruins of the Southwest* has some thirty sites not included in the 2000 edition.

Archaeology is an evolving and dynamic field. That is to say, new fieldwork and analytical methods constantly lead to new findings, interpretations, and theories and our knowledge of the region's deep history increases. This fourth edition incorporates as much of this new research and thinking as I've been able to find. In so doing, I'm indebted to the many working archaeologists who have guided me to sites, pointed me to informational sources, and taken the time to review book chapters and offer corrections and suggestions.

My criteria in preparing this book, in all its editions, have been to highlight only sites that are open to the public, reasonably accessible, monitored and cared for, and (in most cases) interpreted. Not included are sites that require long driving on rutted/dusty/muddy roads (where we all pray never to be stranded) and places that require serious hiking and backpacking to reach. Also left out are sites that only those deeply initiated in archaeology would find meaningful. I remember once going to a large village site that a federal agency wanted me to include in the book. It was a mound along a ridge with no interpretive trail or signage and I was duly impressed. However, while I was there, two tourists from out of state arrived, had a look around, and declared this wasn't "the place"—the ruins they'd been told about must be farther up the road. I assured them that this was, indeed, the place. "Hey, I know a ruins when I see one," one of them said, "and this isn't one." Off they went. I omitted it from the book. Some sites are best left to enjoy their privacy.

This leads to the matter of conservation and protection, which is considered in more detail in the following chapter. We all know how vulnerable many archaeological sites are to vandalism and looting. How does that problem vie with producing a guidebook? The fact is, when responsible people go to many of these sites, their very presence provides a measure of protection, especially in this time of cell phones and digital cameras. Yes, public presence can help protect sites. Several sites in this book, in fact, were recently opened to the public by federal agencies expressly in order to discourage vandalism. And it has worked. On the other hand, there certainly exist remote and little-visited sites that, even though legally open, should not be publicized—the fewer people who know about them, the better off they are. You won't find them here. As you might suspect, I'm not a fan of Internet backpacker guides that provide GPS locations to such remote unprotected archaeological sites.

There is also the matter of public education and appreciation of our cultural heritage. Archaeology needs advocates, especially in these times when federal and state agencies are coming under increased pressure to grant leases for oil, gas, and mineral exploration and drilling. This book and many other informative books on the market help to spread the word that archaeological sites have intrinsic value as part of our national patrimony.

Let me say a few words about my own experience in archaeology. I came to it from an entirely different background—a French literature major and then a French teacher in the East. In 1971, my wife and I made the move to New Mexico, and the following spring I was hired by the School of American Research as the record photographer at the Arroyo Hondo Pueblo excavations near Santa Fe. This was a major archaeological project funded by the National Science Foundation and National Geographic Society. At the time, I had no background in archaeology and only minimal experience doing photography. So I had a steep learning curve and in the process learned something about Southwestern history and culture. This led to my visiting many archaeological places, reading books, talking to archaeologists and Native people, and generally educating myself about the region where I lived.

It was that experience, which continues, that inspired me to write this book's first edition. I like history and detective stories and find the field of archaeology combines them. Many people learn about archaeology through books and libraries and academic courses, but an educational process can also happen on the landscape, by going to the places where people once lived and seeing where events happened and where culture evolved. This can be quite an emotional experience. There are elements of romance, too, and sometimes sadness. Then, too, whatever the history, the places themselves are infused with beauty. All of these things contributed to my photography and writing.

As you visit sites and learn about the past, you may find your interests evolving. The first sites I went to, in 1958, were the stunningly beautiful cliff dwellings of Mesa Verde and the monumental great houses of Chaco Canyon. Wonderful as they are, I now find myself more drawn to unexcavated sites that have not been restored, swept clean, and enhanced for tourists—like that mound I mentioned before. I remember once walking around in a remote area with an archaeologist friend when he suddenly stopped and pointed at the ground, and his eyes lit up. I peered down and spotted a few chips of flint. "Now, that's my kind of archaeology!" he said. Well, I'm not quite there yet.

Whatever your kind of archaeology is, I wish you memorable experiences as you explore the deserts, mesas, valleys, and mountains of the American Southwest and learn about its rich heritage.

Vandalized Fremont petroglyph in Dinosaur National Monument.

Preserving Our Archaeological Heritage

The ancient sites described in these pages represent but a fraction of the archaeological resources that exist throughout the Southwest. Nonarchitectural remains scattered about the landscape, indeed, often are passed by unnoticed by nonexperts. But to archaeologists, every potsherd, projectile point, and manmade alteration of the landscape, however subtle, contributes to the story of our collective past.

How long our archaeological heritage will last is uncertain. To be sure, the ruins we are most familiar with, especially those managed by national and state park systems, are safe. But on both public and private lands, sites of all kinds have been damaged or are threatened by mining, logging, road building, housing developments, off-road vehicular driving, and other consequences of urban and suburban growth. Another problem, of course, is vandalism and looting. Lucrative national and international black markets in antiquities encourage the latter. Happily, in recent years, government agencies have taken proactive measures to stop those who illegally take away our country's patrimony.

So what can *we* do? In the long run, education is probably the most effective approach. The more people who understand, respect, and value our shared history, the safer archaeological sites are. The greatest help in preserving archaeological resources comes from the vast pool of people who love and value our cultural and natural environment. They include hunters, fishermen, ranchers, backcountry hikers, bird watchers, horseback riders, photographers, naturalists, ruins buffs, and many others. Here are some practical measures and precautions we can take as individuals.

1. Be sure when visiting archaeological sites that you and your family and companions do not climb on walls, disturb ruins, touch rock art, or collect artifacts.
2. If you notice signs of recent or current pothunting, vandalism, natural erosion, or any activities proscribed in the Archaeological Resources Protection Act of 1979, make a report immediately to the owner or manager of the property or local law enforcement authorities. Photographs, license numbers, and descriptive information all are useful in apprehending offenders; however, don't place yourself at personal risk in collecting information.
3. Should you become aware of a proposed development or land-disturbing activity that might damage an archaeological site, become an advocate and work with local political bodies and media to find an acceptable way to resolve the problem.
4. When hiking in backcountry, don't upload photographs and locations of unprotected and vulnerable sites to the Internet; the less some sites are visited, the better.
5. Support and/or participate in educational programs that communicate the value of our cultural heritage. This can be done through museums, cultural and civic organizations, or school systems, and can be as simple as telling a scout troop about your visit to Mesa Verde.
6. Become a site steward through one of the federal or state agencies that monitor and manage archaeological sites. Support organizations such as the Archaeological Conservancy (www.archaeologicalconservancy.org), Crow Canyon Archaeological Center (www.crowcanyon.org), American Rock Art Research Association (www.arara.org), and Archaeology Southwest (www .archaeologysouthwest.org).

America's archaeological treasures are sacred to Native Americans, an inspiration to writers and artists, and an irreplaceable source of information for historians, social scientists, students, and tourists. Let's do all we can to help keep them safe and intact. It is my hope that this book will make a small contribution to better understanding and valuing archaeological sites, thereby helping promote the cause of preservation.

ARCHAEOLOGICAL RESOURCES PROTECTION ACT OF 1979

The Archaeological Resources Protection Act (1979), parts of which are listed below, is the most comprehensive and robust federal law protecting archaeological sites. Its provisions contain both criminal and civil penalties for violations, address the problem of buying and selling artifacts illegally taken from public and tribal lands, and reward citizens who provide information leading to prosecutions or convictions.

PUBLIC LAW 96-95, 31 OCTOBER, 1979

To protect archaeological resources on public lands and Indian lands, and for other purposes.

FINDINGS AND PURPOSE

Sec. 2(a) The Congress finds that—

(1) archaeological resources on public lands and Indian lands are an accessible and irreplaceable part of the Nation's heritage;

(2) these resources are increasingly endangered because of their commercial attractiveness;

(3) existing Federal laws do not provide adequate protection to prevent the loss and destruction of these archaeological resources and sites resulting from uncontrolled excavations and pillage; and

(4) there is a wealth of archaeological information which has been legally obtained by private individuals and noncommercial purposes and which could voluntary be made available to professional archaeologists and institutions.

(b) The purpose of this Act is to secure, for the present and future benefit of the American people, the protection of archaeological resources and sites which are on public lands and Indian lands, and to foster increased cooperation and exchange of information between governmental authorities, the professional archaeological community, and private individuals having collections of archaeological resources and data which were obtained before the date of the enactment of this Act.

CRIMINAL ACTS AND PENALTIES

(a) No person may excavate, remove, damage, or otherwise alter or deface or attempt to excavate, remove, damage, or otherwise alter or deface any archaeological resourcc located on public lands or Indian lands unless such activity is pursuant to a permit issued under section 4 of this Act, a permit referred to in section 4(h)(2) of this Act, or the exemption contained in section 4(g)(1) of this Act.

(b) No person may sell, purchase, exchange, transport, receive, or offer to sell, purchase, or exchange any archaeological resource if such resource was excavated or removed from public lands or Indian lands in violation of—

(1) the prohibition contained in subsection (a), or

(2) any provision, rule, regulation, ordinance, or permit in effect under any other provision of Federal law.

(c) No person may sell, purchase, exchange, transport, receive, or offer to sell, purchase, or exchange, in interstate of foreign commerce, any archaeological resource excavated, removed, sold, purchased, exchanged, transported, or received in violation of any provision, rule, regulation, ordinance, or permit in effect under State or local law.

(d) Any person who knowingly violates, or counsels, procures, solicits, or employs any other person to violate any prohibition contained in subsection (a), (b), or (c) of this section shall, upon conviction, be fined not more than $10,000 or imprisoned not more than one year, or both: *Provided, however*, That if the commercial or archaeological value of the archaeological resources involved and the cost of restoration and repair of such resources exceeds the sum of $500, such person shall be fined not more than $20,000 or imprisoned not more than two years, or both. In the case of a second or subsequent such violation upon conviction such person shall be fined not more than $100,000, or imprisoned not more than five years, or both.

REWARDS

(a) Upon the certification of the Federal land manager concerned, the Secretary of the Treasury is directed to pay from penalties and fines collected under sections 6 and 7 an amount equal to one-half of such penalty or fine, but not to exceed $500, to any person who furnishes information which leads to the finding of a civil violation, or the conviction of criminal violation, with respect to which such penalty or fine was paid. If several persons provided such information, such amount shall be divided among such persons. No officer or employee of the United States or of any State or local government who furnishes information or renders service in the performance of his official duties shall be eligible for payment under this subsection.

Acknowledgments

In preparing this guidebook, I have drawn upon the research—field, laboratory, and library—of scores, if not hundreds, of Southwestern archaeologists, historians, and other scholars and specialists. The "suggested reading" sections at the end of chapters reflect some of their published works.

I am especially indebted to those, acknowledged here by name, who have communicated with me personally about what they know, provided obscure informational material, pointed me toward relevant publications and reports, suggested "new" public sites to include, been my guide, reviewed drafts of chapters, and helped me with digital photography challenges. I am deeply gratified by their generously provided assistance, which has helped make the information in this book as accurate and up-to-date as possible.

Thanks to Christopher D. Adams, Charles E. Adams, Larry Baker, Anne Baldwin, Mathew Barbour, Cynthia A. Bettison, Deborah Bigness, Evelyn Billo, Lauren Blacik, Tracy Bodnar, Todd W. Bostwick, Mike Bremer, Ellen Brennan, Catherine M. Cameron, Jane P. Childress, Jeffery J. Clark, Karl P. Cordova, Greg Cross, Merrill Dicks, William H. Doelle, David E. Doyel, Cynthia Dyer, David Eck, Donna Glowacki, Charles Haecker, Cynthia Herhahn, Michael J. Hoogendyk, Jerry Howard, Stance Hurst, Amber Koski, Kristin A. Kuckelman, Donald Lamm, Richard C. Lange, Andrew Laurenzi, Robert Mark, Timothy Maxwell, Roy McKeag, Don Merritt, Paul E. Minnis, Colleen Nicholas, Jason Ordaz, Linda J. Pierce, Peter J. Pilles Jr., Robert P. Powers, Paul F. Reed, Elizabeth Reid, William Reitze, Tim Riley, Deni Seymour, Colleen Spencer, Connie Stone, Ronald H. Towner, Ruth Van Dyke, Mark D. Varien, Judy Vredenburg, James Walker, Barbara Webb, Neil Weintraub, Scott Wood, and Holly Young.

In addition, I thank the following people and institutions for granting me permission to publish their artwork and photographs: Archaeology Southwest, Arizona State Museum, Arizona State University, Mary Beath, Crow Canyon Archaeology Center, Robert A. Ellison Jr., Doug Gann, Vance Haynes, Adriel Heisey, Dennis Holloway, Richard W. Lang, Maxwell Museum of Anthropology, School for Advanced Research, Karen and Robert Turner, University of Utah Press, and Henry Wallace.

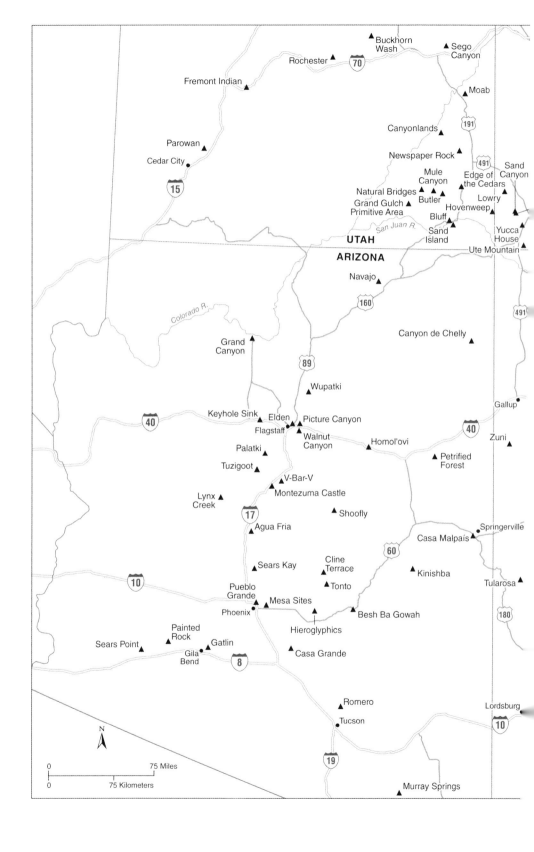

Ancient Ruins and Rock Art of the Southwest

▲ Canyon of the Ancients

Goodman Point

▲ Mesa Verde

Farmington
▲ Aztec
Salmon ▲ ▲ Dinetah

● Alamosa

COLORADO
NEW MEXICO

▲ Rattlesnake

Chimney Rock ▲

Chama Valley ▲

Chaco
Canyon ▲

Pueblo Pintado ▲

▲ Kin Ya'a

▲ Casamero

Jemez ▲
La Cieneguilla ▲

Santa Fe
▲ Pecos

Coronado ▲

Alibates →

Petroglyph ▲

▲ El Morro

Albuquerque ●
▲ Tijeras

Santa Rosa ●

▲ Dittert

Fort Sumner ●

Blackwater
Draw ▲

▲ Salinas

Socorro ●

Lubbock ▲
Lake

▲ Gila Cliffs

Mimbres Valley
▲ Sites

Three Rivers ▲
Petroglyphs

Silver City ●

● Alamogordo

● Las Cruces

● El Paso ▲ Hueco Tanks

Artist's reconstruction of a Paleoindian hunt scene. Drawing by Richard W. Lang.

The First Americans

For generations, researchers have debated when human beings first came to the Americas. Some estimates go back more than twenty thousand years while more scientifically documented ones put the arrival time at twelve thousand or so years ago. Native Americans often say they have been here since "time immemorial" and relate narratives of an emergence into this world from worlds beneath.

On the archaeological side, theories hinge on the validity and interpretation of evidence excavated from sites scattered across North, Central, and South America. The traditional "Clovis first" view holds that immigrants from Asia journeyed in several waves across the Bering land bridge between Siberia and North America. This happened near the end of the last Ice Age when sea levels were lower and shorelines extended farther out from where they are today. Some of the migrants, it is theorized, walked along a narrow ice-free corridor between the Laurentian and Cordillera ice sheets. Scholars increasingly recognize, however, that America's earliest arrivals may have used boats, traveling from Asia (or even possibly Europe) along the edges of ice fields and coastlines where abundant seafood was available.

Known Paleoindian sites are scarce for most are either deeply buried or already have been lost to natural erosion. The site that first demonstrated the antiquity of human presence in North America was found near the town of Folsom, New Mexico. There, in 1906, George W. McJunken, an African American cowboy born in slavery in Texas, noticed the bones of a long-extinct species of bison (*Bison antiquus*) eroding from an arroyo bank. Later, the archaeological community became excited when investigators found a fluted spear point embedded in one of the animal's bones and dated it to between 10,900 and 10,200 years ago. The Folsom site, by establishing a widely accepted chronology of human presence in North America, became famous.

Paleoindian spear points. Left to right: Clovis, Folsom, and Plainview points.

Soon a similar discovery at Blackwater Draw (p. 3) near Clovis, New Mexico, pushed the date back to more than 12,000 years ago. Folsom, Clovis, and other Paleoindian peoples were nomadic, depended heavily (though not exclusively) on big-game hunting, and excelled at blade technology. Their sites span the continent. In recent decades, some discoveries indicate the existence of pre-Clovis people in the Americas. This is an exciting, controversial, and fast-evolving field of research: stay tuned.

At the end of the Pleistocene epoch, the Southwest's climate grew warmer and drier and many New World megafauna—mammoths, prehistoric bison, and giant sloths, for example—vanished. After 5500 BCE, small bands of Archaic-period foragers moved from camp to camp across the Southwestern landscape as they pursued a seasonal round of hunting game and collected wild edible plant foods.

Eventually, knowledge of growing corn and other plants spread north from Mexico and a more settled way of life in the Southwest replaced that of mobile hunter-gatherers. The timing of this agricultural transition varied regionally. Around the Four Corners, it happened between around 1000 BCE and 500 CE; that is, from late Archaic to early Basketmaker times. In southern Arizona, it occurred more than a millennium earlier, but in the Rio Grande Valley it came later.

It is important to remember that it is the Euro-American scientific tradition that constructs a chronological sequence of cultural periods. How Native Americans once identified and differentiated themselves, community to community and region to region, we will never know. Today, the Hopi tell of only two groups, the Motisinom (pre-agricultural hunter-gatherers) and the Hisat'sinom (ancestral farmers). Their traditional knowledge, like that of other tribes, comes from narratives passed down orally from generation to generation. Archaeologists, in contrast, study physical objects—from stone tools to potsherds to plant remains—that they excavate or collect at sites. If and when these different knowledge traditions can be combined, a fuller, multidimensional picture of the past will emerge.

BLACKWATER DRAW ARCHAEOLOGICAL SITE AND MUSEUM

The Blackwater Draw National Historical Landmark is located near Portales, New Mexico, 5 miles north of the intersection of NM 467 and US 70 (Address: 508 Route 467). The museum is on the campus of Eastern New Mexico University at 1500 South Avenue K, Lea Hall, room 163, in Portales. The site and museum are open from Memorial Day through Labor Day and on weekends in April, May, September, and October. They are closed on Mondays. Information: (575) 35t6-5235 (site); (575) 562-2202 (museum); www.enmu.edu/blackwaterdraw. Entrance fee.

Far out on the arid plains of eastern New Mexico, in a region known as the Llano Estacado, is the famous site of Blackwater Draw, or more technically, Blackwater Locality No. 1. This is where archaeologists first discovered evidence of the existence of the Clovis culture, long thought to be the oldest in the Americas.

In situ bone bed at Blackwater Draw.

A mile-long path leads through the site and around the gravel quarry in which the ancient remains were found. You can view a Clovis-era well and enter a building in which archaeological excavations at different levels were left intact. Interpretive signs are situated along the trail.

When Clovis people hunted here twelve thousand years ago, the place was a shallow, marshy, spring-fed pond surrounded by expanses of grasslands and limber pine forests. This habitat supported large grazing animals, or *megafauna*, such as Columbian mammoths, camelids, and horses, as well as their predators, including saber-toothed cats, dire wolves, and people. As archaeologists reconstruct the scene, hunters hid around the waterhole in wait for animals and ambushed them using spears when they came to drink. Flight was hindered by the water, mud, and underbrush.

After killing and butchering a beast, the hunters carried the edible and accessible parts to their camp. Some parts remained submerged, often including spear points (usually snapped off by striking bone) and stone knives. Later, Folsom and Archaic hunters enacted similar hunts with bison. Over the subsequent centuries, 15 feet of sediment accumulated, sealing in the detritus to form a stratified archaeological record. When the climate warmed and dried, the former pond became a grassy depression in the wide reaches of New Mexico's buffalo plains.

The full realization of Blackwater Draw's archaeological potential began in 1932 under the direction of Edgar B. Howard of the University of Pennsylvania Museum of Archaeology and Anthropology. Although the site contains four Paleoindian components, what gained it fame was the discovery, beneath the Folsom layer, of distinctively styled fluted spear points among mammoth bones. They were radiocarbon dated to between 11,040 and 11,630 before the present. Most common were bison kill sites of the Folsom period. Investigators also found campsites with other types of tools and a dozen hand-dug wells from various periods. The one still visible along the trail is thought to be the earliest evidence of a water-control mechanism in North America.

Archaeological research continued at the site, except for a hiatus during World War II. After the war, scientific and business interests clashed when the quarrying of gravel, which lay beneath the cultural layers, began destroying parts of the site. By the late 1950s, heavy earth-moving equipment, combined with hydraulic suction pumps and blasting, were removing two hundred to four hundred cubic yards of sand, gravel, and overburden daily. The sight of dirt piles covered with crushed bone attracted local collectors.

In 1962, archaeologists uncovered five mammoths and a bison along with stone weapons and tools, motivating the New Mexico legislature to appropriate $100,000 to acquire and preserve five acres of the site. Preservation efforts collapsed, however, when the mining company raised the selling price to $300,000. Archaeologists then salvaged what they had already found. In addition to archaeological research, paleo-ecological studies have been conducted to better understand the ancient environment.

The Blackwater Draw site was declared a National Historic Landmark in 1961, and in 1978 Eastern New Mexico University purchased 157 acres. Thankfully, a portion of it near the original pond's outlet was still undisturbed and research continues there.

The Blackwater Draw Museum has information about the site, displays of projectile points and other artifacts, and reconstructions of archaeological and geological deposits and dioramas. Some publications relating to the site are for sale. A highlight for kids is a full-scale model of a mammoth's head complete with long curving tusks.

There are abundant travel services in the towns of Clovis and Portales.

Suggested Reading: *The History of Blackwater Draw*, Eastern New Mexico University, Portales, New Mexico, undated.

LUBBOCK LAKE NATIONAL HISTORIC LANDMARK

Lubbock Lake Landmark is at 2401 Landmark Drive in Lubbock, Texas. This is just north of the 289 Loop and the Clovis Highway (US 84). There is an exit from 289. Information: (806) 742-1116; www.lubbocklake.musm.ttu.edu. Entrance fee.

Like those of Blackwater Draw, the Paleoindian remains in Yellowhouse Draw, on the northwest edge of Lubbock, are of great importance to archaeologists. When you come here, be sure to leave enough time to walk the half-mile loop trail around the archaeological area and see the excellent museum, which features dioramas, visual aids, explanatory texts, and artifacts recovered from the site. The museum's staff also is present to answer questions. Besides the site and museum, there are a short, handicapped-accessible nature trail and a longer hiking trail. In summer, archaeologists and volunteers are actively excavating the site and tours of the work in progress can be arranged.

The Lubbock Lake site, on the Southern High Plains, is remarkable in that it consists of a series of separate geologic levels through time, each containing distinct artifacts and animal species. The Paleoindian strata (10000–6600 BCE) begin with the Clovis culture and continue through the Folsom, Plainview, and Firstview periods. Later come the Archaic (6500 BCE–1 CE), Ceramic (1–1500 CE), Protohistoric (1500–1700), and Historic (1700–present) levels. Researchers have recorded twelve thousand years of human occupation at this site. When I visited in 2014, the broken bones of an extinct Pleistocene-era species of bison were visible in the cut bank of the draw.

How did this site come about? Briefly, a meandering tributary of the Brazos River, known as Yellowhouse Draw, traversed this landscape. It no longer flows through the Lubbock Lake landmark due to drought and a lower water table, but it did so for many millennia. At the site, it made a bend where a natural spring also occurred, forming a small lake. Its level fluctuated depending on rainfall and

Diorama of a Paleoindian bison kill, Lubbock Lake Museum. Courtesy of Lubbock Lake National Historic Landmark, Museum of Texas Tech University.

sometimes even sank below ground. The water attracted animals—Columbian mammoths, bison, camels, short-faced bears, horses, and other game—and their presence drew human hunters.

There is another critical dimension to this story, however. The stream bed gradually filled with sediments, sometimes carried by the flowing water, sometimes blown in by wind or eroding from the banks. As noted on the landmark's official website, "Each layer represents a different time period, water regime, suite of plants and animals, group of peoples, and climate and environment covering the past 12,000 years of history and prehistory." Over time, members of the succeeding cultures killed bison and other animals, butchered them on the spot, broke up and piled the bones, and retouched their tools. In the process, they created a superb archaeological record.

In the 1930s, before archaeologists knew about the significance of this site, the city of Lubbock conducted dredging here in an attempt to revive the old springs. During this process, two young boys found a Folsom spear point and brought it to the attention of a Texas Tech archaeologist. That was the beginning, and archaeological research has been ongoing since. Today, the Lubbock Lake Landmark Regional Research Program carries out research not only here but at other sites across the Llano Estacado, the 3,000- to 5,000-foot escarpment extending from northwestern Texas into eastern New Mexico.

While in Lubbock, a visit to the Museum of Texas Tech University will be of interest. Also, Blackwater Draw (p. 3), where the first Clovis site was discovered, is a two-hour drive to the east near Clovis, New Mexico.

Suggested Reading: *Lubbock Lake Landmark*, compiled and edited by Mindy Myers, Eileen Johnson, Susan Shore, Vance T. Holliday, and Susan Rowe, Museum of Texas Tech University, Lubbock, Texas, 2012. *Archaeology on the Great Plains*, edited by W. Raymond Wood, University Press of Kansas, Lawrence, 1998.

ALIBATES FLINT QUARRIES NATIONAL MONUMENT

Alibates Flint Quarries is near Fritch, Texas, about 35 miles northeast of Amarillo. From Fritch, drive 7 miles south on Texas 136 and turn west on Cas Johnson Road. Five miles on, you will come to the monument's contact station. Guided walking tours leave here at 10 a.m. and 2 p.m. from Memorial Day to Labor Day and off-season by appointment. Information: (806) 857-3151; www.nps.gov/alfl/index.htm.

––––––––––––––––

The making of tools from stone was the first technology developed by humans, who discovered that certain stones, when fractured in the right way, acquired a sharp edge that could be used to chop, scrape, or cut. Later flint knappers learned to chip flakes off both sides of the stone to produce "bifaces" such as knives, spear points, and arrowheads.

Alibates Flint Quarries is one of the few places in the Southwest where you can see where ancient Indians quarried stone to make weapons and tools. Twelve thousand years ago, some of America's earliest pioneers discovered rock outcrops along the bluffs on the north side of the Canadian River containing nodules of chert (popularly called flint) of the highest quality for tool making. They occurred in a thick layer of silicified dolomite, a Permian-age sedimentary rock resembling limestone. Long ago in geologic time, mineral-bearing water had seeped into the dolomite, replacing it with very hard, fine-grained quartz. Petrified wood is formed by a similar process. Chert's molecular structure causes it to make conchoidal, or shell-like, flakes when fractured. This characteristic allows knappers to fashion sharp-edged tools and weapons.

Alibates flint had another quality—its rainbow colors, which range from creamy whites to deep reds and browns to translucent hues of gray, blue, and purple. A single flake can be banded in all colors; little wonder its appeal was widespread. Archaeologists have turned up lance points made of Alibates flint at mammoth and bison kill sites dating from the Clovis and Folsom periods (see p. 1). Archaic hunters also prized this stone, as did later Pueblo farmers and the nomadic Great Plains tribes even into the nineteenth century. Not surprisingly, Alibates flint was traded widely through the Southwest and beyond.

Between around 1200 and 1450 CE, several Puebloan-style villages thrived near the quarries. (Archaeologists refer to these sites as the "Panhandle Aspect of the Antelope Creek Focus of the Plains Village Culture.") The Alibates Ruin, located

less than a mile from the quarries, contained a substantial block of contiguous, square, rectangular, and circular rooms of stone masonry construction. Its occupants farmed along the Canadian River and its tributary creeks, quarried flint, and participated in a far-reaching trade network.

When Coronado searched the plains for the legendary Cities of Gold in 1541, he encountered bands of nomadic Apache in the Texas Panhandle. In the eighteenth and nineteenth centuries, Comanche Indians trailed buffalo herds in this region. These tribes, too, quarried Alibates flint to fashion their weapons; that is, until metal became readily available.

Do not expect to see large-scale excavations at the Alibates site: its miners used only hand tools to dig the precious stone. They discovered, however, that the buried chert was of higher quality than the weathered nodules on the surface of the ground. Hundreds of pits covering approximately three hundred acres along a ridge top have been recorded. They range from 5 to 20 feet in diameter and are rimmed by mounds of lithic rubble, or tailings. Over the ages, they were filled with windblown topsoil such that they appear today as shallow depressions.

Quarry tours last approximately two hours. Your guide will lead you up a trail to the ridge and provide information on the geologic aspects of the site, flint-knapping methods, and the prehistoric cultures of the Texas Panhandle region. Along the way, you'll see chert nodules of various sizes and colors, many partially worked cores, and an abundance of colorful chips and flakes. All this debitage represents rejected material that ancient knappers left on the ground. This is one type of litter to be grateful for!

Most people assume that the word Alibates is a Spanish term, but, in fact, an American cowboy settled here in pioneering days and his name was Allen "Allie" Bates.

Suggested Reading: *Alibates Flint Quarries National Monument*, by Conger Beasley Jr., Western National Parks Association, Tucson, Arizona, 2001.

MURRAY SPRINGS CLOVIS SITE

Murray Springs Clovis Site National Historic Landmark is near Sierra Vista, Arizona. From the intersection of Arizona 90 (Fry Blvd.) and Arizona 92 in Sierra Vista, drive 4 miles east on 90, then turn north on Moson Road. Go 1.1 miles, then turn east (right) on the entrance road to the site. Information: (520) 439-6400; www.blm .gov/az/st/en/prog/cultural/murray.html.

———————

Most evidence of the Clovis culture found in North America consists of isolated (usually broken) spear points, stone artifact scatters on the ground, or flint quarries. Buried stratified sites are rare, and Murray Springs is an important one. What is more, it is open to the public and has an easy loop trail along which the Bureau of Land Management (BLM) has installed informative signs. The ⅓-mile

Chert nodules at Alibates Flint Quarry.

trail passes areas along Bison Kill Creek where, from 1966 to 1971, investigators unearthed a wealth of Clovis-period artifacts. Bruce B. Huckell, who co-edited the report on Murray Springs, stated that the site's assemblage "constitutes the largest single sample of Clovis flint knapping activity yet known from the western United States."

Murray Springs was discovered in 1966 by C. Vance Haynes Jr. and Peter Mehringer Jr. of the University of Arizona. The following year, with support from the National Geographic Society and the National Science Foundation, Dr. Haynes directed scientific excavations, which continued for five field seasons. Murray Springs is one of a dozen Paleoindian sites found in the San Pedro River Valley, which has a greater concentration of Clovis sites than any other part of the country. Another well-known one, also managed by the BLM, is the Lehner Mammoth Kill National Historic Site.

In the late Pleistocene, when the climate was cooler and wetter, this landscape was lush and saw an abundance of grazing animals, including mammoths. Haynes wrote that this area was "a spring field where water oozed from grass- and sedge-covered slopes to feed the shallow brook of Bison Kill Creek." Even today, in a different climate, the desert here can become a jungle with many varieties of perennial plants in bloom and producing flowers and fruit.

During the excavations, archaeologists found the bones of eleven prehistoric bison, three Columbian mammoths, early types of horse and camel, and the jaw

Peggy E. Davis excavating in Area 2 of the Murray Springs Clovis site. Courtesy of Vance Haynes.

bone of a dire wolf. Associated with these remains was a Clovis hunting camp with fireplaces, where researchers unearthed a trove of stone tools and weapons: scrapers, knives, projectile points, and waste flakes. Many of the objects lay on the surface of the hunters' campsite, undisturbed for about 13,000 years. Among the buried artifacts found adjacent to an adult female mammoth was a unique tool fashioned from mammoth bone, which some archaeologists think Clovis people used to straighten spear shafts.

According to the researchers' reconstruction, a group of Clovis people, perhaps a single social unit, came here to hunt, killing one mammoth along the stream and scavenging another that apparently had died of natural causes. They then carried the animal parts to a flat area nearby, where they made camp and set about the task of butchering. As their knives grew dull, they resharpened them or made new ones, in the process creating thousands of waste flakes, or "debitage." Haynes thinks the Murray Springs site probably was occupied for only a few years.

As you go along the trail, you will come to a place where you can clearly see in the arroyo cut what scientists call the "black mat." This is a distinct thick algal layer visible in the arroyo bank beneath which, here and elsewhere, Clovis sites have been found. It was formed soon after the Clovis period by algae growing along streams and in wetlands. Interpretive signs along the path point out the places where mammoth bones were found and where the hunters made their campsite. Don't expect to see actual fossil bones or spear points here: they were collected and archived years ago. In 2012, this site was designated a National Historic Landmark.

Suggested Reading: *Murray Springs: A Clovis Site with Multiple Activity Areas in the San Pedro Valley, Arizona*, C. Vance Haynes Jr. and Bruce B. Huckell, editors, University of Arizona Press, Tucson, 2007.

SAN RAFAEL SWELL SITES

Travelers have long extolled the scenic beauty of the San Rafael Swell in eastern Utah. This region extends from Dale in the west to Green River in the east and from Price in the north to Hanksville in the south and is divided by Interstate 70. Some sixty million years ago, pressures deep within the earth pushed up overlying layers of sandstone to form a dome. This vast anticline of colorful sandstones, cut by rivers and canyons, is of compelling interest to geologists as well as to archaeologists.

Travel services are available in Green River, Price, and Castle Dale. The Prehistoric Museum in Price has fine anthropological and cultural exhibits, including an outstanding collection of Fremont clay figurines. The Museum of the San Rafael in Castle Dale has archaeological exhibits donated by local citizens. Here you also can obtain directions to the Rochester Creek Rock Art Panel and other nearby sites. The Cleveland Lloyd Dinosaur Quarry, located between this site and Price, makes another interesting side trip.

Information: (435) 781-4400 (BLM in Green River); (435) 636-3600 (BLM in Price); www.blm.gov/ut/st/en/fo/price/recreation/SanRafaelDesert.html.

The San Rafael Swell contains evidence of several cultural traditions, including Barrier Canyon Archaic, Fremont, and Ute, with possible Basketmaker II influences, as well. Compared to the Mesa Verde and Chaco regions, relatively little archaeological research has been done. In recent years, however, the College of Eastern Utah has made the San Rafael Swell a focus of investigations. This is important and timely considering the current interest of energy companies to exploit the area's potential oil and gas reserves. The Bureau of Land Management manages the area.

Travel around parts of the swell is on secondary dirt roads for which a high-clearance, four-wheel-drive vehicle is advisable. Particular caution must be taken during stormy weather when flooding can render roads impassable. This section will highlight two outstanding and easily accessible sites along well-maintained gravel roads. To find other sites, such as Black Dragon and Head of Sinbad, obtain a detailed large-scale map. Several are available, one of which is indicated below.

Native American sites in the swell include hunting camps, farming villages, stone quarries, and rock art galleries. It is the Archaic and Fremont petroglyph and pictograph panels, however, that are most visible to visitors. Some date to before 1,500 years ago, when mobile bands of Desert Archaic people roamed the land on their seasonal rounds of hunting and foraging. Scholars have noticed similarities in the styles and themes of the rock art of these ancient groups, pointing out a possible ideographic system extending through time and space. The people of this region may represent a transitional stage between the Barrier Canyon Archaic and Fremont cultures. Both styles can be seen in some panels, but much of the imagery has its own distinct San Rafael character. From archaeological evidence and ethnographic analogy, researchers think the San Rafael people gathered periodically in specified locations to trade, conduct religious ceremonies, and enjoy social interaction. Such gatherings may have provided the context for producing the rock paintings that we find so impressive.

Suggested Reading: *San Rafael Swell: Trails Illustrated Topographic Map, 712,* published by National Geographic Maps, Washington, D.C., 2005. www.natgeomaps .com/ti_712.

Buckhorn Wash Pictographs

The Buckhorn Wash Pictograph Panel is located between Price and Green River, Utah, 22.5 miles east of Castle Dale. From Castle Dale, go 1 mile north on Highway 10 and turn east on a major unpaved road designated "San Rafael Recreational Access." Continue for 22 miles to the pictograph panels, which are along the road. A couple of miles before you reach the site, you will see a pull-off on the left and a trail leading to a cliff along which there are several petroglyph panels.

From the town of Green River, drive 30 miles west on Interstate 70 and take exit 129, then continue 27 miles north on a well-maintained gravel road to the panel. Information: (435) 636-3600.

———————————

Archaic pictographs at Buckhorn Wash.

Some years ago, the Buckhorn Wash Pictograph Panel was a notorious example of archaeological vandalism. For generations, passersby had defaced the site with bullet holes, spray paint, chalk, and even axle grease from wagons. Happily, as part of the 1996 Utah Centennial Celebration, local preservationists arranged to have the panel restored. As a result, we are now able to appreciate the stunning beauty of these extraordinary ancient paintings.

While rock art is inherently hard to date, researchers estimate the Buckhorn Wash paintings to be 1,500 to 3,000 years old and to exemplify a version of the Barrier Canyon rock-art style found in eastern Utah and in Canyonlands National Park (p. 17).

The creators of this artwork were Archaic folk who roamed over a wide territory and lived by foraging, hunting, and fishing. The panel is more than a hundred feet long and includes groups of life-size anthropomorphic figures that have a supernatural or ceremonial appearance. Their strangely elongated bodies seem to hang suspended in lithic space. Their hands and feet, if they are shown at all, are small, stick-like, and useless. One large figure with wings resembles an angel while others are accompanied by tiny bird or animal figures. The pictures are painted mostly in reddish pigments made from iron oxide.

Scholars often describe otherworldly figures such as these as shamanic, suggesting that they communicate the transformations that shamans undergo while in a trance and as part of their healing and religious ceremonies. Shamans played in pre-agricultural societies, and still play, an important spiritual role, and a part of their practice involves leaving their physical form to make contact with super-natural powers beyond this world.

The panel appears on the face of a reddish sandstone cliff along the roadside, 4 miles above the confluence of Buckhorn Wash and the San Rafael River.

The Bureau of Land Management maintains an attractive campground where the road crosses the San Rafael River.

Rochester Petroglyph Panel

A portion of the Rochester Petroglyph Panel.

This rock art site is easily accessible from Utah 10. The turnoff is to the east, 11 miles south of Ferron and 3.5 miles north of Emery. It is between mileposts 16 and 17 and marked "Moore." At a half mile, turn right on a graded gravel road and continue 3.5 miles to the trailhead. It is about a 15-minute walk to the site on a rough trail. A short distance beyond halfway, where the trail forks, keep to the right. (The left fork leads down to the Muddy River.) The rock art panel is on a rocky point ahead.

———————

This is a large, densely packed collection of Archaic and Fremont petroglyphs that include some very unusual images. Centrally positioned is a rainbow-like arch of eight carefully pecked parallel lines. Beneath it a recumbent human male figure has an erect phallus directed into a squatting female figure. Of a less erotic nature are numerous anthropomorphs in the Fremont style. There are bighorn sheep—some with big square bodies, others depicted as stick figures—and there are abstract designs. Most surprising, however, are numerous fantastic animals, made prehistorically. One resembles an alligator; another looks like a hippopotamus. Others are purely imaginary, even nightmarish. They appear highly aggressive with open mouths and bared teeth. What cultural tradition do they come from and what do they mean? No one knows. Just around the corner from the main panel is another smaller one, and along the trail, you will find a few more glyphs.

SEGO CANYON ROCK ART SITE

The Sego Canyon Rock Art Site is just north of Thompson, Utah. From Green River, follow Interstate 70 east for 25 miles to the Thompson Springs exit (187). Drive through this settlement across the railroad tracks and 3.5 miles farther to the parking area at the site. Information: (435) 259-2100; www.blm.gov/ut/st/en/prog/more/cultural/archaeology/places_to_visit/sego_canyon.html.

———————

This rock-art site is exceptional in that it includes panels from three distinct Native American groups: Archaic, Fremont, and Ute. It is only minutes off a major highway and requires no hiking. To see it will introduce you to a variety of regional rock-art styles.

The largest panel has rock paintings, or pictographs, in the Barrier Canyon style and so has similarities to those found in Canyonlands and the San Rafael Swell (pp. 17 and 11). The haunting anthropomorphs in the panel poignantly express the mystical or otherworldly character of this type of very old Southwestern iconography. Experts surmise that they represent the visions shamans experienced while in a trance state of supernatural beings with whom they came in contact. Through out-of-body ritual experiences, they gained the power to heal and bring well-being to their community.

The many tall, broad-shouldered figures are painted in reddish pigments made from iron oxide (hematite). Notice the curved horns or antennae and round,

Paintings in the Barrier Canyon style at Sego Canyon.

oversized, staring eyes or eye sockets. Absent arms and legs, their heavy floating trapezoidal bodies give the figures a spectral appearance. Of this rock art, Polly Schaafsma has written, "Artists of the Barrier Canyon Anthropomorphic Style focused primarily on the emotional impact of their work." In this regard, the Sego Canyon images certainly succeeded.

The Fremont panel depicts triangle-shaped human figures wearing elaborate headdresses, necklaces, and pendants. These figures, too, lack arm and leg appendages. The similarities between the Barrier Canyon and Fremont styles suggest a cultural link or sequence between these two regional groups. In the first panel, petroglyphs are superimposed on painted figures. Also included in the panel are fat-bodied bighorn sheep and a variety of designs.

The Ute Indians were relative latecomers to the region, having moved here, it is thought, from the Great Basin around the time the Fremont archaeological culture vanished. Researchers have speculated that the Utes, who are Numic speakers, pushed the Fremont out, or that the two groups merged. After Spanish settlement of northern New Mexico in the seventeenth century, some Ute bands began to acquire horses and soon excelled in horse breeding and riding. Then their hunting and gathering territory expanded and they began raiding their neighbors with impunity. The Ute pictograph panel at this site shows horses and riders as well as two imposing standing human figures and two large round white shields decorated in red.

The paintings at Sego Canyon suffered badly from vandalism but, thankfully, were restored by a professional art conservator. The Bureau of Land Management built a parking area, landscaped the site with pathways and rail fences, and installed interpretive signs. There are also picnic tables. A few yards beyond the turnoff to this site and across the road (not on BLM property) are more pictographs of large figures.

Thompson is a tiny settlement that once saw more prosperous days. Its now-closed café appears in the popular movie *Thelma and Louise*. The nearest towns with travel services are Green River and Moab.

CANYONLANDS NATIONAL PARK

Canyonlands National Park covers 338,000 acres along the Colorado and Green rivers in southeastern Utah. The park is divided into districts. To access the Needles District, follow US 191 north from Monticello or south from Moab, then take Highway 211 west to the park entrance. To reach the Island in the Sky District, drive southwest on Utah 313. The turnoff is about 11 miles north from Moab on US 191. Horseshoe Canyon (also known as Barrier Canyon) is a separate unit of the park west of the Colorado River. To reach it, follow Utah 24 south from Interstate 70 west of Green River. After 24 miles, turn east on an unpaved road and continue to the edge of Horseshoe Canyon, from where you will continue on foot. Large-scale maps of Canyonlands are available on Canyonlands' website, and the Indian Country Guide Map is useful. Information: (435) 719-2100 (park administration); www .nps.gov/cany/index.htm. Entrance fee.

Canyonlands National Park is world-renowned for its spectacular desert-canyon scenery, which is best experienced by hiking, on horseback, or jeeping in a high-clearance, four-wheel-drive vehicle. At first glance, this arid, eroded landscape appears inhospitable to human life; however, human beings have lived in or traveled through these canyons for millennia and left their marks.

The first people here—at least, of whom archaeologists have found evidence—were nomadic hunter-gatherers from the late Archaic period. In certain locations, they painted and pecked stunning images on rock-shelter walls and cliff faces. This artwork, which is believed to have been done between 1,500 and 3,000 years ago, is some of the finest to be found in North America. Most impressive are elongated, ghostlike, anthropomorphic figures, which often are associated with depictions of animals and birds.

Academics generally agree that this is the work of shamans who, through art, were trying to communicate their experiences while on ecstatic, trance-induced journeys to the spirit domain. Shamans were (and in some places still are) key figures in some tribal societies around the world. Polly Schaafsma, a noted anthropologist and rock-art scholar, has written, "Shamans would have been held responsible for effecting a balance with the cosmos and played important roles

The "Ghost Panel" in Barrier Canyon.

in curing as well as in the social and economic welfare of the early people on the Colorado Plateau."

In addition to the panels of rock art, researchers have found the remains of Archaic-period campsites going back some six thousand years and usually located near sources of water. The Green and Colorado rivers flowed year round; lesser drainages ran off and on; and a few springs and seeps existed. Archaic folk exploited a variety of food and medicinal and lithic resources in the canyons while on their seasonal rounds. The big rock-art panels probably were created in places where groups gathered periodically to socialize and conduct religious ceremonies.

Ancestral Pueblo Indians also lived in Canyonlands, especially between around 950 and 1250 CE. They, too, hunted animals and foraged for plant food, but they also grew gardens of corn, beans, and squashes where water was available. Their settlements are found near springs and intermittently flowing streams. When drought struck in the late thirteenth century, everyone evacuated this region and never came back.

Three rock-art sites in Canyonlands are worth special mention here. Best known is the Great Gallery in Horseshoe Canyon, which is noted for its life-size anthropomorphic figures in the Barrier Canyon style. The 6-mile round-trip hike to it should be done in a day as camping is not permitted. Another site, known as the Harvest Scene, is in the Maze District. To reach it involves a longer hike on the Pictograph Fork Trail. Also well known are several painted panels of faces in Salt Creek Canyon in the Needles District. The hike to see these is even longer. Details about all hikes, and backcountry permits, should be obtained from Canyonlands National Park, whose website contains maps and descriptions.

The rock-art sites in Canyonlands are fragile national treasures that have endured for thousands of years. Please be sure that everyone in your group is respectful and does not touch or in any way damage them. Report any preservation problems to park officials. Also, remember that hiking and jeeping in remote desert environments involve risks. Prepare wisely, drive cautiously, and be sure you know how to change a flat as towing charges are high.

Green River and Monticello have travel services, and Moab is a major travel and tourist center where you can arrange for raft, jeep, and bicycle tours.

Suggested Reading: *Cultural Resource Inventory in the Salt Creek Pocket and Devils Lane Areas, Needles District, Canyonlands National Park*, by Betsy L. Tipps and Nancy J. Hewett, National Park Service, Denver, Colorado, 1989. *The Archaeology of Horseshoe Canyon*, an online collection of articles available at www.cnha.org/pdfs/HorseshoeBook.pdf, compiled by Gary Cox and Neal Hervert, Canyonlands Natural History website, 1998.

The Mogollon

∋I∈

Anthropologists often cite several seminal agricultural cultures in the American Southwest: the Mogollon (*mug-ee-yone*), Hohokam, and ancestral Pueblo, or Anasazi. Sometimes a fourth, the Patayan, in west-central Arizona, is included. Puebloan sites are best known by the general public since so many have visible aboveground architecture. For most of their history, the Mogollon lived in pithouse settlements in hilly, forested regions. Their habitations, made of earth and wood, are the least visible on the landscape today, and it follows that they are little appreciated by the public.

The Mogollon were "discovered," as it were, in the 1930s, and even then, when the first book about the culture appeared (*The Mogollon Culture of Southwestern New Mexico*, by Emil Haury), its conclusions were not accepted by many established archaeologists. It was called "one of the most provocative publications in the history of southwestern archaeology because it created an intellectual schism that lasted for more than twenty years." That controversy, however, is long over.

Ancient Southwestern cultures are sometimes named for rivers—the Fremont, for example—or other topographical landmarks or names told to Europeans by neighboring Native American groups. "Anasazi" is an example. "Mogollon" is the designation of a mountain range, which was named for a New Mexico governor of little consequence.

The Mogollon lived in the wooded highlands of east-central Arizona and west-central New Mexico and extended southward into northern Chihuahua, Mexico. Around 200 CE, in the late Archaic period, they emerged from the existing pre-ceramic Cochise culture of hunter-gatherers. The Mogollon are credited with having practiced agriculture and made pottery very early. Excavations of their scattered hilltop hamlets have turned up a plain brown or red-on-brown style of pottery constructed using the coil-and-scrape technique. Later on, they made black-on-white types. For many generations, they lived in round or oval pithouses and subsisted on hunting (especially deer), foraging, and cultivating corn in small garden plots.

Mogollon culture evolved over time, and archaeologists recognize considerable diversity between different areas. Anthropologist J. J. Brody wrote, "Diversity rather than homogeneity seems to characterize the later Mogollon peoples" (*Mimbres Painted Pottery*, 2004). As they thrived and their settlements swelled, they shifted their settlement from high places to valleys. Great kivas appeared, presumably to serve as community gathering places, and they depended increasingly on corn for their sustenance. After around 1150, the Mogollon came into frequent contact with Hohokam and ancestral Pueblo Indians and their culture became even more diverse. At the end of the thirteenth century, during the Great Drought, Puebloans from the Four Corners region migrated south and joined the Mogollon. Immigrants from the Kayenta region, for example, created a 70-room enclave in the 800-room village of Point of Pines. The site of Kinishba (p. 41),

Classic Mimbres bowl excavated at the Mattocks site. This bowl was depicted on a U.S. postage stamp in 2004. Courtesy of the Maxwell Museum of Anthropology, University of New Mexico. © University of New Mexico.

dating to the 1300s, exemplifies how the growing population concentrated in a large village. Puebloan influences are evident in the architecture of sites like Casa Malpais (p. 39), Gila Cliff Dwellings (p. 28), and Kinishba. The Mogollon also had ties to the south, especially with the dynamic trading center of Paquimé in Casas Grandes, Mexico (p. 36).

One well-known Classic Phase branch of the Mogollon culture is the Mimbres, whose painted pottery is world renowned. For more about the Mimbres here, see the "Mimbres Valley Sites" section, which follows. After 1050, some Mogollon lived in arid lands south and east of the mountains. Their "Jornada Style" rock art differs from the Mogollon Red Style and often resembles Mimbres art. By the mid-fifteenth century, for reasons little understood, the Mogollon (archaeologically speaking) had disappeared. It seems many joined western pueblos, such as the Zuni and Hopi villages, and others may have migrated to the Rio Grande Valley. The sites you can visit today tend to be late in the Mogollon cultural sequence when, influenced by their northern Pueblo neighbors, they built aboveground stone-masonry villages and lived in cliff dwellings.

MIMBRES VALLEY SITES

The Classic Mimbres, a branch of the widespread Mogollon culture, thrived in the environs of the Mimbres River in southwestern New Mexico between about 1000 and 1130 CE. This river rises in the Black Range northeast of Silver City and flows southward, sinking underground near Deming, except when high water carries it into Chihuahua, Mexico. "Mimbres" is a Spanish word meaning "willow," and the term was given to the river and valley due to the abundance of willows and cottonwoods.

The Mimbreños, as the people are often referred to, lived in agricultural settlements, their heartland being from north of the present-day town of Mimbres, along New Mexico 35, southward along NM 61 to around Deming. Some nine hundred Mimbres archaeological sites are known, including some hundred villages densely packed along the valley. The people raised corn, beans, squash, sunflowers, cotton, and other crops; hunted game; and foraged for edible wild plants. They dug canals off the river to irrigate their fields.

Their house structures, built of river cobbles laid up in mud mortar and wood timbers, were less strong and enduring than those of their northern neighbors; after being vacated they melted back into the terrain, forming subtle mounds and depressions on the landscape. Roomblocks enclosed plaza areas where, presumably, the inhabitants held communal functions. Settlement in the valley by pit-house-dwelling Mogollon ancestors of the Mimbres goes back to around 550 CE, and even older hamlets are located on nearby hilltops. The valley's population reached an estimated peak of 3,000 to 4,000 people in the late 1000s. Research in recent decades has demonstrated that the Mimbres did not vanish after 1100 but, rather, moved into new areas in eastern Arizona, across the Rio Grande, and south in Chihuahua, Mexico. In this later period, the Postclassic phase, they no longer made the pottery for which they are noted.

In the nineteenth and twentieth centuries, Euro-Americans settling this region dug into the village mounds and discovered the extraordinary painted ceramics that Mimbres potters had made. What followed were decades of pot hunting on both large and small scales and an inflating market for Mimbres pots. This looting activity, which became part of the local culture and economy, went on until nearly all Mimbres villages were damaged or completely destroyed. This emergency was the catalyst for the founding of the Archaeological Conservancy in 1979.

The Mimbres Valley has a history of scientific archaeological research, too, beginning in the early twentieth century and continuing, with lapses, until recent times. Thankfully, numerous museums today hold considerable collections of Mimbres pottery, and there are books illustrating Mimbres ceramic creativity.

Long after the Mimbres culture had disappeared, Apaches lived in this region. Being nomadic, their sites are much less visible than the farming villages. However, like all Southwestern groups, they left traces of their presence in the form of rock art. The three sites in the valley briefly described here are open to the public. Directions to them are provided using mileposts along New Mexico 35.

Mimbres Culture Heritage Site

This prehistoric village, commonly known as the Mattocks Ruin, is located on Sage Drive just east of Highway 35 near milepost 4. As you drive north on NM 35, turn right on Sage Drive to the entrance and parking lot. The turn is 1 mile south of the Mimbres post office. Information: www.mimbresculturesite.com. Donation requested.

———————

The Mattocks Ruin, which is owned by the Wilson Education Foundation, was opened to the public with an interpretive trail in 2013. The site also includes two Territorial-period adobe ranch houses, and a museum is planned. High on the walls of one of the old buildings, you can see small rectangular gun ports, which were built for defense against Apaches. Signs with information about the Mattocks Ruin, layouts of roomblocks, and archaeological research are situated along the trail, which is wheelchair accessible.

A visit to this ancient pueblo site offers a very different experience to someone who has seen and been impressed by cliff dwellings and multistory stone pueblos in the Four Corners region; at first glance, indeed, you might think it is just an overgrown field. But it was a large village and in its day it would have impressed. Its first inhabitants were pithouse dwellers between about 750 and 1000 CE. The remains of their living and storage rooms lie beneath roomblocks of the later Classic Mimbres period. The people of this time left around 1130.

The Mattocks Ruin was partially excavated between 1929 and 1931 by archaeologists from the Logan Museum of Beloit College. In the mid-1970s, the

The Mattocks site.

Mimbres Foundation, which owned the site, conducted further research here and at other sites in the valley. Some of the pueblo remains scientifically unexcavated, although it was damaged by looters.

PICTOGRAPH CANYON

A short easy trail on the west side of NM 35 leads to several interesting panels of rock paintings. Between mileposts 22 and 23, look for a small parking area on the west side of the road. The Gila National Forest plans to make trail improvements and install an interpretive sign by 2016. Until that is accomplished, however, the trail up the canyon is not hard to follow. In stormy weather, be alert for stream flooding.

————————

As you make your way up the trail about a hundred yards, you will come to several red-painted stick figures on the cliff on the left and, a short distance beyond them, two closely associated panels. The first shows an unusual reticulated vertical figure in red pigments. What it depicts is uncertain; however, some speculate that it shows a net trap holding a caught deer. At close inspection you can make out what appear to be legs dangling from the bottom and a possible deer's head projecting from one lower corner.

Reticulated painted figure, Pictograph Canyon.

Just to the right of the netlike figure, there is a cluster of carefully executed striped handprints. In her book, *Rock Art in New Mexico*, anthropologist Polly Schaafsma ascribes all the pictographs at these sites to Apaches. In the late 1800s, this country was a stronghold of the Warm Springs band of Chiricahua Apache. Some of their leaders—Mangas Coloradas, Cochise, Victorio, and Geronimo, for example—became legendary figures of Indian resistance to Euro-American expansion in the Southwest. Others think the stick figures are Apache, but the other panels may be of much earlier origin and are in the Mogollon Red Style.

Vista Village

Vista Village is located along NM 35 near milepost 24. The site overlooks Lake Roberts.

Vista Village is a long-occupied Mogollon-Mimbres settlement on a hill above Sapillo Creek, not far north of the Mimbres Valley. As you drive up the valley, this is the third public archaeological site you can stop to see. From the parking area, a short paved walkway leads to the site's mounds and depressions.

For three summer field seasons between 1992 and 1995, archaeologists Cynthia A. Bettison and Barbara Roth co-directed excavations here. Since archaeologists' attention had long been focused on large sites in the Mimbres Valley, Bettison and Roth were eager to learn more about a small upland village to see how it compared. Of particular interest to them was when people lived here, whether they used the site seasonally or permanently, and how it related to others in the area. They and their students excavated six pithouses and a part of a great kiva and did some other testing.

View of Vista Village showing the great kiva depression.

Vista Village consisted of a dozen or so pithouse rooms in three roomblocks, a great kiva, a "semi-subterranean civic-ceremonial room," and a plaza area. For a small settlement, it was long-lived. Sometime after 550 CE, its first occupants built pithouse rooms, probably using them seasonally while they hunted and foraged in the mountains. They typically housed a single family. It's hard for us to visualize an underground dwelling, but as anthropologist Patricia A. Gilman, a Mimbres specialist, has described them, "From the ground surface, deep pit structures looked like low earthen igloos."

Two hundred years later, it appears, Vista Village folks were living here on a more permanent basis, sustaining themselves to a greater extent by farming. They continued living in pithouses until around 1000. Along the way, they constructed a great kiva, which you will see at the end of the paved pathway as a large depression in the terrain. This rectangular structure had cobble and adobe walls, an adobe bench, and a clay-lined hearth. The researchers found evidence that it was ritually dedicated at the time of construction. This was a common practice of the time. Later, when it ceased to be used, it was ritually closed with exotic items, including turquoise and quartz crystals, being buried as offerings in a pit in the middle of the floor.

Vista Village also was occupied during the Classic Mimbres period between 1000 and 1150. At this time, its inhabitants probably lived in the pueblo year-round and depended more on growing corn. They also converted a pithouse room into a civic-ceremonial room.

When you reach the top of the knoll where Vista Village sits, you can look down on Roberts Reservoir and across to the Gila Wilderness. Most of the hilltops in view have sites on them and, like Vista Village, most were plundered in the past.

A short drive beyond Vista Village, at the end of NM 15, is Gila Cliff Dwellings National Monument and two related sites. The best place to find lodging and other travel services is Silver City.

Suggested Reading: *Mimbres Lives and Landscapes*, edited by Margaret C. Nelson and Michelle Hegmon, School for Advanced Research Press, Santa Fe, New Mexico, 2010.

GILA CLIFF DWELLINGS NATIONAL MONUMENT

Gila Cliff Dwellings is located at the end of New Mexico 15, 44 miles—much of the way is slow driving—north of Silver City, in southwestern New Mexico. Information: (575) 536-9461; www.nps.gov/gicl/index.htm. Entrance fee.

———————

When you first come to this monument, go to the visitor center to check in and see the museum and introductory video. Then proceed to the nearby scenic trail to the cliff dwellings. In the shade of tall pines, the trail crosses the West Fork of the Gila River, winds along a small stream, and climbs to the dwellings where you can explore many of the stone-masonry rooms set in deeply recessed caves. The architecture is remarkably well preserved, and you will get a sense of how it might have been to live here seven hundred years ago.

The trail is maintained but rough, sometimes muddy or icy, and there is a 175-foot elevation gain to reach a series of caves with dwellings. When you arrive at the cliff dwellings, notice how the house walls do not reach quite to the cave ceilings to allow smoke from interior hearth fires to escape and that the dwellings face south to allow passive solar heating in winter. From the cliffs, the trail loops around by a different way to the river and parking area. You should plan about an hour for the walk, longer for a more leisurely sightseeing and cultural experience.

The first people to take shelter in the caves here were Archaic-period hunter-gatherers. After around 200 CE, Mogollon settlements appeared in the region—clusters of semi-subterranean dwellings made mostly of wooden structural members covered with dirt. It is a surprise to find cliff dwellings in Mogollon country. According to researchers, Mogollon people, perhaps drawn by the reliable water in the Gila River, moved here from the Tularosa area around Reserve, New Mexico, 40 miles to the west. Around 1270 CE, they began constructing their homes in the style of the ancestral Puebloan peoples to the north with whom they had relations. In addition to providing good shelter, the cliff dwellings were effective for defense and they did not impinge on valuable farmland.

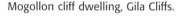
Mogollon cliff dwelling, Gila Cliffs.

Around the world, cultures and societies influence their neighbors. People travel, migrate, carry on trade, learn each other's language, and sometimes marry into each other's communities. In so doing, they exchange ideas and add to their knowledge of many subjects from religion to technology. In the 1200s, the ancestral Pueblo people who lived north of the Mogollon were expanding beyond their original boundaries, carrying with them many of their own ideas and practices, including building cliff dwellings.

Archaeological explorations, surveys, and a few limited excavations have taken place in and around this small park ever since Adolph F. Bandelier was here in 1884. But research has been sporadic and inhibited in its results by generations of relic collecting and vandalism by early American settlers, soldiers, and miners.

Excavations have turned up the remains of corn, three varieties of squashes, and five types of beans, as well as mule deer and, surprisingly, even bison. Wild edible leafy plants, nuts, fruits, and tubers, which people collected according to the season, made for a healthy, well-rounded diet. Weather and climate, however, did not always accommodate, and the inhabitants of the cliff dwellings left within a generation or two. It is not known where they went; however, some clues indicate that some migrated north up the Rio Grande Valley to integrate with Pueblo peoples already there.

The Gila headwaters have three branches—East Fork, Middle Fork, and West Fork—and cliff dwellings, as well as rock art, exist along all three. Although the largest are on the West Fork within the monument, the wider area contained a scattered community of people. The park is adjacent to the vast Gila and Aldo Leopold Wilderness Areas, a beautiful and remote part of the Southwest that attracts many people to hike, ride horseback, camp, fish, and hunt.

On your way from the visitor center to the cliff dwellings trailhead, you will pass two other archaeological sites. The first, on the left, is a place where, prior to the building of the road in 1966, there were the remains of ancient pithouses, a small stone-masonry pueblo, and a historic homestead. It is known as the West Fork site. The Native American occupation of the site spanned eleven centuries, from 200 to 1300 CE. In 1883, a member of archaeologist-explorer Adolph F. Bandelier's party, named John Williams, built his home here. The Park Service has marked the outlines of the pueblo on the ground and put up interpretive signs.

A short distance farther, you will come to the Lower Scorpion Campground, which has a parking lot and latrine. Here there are two archaeological sites to see. A short left-hand trail goes to a small masonry house under a rock overhang. It has several rooms and what appears to be a plaza area in front. Another path, to the right in the parking area, leads to several pictograph panels in the Mogollon Red Style. Along the way it also passes a double grinding slick on a boulder. Both these sites are rewarding to explore and are open all the time.

There are a few travel and tourist services along highways 35 and 15, especially in summer, but Silver City is your best bet for restaurants and lodging. Gas stations are scarce so be sure to have a full tank when you go to Gila Cliffs. When

Small cliff dwelling at Lower Scorpion Campground.

in Silver City, the museum at Western New Mexico University, which has a fine collection of Mimbres pottery, is worth visiting.

Suggested Reading: *Gila Cliff Dwellings National Monument*, by Laurence Parent, Western National Parks Association, Tucson, Arizona, 2004.

THREE RIVERS PETROGLYPH SITE

At Three Rivers, an intersection along US 54, 30 miles north of Alamogordo, New Mexico, turn east on route B30 and proceed 5 miles to the entrance to the Three Rivers petroglyph site parking lot. From there, one trail leads through the petroglyph area and another to a pithouse settlement. Information: (575) 525-4300; www .blm.gov/nm/st/en/prog/recreation/las_cruces/three_rivers.html. Fee area.

This rock art site contains some twenty thousand petroglyphs that Jornada, or Desert, Mogollon people pecked on boulders scattered over some 50 acres between around 900 and 1400 CE. When you explore this collection and its landscape, you may wonder why and why here. It's puzzling for the glyphs seem to be in the middle of nowhere. However, they weren't for people who were living in nearby pithouse settlements that have long since collapsed and melted into the ground. Such is the natural life cycle of homes built of wood and mud in open country. A trail east of the picnic area leads to one site, which was occupied for about four centuries. It was partially excavated in 1976.

The petroglyphs are scattered along a ridge near the western base of the Sacramento Mountains. As you walk along the trail through the site, you will be struck by the views toward the mountains and over the Tularosa Basin. You'll find this to be not only an anthropologically interesting experience, but quiet and scenic as well. As you observe the ancient markings, remember that not far away, in the early morning hours of July 16, 1945, an awesome and history-making explosion occurred at a site called Trinity on the White Sands Missile Base.

Desert Mogollon Indians made these glyphs by chipping designs in the patina of rocks using hammer and chisel stones. It was a slow, delicate process with no erasing mistakes. The pictures depict animals, birds, fish, reptiles, insects, and plants, as well as geometric and abstract designs. Some petroglyphs resemble the paintings on Mimbres pottery, indicating a cultural relationship between the two groups.

Many of the petroglyphs are close at hand along the trail and easy to see and photograph. Others are off-trail and harder to find. The walk here can be hot and windy. And one should keep a wary eye for rattlesnakes, especially when straying from the main trail, which is a half mile in length. You will need a minimum of an hour here, longer if you explore in more detail.

The Bureau of Land Management, which manages the site, has a parking lot, picnic tables, barbecue pits, drinking water, and toilets. Overnight camping is permitted. A National Forest Service campground is located several miles farther

Petroglyph in the Jornada Mogollon style at the Three Rivers site.

up the road, and travel facilities are available in the towns of Alamogordo and Carizozo. Other nearby points of interest are White Sands National Monument and the historic town of Lincoln.

Suggested Reading: *Archaeological Survey, Three Rivers Drainage, New Mexico*, by Mark Wimberly and Alan Rogers, El Paso Archaeological Society, El Paso, Texas, 1977.

HUECO TANKS STATE PARK AND HISTORIC SITE

From El Paso, Texas, drive 24 miles northeast on US 62/180, then north on Ranch Road 2775 for another 8 miles. Information: (915) 857-1135; camping reservations: (800) 792-1112, option 3; tour and camping reservations: (915) 849-6684; website: tpwd.texas.gov/state-parks/hueco-tanks. Entrance and guided-tour fees.

———————

Hueco Tanks is a park with several attractions, one of which is its unusual rock art. Most visitors, however—especially on holidays and weekends—come for bouldering or rock climbing on the park's three impressive volcanic hills. If your interest is mainly to see the ancient paintings and petroglyphs, try to visit on a day of low attendance.

Hueco is a Spanish word for a hollow in rock formations where rainwater collects. Similarly, "tanks" is a commonly used term in the West with a similar meaning. The granite-like outcrops here have many huecos, which trap and hold water runoff; thus, it was a popular place for people to come and quench their thirst. Native Americans, not surprisingly, have known of these water sources for millennia.

Between around 6000 BCE and 450 CE—the Archaic Phase—nomadic groups hunted and foraged and made their camps in this region. The early marks they made on the rocks tended to be abstract motifs such as circles, dots, zigzags, and parallel wavy lines. Later, they incorporated human-like and animal figures and hunting scenes. The anthropomorphic figures have some of the attributes (broad shoulders, horned headdresses, small heads and limbs) of Archaic rock art in southeastern Utah and the lower Pecos River region of south Texas, suggesting widespread cultural commonalities.

Of great interest in Hueco Tanks are the finely executed masks painted by Indians of the Jornada Mogollon culture, probably in the 1100s and 1200s. About two hundred have been recorded, though some are very faint. Both linear and solidly painted masks are found on the walls and ceilings of rock shelters and caves. The artists liked the faded red color made from iron oxide pigments but also painted in black, white, brown, green, and various shades of ocher. The linear masks show an outlined head with facial features and headdress. The solid masks, on the other hand, depict only the painted mask with empty or negative spaces left for the eyes. Thus, the person or spirit behind the mask is left to the viewer's imagination. Many of these paintings are found in dark hidden recesses in the rock, where they have remained well preserved for many centuries.

Anthropologists have identified representations of two Mesoamerican deities among the Mogollon masks here. One is the Rain God known as Tlaloc, who has a large trapezoidal head with goggle eyes sitting on a chunky, armless, decorated torso. The effect is disturbing. Some masks also depict Quetzalcoatl, the multi-faceted Mexican deity, which often has a plumed or horned head on a serpent's body. In the Cave of the Masks, the feathered plume or curved horn appears as a bent-over hat.

Wide-ranging bison hunters of the Southern Plains—Apaches, Comanches, and Kiowas—also camped at Hueco Tanks, especially in the eighteenth and nineteenth centuries, and they also made pictures on rock. Comanche Cave, for example, contains paintings of lines of dancers and a large decorated shield.

In the 1970s, archaeologists made test excavations in the flats near the base of the hills where they had noticed many artifacts lying on the ground. What they unearthed were pithouses and water diversion features, which they attributed to the Dona Ana phase of the Jornada Mogollon culture, dating from circa 1150 to 1300. It is assumed that additional surveys and tests would reveal more such hamlets in the area and it was these part-time farmers who painted the masks and Tlaloc figures.

In 1857, Congress authorized the establishment of a mail service across the West and John Butterfield and his partners in the Overland Mail Company won the contract. At considerable expense, Butterfield developed a 2,795-mile-long wagon road from St. Louis to San Francisco with relay stations built and manned along the way. At these stops, the stage coach drivers could get fresh horses and the passengers could have a brief rest and a meal. It was John Butterfield who famously declared, "Remember, boys, nothing in God's earth must stop the United States mail!" Being federally sponsored, the service was interrupted by the Civil War and not revived after the war ended. You can see the remains of a Butterfield Trail station in this park.

In addition to viewing pictographs or rock climbing, you can arrange to join a guided nature and bird-watching tour. To do this, contact the park in advance for current information about tour details and to make a reservation. Customized tours also can be arranged for groups. Make reservations well in advance to use the campground. The nearest motels, restaurants, and markets are along route 62/180 on the east side of El Paso. In 1998, Rupestrian Cyber-Services mapped and digitally photographed about fifty rock art sites in the park. Some of their digitally enhanced images can be viewed at www.rupestrian .com/hueco-tanks.html.

Suggested Reading: *Rock Paintings at Hueco Tanks State Historical Park*, by Kay Sutherland, Texas Parks and Wildlife Department, Austin, 1995. To read this publication online, go to the park's website and click on the link "Rock Paintings at Hueco Tanks."

Pictographs at Hueco Tanks.

CASAS GRANDES

The ruins of Casas Grandes (Paquimé) are located just outside Casas Grandes, Chihuahua, Mexico, and near the city of Nuevo Casas Grandes. This is approximately 180 miles southwest of Ciudad Juarez, Chihuahua, and El Paso, Texas, along Mexico 2 and 10, and 100 miles from the U.S.-Mexico border at Columbus, New Mexico. Crossing the border at Columbus is easier and faster than at El Paso. You will need a current passport to return to the United States. Check Mexican regulations regarding what documents you need to drive a vehicle into Mexico. Entrance fee.

―――――――――

What we in the United States consider the "Southwest" is to Mexicans the "Northwest." Prehistorically speaking, the national frontier is meaningless; however, from an archaeological viewpoint there is a difference because so much more research has taken place on the north side of the border than the south. A notable exception is the large urban site of Casas Grandes and its core city, Paquimé. Intensive excavations were conducted here between 1958 and 1961 by the Amerind Foundation of Dragoon, Arizona, under the direction of the late Charles C. Di Peso and Eduardo Contreras as the Mexican governmental representative. Mexican and American investigators have done more research since, focusing especially on sites in Casas Grandes' environs.

Paquimé, which thrived between 1150/1200 and the late 1400s CE (the Medio period), was a major population, cultural, and economic center with far-reaching influence. In size and technological achievements, it is certainly the equal of Southwestern centers such as Chaco Canyon (p. 121). Half a century ago, Di Peso

The ruins of Paquimé, Casas Grandes.

argued that the city was ruled by a group of entrepreneurs who represented Mesoamerican trading guilds far to the south. These *puchtecas* forged local support into political power to eventually dominate a vast area of northwestern Chihuahua, northeastern Sonora, and even into the American Southwest. He compared Casas Grandes' trading empire to that of the Hudson Bay Company in Canada in the nineteenth century.

Science evolves and archaeologists who have more recently conducted research in the Casas Grandes region have come to different conclusions. After reevaluating Di Peso's findings and investigating hundreds of sites in the vicinity of Casas Grandes and in the surrounding region, they think this urban center, rather than being a Toltec outpost, was a local development that emerged from existing communities in the basin and nearby uplands. Current thinking also minimizes the importance of trading. That is not to say, however, that Casas Grandes did not have links to the south; the presence of ball courts, particular architectural features such as colonnades, and Mesoamerican iconography all point southward as do goods such as a ton and a half of shell, many copper artifacts, and the remains of hundreds of macaws. Especially distinctive among crafts made at Casas Grandes are its ceramics, which, five centuries later, inspired the potter Juan Quesada of Mata Ortiz to revive and elaborate on the tradition.

Paquimé grew to become a city with marketplaces, warehouses, and apartment buildings as well as public architecture: plazas, ceremonial mounds, and ball courts. The large basin in which Casas Grandes is centered provided many natural resources to sustain its population. City engineers built an aqueduct from a spring to the northwest to a reservoir from where the water was dispersed in underground stone-lined channels to the main house clusters. Other system features included drainage tunnels and subterranean walk-in cisterns. Aviculture, evidenced by the remains of turkey and macaw pens along the edge of plazas, became a lucrative and prestigious part of the economy and ritual life of the people.

Sometime after 1400, civil construction ceased and Casas Grandes' once impressive buildings began to fall into disrepair. The good times were over. Did trading problems cause the economic slump? Was it drought, or a popular revolt? To date, archaeology has revealed no definitive answer. Whatever happened, when European explorers first entered Casas Grandes' domain more than a century later, they found the city in ruins—the main construction material was adobe—and the inhabitants of the valley living a very different lifestyle.

Thanks to the region's arid climate, the massiveness of Paquimé's rammed-earth structures, and restoration work by the Mexican government, this UNESCO World Heritage archaeological site and its museum offer much to marvel at and you will gain a sense of the power that Casas Grandes once enjoyed. Plan a couple of hours here.

West of Casas Grandes in the Sierra Madre Mountains are several cliff dwellings maintained by the Mexican government for tourists. To appreciate present-day, small-town Mexican life, take a stroll around the historic plaza of Casas

Grandes. There are both Mennonite and Mormon communities near Nuevo Casas Grandes and the flourishing pottery-making village of Mata Ortiz is only a short drive away. In Nuevo Casas Grandes you will find lodgings, restaurants, and many other services.

Suggested Reading: *Casas Grandes: A Fallen Trading Post of the Gran Chichimeca,* 3 vols., by Charles C. Di Peso, Northland Press, Flagstaff, Arizona, 1974. Also *Casas Grandes and Its Hinterlands: Prehistoric Regional Organization in Northwest Mexico,* by Michael E. Whalen and Paul E. Minnis, University of Arizona Press, Tucson, 2001.

TULAROSA CREEK PETROGLYPHS

The Tularosa Creek rock art site is near Reserve, New Mexico. From Reserve, take New Mexico 12 north about 9 miles. On the east (right) side of the highway, you will see a trail sign (two figures hiking). Turn here and then turn right on Forest Trail 616 and proceed to the parking area and trailhead. (Note: if you go too far on 12, you'll pass an RV park on the left.) There is an informational kiosk where the trail starts. The ¾-mile hike to the petroglyph panels, which goes up and over a hill, is of moderate difficulty.

––––––––––

Shortly before you reach the petroglyph panels, you'll pass a historic log cabin, which was part of the old Tularosa Ranger Station. The cabin was built in 1905 and used for twenty-three years, after which it began to deteriorate. When its historic significance was recognized, the Forest Service stabilized and restored it and archaeologists conducted excavations; they recovered bottles, metal fragments, stamps, and paper documents. There are pueblo sites in the surrounding area that are thought to be contemporaneous with the rock art panels. Some of these sites were excavated in 1907 as part of the salvage project associated with construction of Highway 12. It is interesting to note that the original cost of building the cabin was $50, whereas the stabilization and restoration work in the 1990s cost $7,000.

Continue beyond the cabin and you will come to the petroglyphs. The main panels, which are on this side of the river, extend for some distance along a cliff. They are Mogollon and, if potsherds found in association with the rock art are a reliable indicator, they date to between 900 and 1100 CE. A few are later Puebloan. There are many representational figures and abstract designs here. In the former category are anthropomorphic stick figures, footprints, lizards, and a flute player on his back. Particularly interesting are a line of human figures holding hands and several depictions of eagles with outspread fringed wings. The abstract designs include concentric circles, grids, rakes, wavy lines, double spirals, and outlined crosses. Some of the figures are deeply incised in the rock.

The Forest Service has developed a trail to the Apache Creek rock art site. To reach it, proceed along Highway 12 to Apache Creek Junction, then turn right (east) on Forest Road 94. This is between mileposts 15 and 16. Go half a mile

Ancestral Pueblo images at the Tularosa Creek site.

beyond the Apache Creek campground and turn left on FR 4033R, which leads to the parking area and trailhead. The half-mile loop trail winds up a hillside and along the base of a basalt escarpment where you'll walk by a scattering of petroglyphs, some faint, some distinct.

In the town of Reserve, you'll find a café, two motels, a store, and gas stations. Silver City is about an hour and a half drive away, a scenic drive along the San Francisco River.

CASA MALPAIS ARCHAEOLOGICAL PARK

Casa Malpais Archaeological Park, in Springerville, Arizona, is open to visitors by guided tours, which are offered thrice daily, Tuesday through Saturday, from March through November. They start at the visitor center and museum at 418 East Main Street at (as of this writing) 9 and 11 a.m. and 2 p.m. Advance reservations are advised and participants should arrive fifteen minutes early to view a short video presentation. Information: (928) 333-5375; www.casamalpais.org/. Tour fee.

Casa Malpais (literally, "badlands house") was the home of Mogollon Indians from about 1250 to 1340. The site is on ancient lava-flow terraces in one of the largest volcanic fields in the United States. Between Springerville and Show Low, there are some four hundred volcanic cones, some of which are being quarried for cinders. Basalt rocks and boulders made up the building blocks for the walls of the rooms, which, in some places, overlie filled-in fissures in the lava bedrock. Researchers think that while the pueblo's construction crews were at work, they lived in some of these subterranean fissures. Later, being cool and dry, they became storage cellars. According to stories passed down, early settlers found burials deep down in these cracks. All these aspects make Casa Malpais one of the more unusual sites in the Southwest.

The hour-and-a-half, three-quarter-mile tour goes up to a terrace, which the Casa Malpais inhabitants cleared of rocks and may have used as a plaza and for farming. You will then walk up to a second terrace and to the great kiva, a tour highlight. Its large rectangular interior space is contained by high, massive rock walls. The Indians probably gathered here for communal activities such as ceremonies and trade fairs. Near it are the remains of a sixty-five-room pueblo, nine rooms in which were excavated in the 1990s and have since been partially filled in with dirt to preserve them.

Along the trail, you will pass by a number of petroglyphs, some of which have been interpreted as summer solstice or equinox markers. One of them shows a graceful, symmetrical feather-like design that at noon of the summer solstice is bisected by a shadow. The trail then ascends through a modified fissure to the top of the mesa. At this high point, you will enjoy a sweeping view over the

Excavated kiva at Casa Malpais.

archaeological site and landscape. On the way back, you'll enter a large circular stone-walled enclosure with four doorway openings. The function of this structure and the space within is unclear, though some believe that it, too, served as a prehistoric solar calendar or astronomical observatory.

In the late 1600s, nomadic Apaches moved into this region to take advantage of the good hunting and foraging along the Little Colorado River. In the nineteenth century, European American settlers were drawn to the fine stock-grazing potential here. Predictably, as the town of Springerville grew, artifact collectors and vandals had their way with Casa Malpais, but even so, the site as a whole remains remarkably intact and is a source of much interest to researchers and visitors. Ancient pots, jewelry, stone tools, and other artifacts unearthed during the archaeological excavations are on display in the museum, which also has exhibits of historical items from the area and art.

Springerville has several motels and restaurants, as well as stores and other travel services. Homol'ovi State Park (p. 150) and Petrified Forest (p. 155), along Interstate 40, are worth visiting while you are in the area.

KINISHBA RUINS

Kinishba is near Whiteriver, Arizona, on the White Mountain Apache reservation. To visit the site, go first to the Fort Apache Museum and Cultural Center in Fort Apache, 4 miles west of Whiteriver along Arizona 73, to obtain a permit, trail guide, and directions. Information: (928) 338-4625; www.wmat.nsn.us/fortapachepark .htm. Admission fee.

The ruins of Kinishba, less than 2 miles off Highway 73, consist of the remains of a large late Mogollon village. The site is owned and managed by the White Mountain Apache Tribe with assistance from the Hopi Tribe and Zuni Pueblo. From the site's parking area, you should plan about forty-five minutes to tour the site along its interpretive trail.

Like so many archaeological sites in the Southwest, this one was first scientifically recorded, in 1883, by the intrepid anthropological explorer Adolph F. Bandelier. Of course, it was well known by Apache and Pueblo people before then. In 1931, the archaeologist Byron Cummings of the University of Arizona began a nine-year multifaceted project at the site with crews made up of university students and Apaches. In addition to researching Kinishba's history, Cummings wanted to train students in archaeology, provide employment for local Apaches, restore a portion of the pueblo, and create tourist income for the tribe. It was an idealistic and ambitious plan that he almost accomplished. Unfortunately, events beyond his control caused it to fail.

Cummings believed Kinishba to represent "the highest development" of ancestral Southwestern culture, and the wealth of artifacts he collected at the site demonstrates the skills, artistic sensibilities, and heterogeneous character of the

Kinishba as it appeared in 2014.

village's artisans. They exchanged ideas and goods with all their neighbors: Kayenta communities to the north; Tularosa people to the east; the Hopi pueblos of Sikyatki and Awatovi; and Salado and Hohokam traders from the lower Salt and Gila valleys to the south. Its post-1200 buildings show the influence of Pueblo stone-masonry architecture and the archaeologist Erik K. Reed classified it as "western Pueblo."

Kinishba was inhabited from the mid-eleventh to mid-fourteenth centuries. Its inhabitants farmed corn, beans, and squash (the "three sisters") on arable fields sloping southeast to the White River. At its peak, around 1325, the town had several compact, multistory apartment houses built of stone. These had an estimated six hundred ground-floor rooms; it was a big village. The buildings were built on top of an older, collapsed settlement, and the presence of numerous pithouses showed an even older Basketmaker occupation.

Byron Cummings and his crews excavated one apartment block with more than two hundred rooms. He also built a research and exhibition complex that he envisioned would be the core of a model educational park. He hoped that professionals and laypeople would come to tour the site, relax under shade trees in a park, see Kinishba's art and artifact collections in a modern museum, and enjoy a contemporary Native American arts-and-crafts center.

What happened, before his dream could be fulfilled, was World War II. Understandably, public interest and funding were diverted from his enterprise. Today, Kinishba's restored roomblock and cultural center are in a state of progressive deterioration and the site is little known by the general public. To the serious archaeology student, however, this site represents an important example of Western Pueblo culture and should not be forgotten.

Byron Cummings with pottery from Kinishba. Courtesy of the Arizona State Museum, University of Arizona. Tad Nichols, photographer.

As a matter of safety, when you walk around Kinishba, stay clear of its unstable walls. The printed trail guide will inform you of features along the trail. White-river has a hotel, places to eat, and gas stations. While here, you should visit the tribal museum and walk around the grounds and buildings of old Fort Apache.

Suggested Reading: *A Prehistoric Pueblo of the Great Pueblo Period*, by Byron Cummings, University of Arizona, Tucson, 1940.

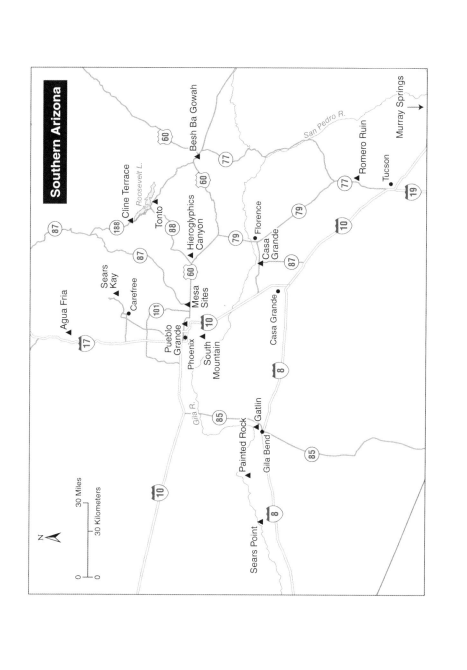

Southern Arizona

N

0 30 Miles
0 30 Kilometers

Agua Fria

Sears Kay

Carefree

Pueblo Grande

Phoenix

South Mountain

Mesa Sites

Casa Grande

Gila Bend

Gatlin

Painted Rock

Sears Point

Cline Terrace

Roosevelt L.

Tonto

Hieroglyphics Canyon

Besh Ba Gowah

Florence

Casa Grande

Romero Ruin

Tucson

Murray Springs

San Pedro R.

Gila R.

The Hohokam

⊐⊱⊰⊏

Centered in the Phoenix Basin of south-central Arizona, the Hohokam were a seminal Southwestern culture with widespread influence. These ancient Indians are remembered especially for their construction of some 500 miles of canals, the building of ball courts and platform mounds, and the manufacture of finely crafted jewelry, pottery, and mosaics. In addition, they developed a widespread trading network that reached into Mexico and to the Pacific Coast.

The word "Hohokam" is an Anglicization of the O'odham word *huhugam*, which, according to Tohono O'odham tribal elder Daniel Lopez, means "something that is all gone, such as food or when something disappears." It also "is used to refer to those people who have disappeared."

Hohokam culture emerged about 450 CE and lasted for a millennium. Along the way, it was influenced in many ways by West Mexican culture. The Hohokam were probably the descendants of Cochise hunter-gatherers who had lived in the region for thousands of years. Around four thousand years ago, these semi-nomadic people began to cultivate corn and a few centuries later were building irrigation ditches and living in hamlets. As their population increased and their society grew more complex, they began to acquire cultural attributes that archaeologists recognize as "Hohokam."

Canal building began early in the Hohokam sequence and expanded until farmers were irrigating as many as 100,000 acres. Some trunk canals were 50 feet wide at the bottom and reached more than 20 miles in length. Villages were spaced at regular intervals along the canals, creating a complex, interlocking social and economic system. To build, maintain, and supervise the waterworks and control the society suggests a sophisticated level of civic management and the existence of a complex bureaucracy ruled by an elite class. The results were successful and long-lived; the Hohokam brought water into desert lands and produced agricultural surpluses for export.

Early in Hohokam history, most common people lived in single-room huts or field houses made of a pole and brush framework covered with mud. Often they arranged their homes around a central courtyard. In the later Classic period, they built more substantial houses of adobe, placed around a central space that was enclosed by a wall. Towns such as Pueblo Grande and the Gatlin Site (pp. 48 and 59) had many such compounds clustered around a platform mound. Archaeologists have recorded 120 of these massive earthen structures. They vary in size, some containing only 2,500 cubic feet of fill, others half a million. There were houses on top of the mounds with views over the surrounding community, and it seems clear that they were used to hold ceremonies. Such rituals must have been amazing to behold.

Another form of monumental public architecture in Hohokam society was the ball court, of which the remains of more than two hundred exist, one even as far away as Wupatki National Monument (p. 161), near Flagstaff. The builders dug large oval depressions and piled the excavated dirt around the edge to form raised embankments. Like the mounds, they vary in size but some reached 250 feet in length and 90 feet in width. Most were built after 900 CE and were no longer used after 1100. The ballgame originated in Mesoamerica; in the sixteenth century, Spanish conquistadores witnessed Aztecs playing the game. Players on two teams tried to put a rubber ball through a stone hoop without using their hands or feet. Three rubber balls have been recovered in the Hohokam region.

The ball court at Wupatki National Monument.

Hohokam pottery display, Pueblo Grande Museum. Left: Santa Cruz Red-on-buff vessel; right: Sacaton Red-on-buff bowl.

The Hohokam were highly skilled craftspeople producing a fine Red-on-buff style of ceramics including fascinating figurines and masks. They fashioned paint palettes, bowls, censers, and a variety of stone tools and weapons. They also excelled in the production of shell ornaments such as beads, rings, bracelets, and pendants. The shells were imported from the Gulf of California, then etched by artisans using an acid solution made from fermented saguaro juice. This was a uniquely Hohokam art form.

While we are inclined to praise cultures for artistic creativity, we have only to drive into the Sonoran Desert in summer to realize the chief accomplishment of the Hohokam: surviving in a desert. Their knowledge of how to do this, combined with an innovative approach to dealing with heat and aridity, allowed them to prosper. They harnessed the region's precious water resources to successfully cultivate corn, beans, squash, cotton, and agave. They harvested wild plants with nutritious or healing qualities, collected cactus fruits, and hunted birds and mammals.

Hohokam culture ended sometime after 1450 but, to date, archaeological evidence is indefinite as to why this happened. Some researchers blame devastating floods, others a revolt against oppressive leadership, and still others European-introduced diseases. O'odham stories speak of conflict and strife. For a culture to collapse does not mean a people vanishes: the Akimel O'odham (Pima), Tohono O'odham (Papago), and Maricopa Indians, who today live in southern Arizona and whom Spanish explorers met in the late 1600s, may well be the descendants of the Hohokam.

Suggested Reading: *The Hohokam Millennium*, edited by Suzanne K. Fish and Paul R. Fish, School for Advanced Research Press, Santa Fe, New Mexico, 2007.

PUEBLO GRANDE MUSEUM ARCHAEOLOGICAL PARK

The Pueblo Grande Museum Archaeological Park is at 4619 East Washington Street (corner of 44th Street) in Phoenix, Arizona. It is close to Sky Harbor International Airport. Public transportation on Valley Metro Light Rail also goes to the museum. The museum and site are open daily except between May and September, when they are closed on Sundays and Mondays. Contacts: (602) 495-0900; (602) 495-0901; www.pueblogrande.org. Entrance fee.

    The Pueblo Grande platform mound and part of a residential compound are what remains of a Hohokam town that existed in what is now Phoenix between about 450 and 1450 CE. Today, a ¾-mile trail winds through the site, up on the mound, and to some house replicas and a stabilized ball court. The museum contains exhibits relating to the Hohokam, other past and present Indian cultures of southern Arizona, and archaeological methods. Also, you can watch a film about the Hohokam culture.

    Both Pueblo Grande and Phoenix owe their existence to the nearby Salt River, which rises in the White Mountains of east-central Arizona and empties into Roosevelt Reservoir in the Tonto Basin; unless, that is, it becomes full enough for its spillways to be opened. Both ancient and modern canals are visible from the top of the platform mound.

Pueblo Grande platform mound.

At its peak in the 1300s, Pueblo Grande covered about two square miles. It had adobe residential compounds; a "big house" similar to Casa Grande (p. 57); a 25-foot-high platform mound, which was football-field size and covered with houses; a couple of ball courts; and hundreds of small stick-and-mud dwellings. This large community was situated at the headwaters of a major canal system, which directed Salt River water to some 10,000 acres of corn, beans, squash, and cotton. Its residents also hunted local game and fished in the river.

Beneath the buildings, streets, and parks of Phoenix lie many other archaeological sites, most of which have never been—and probably never will be—investigated. In the last century, when Euro-American settlers discovered the rich agricultural potential of the Phoenix Basin, they put the Pueblo Grande area under cultivation to produce cotton. Even the three-story big house was razed, its bulk used as fill to level fields. The platform mound, which contained some 32,000 cubic yards of fill, was spared—it simply was not feasible to level it. Besides, it is retained by a massive wall built of river rocks and hardened chunks of caliche. Although the mound was built over many generations, one researcher estimates that it would have taken a hundred workers twenty-four months to complete.

Houses and other specialized structures stood on and around the mound to form a residential and ceremonial compound that was itself walled in. Who lived within this special area has puzzled researchers, but it likely was members of an elite or priestly class who derived their power through control of the canals and success as traders and merchants. The size and prominence of their dwellings reflected their status.

At Pueblo Grande, one cannot but be impressed by the stark contrast between the centuries-old ruins and the modern city. As you watch cars, trains, and jumbo jets moving across and over the site (outside the archaeological park), you are reminded of the ephemeral nature of culture and civilization.

Since Adolph F. Bandelier first visited this site in 1883, many archaeologists have probed its secrets. Between 1988 and 1990, to make way for the Hohokam Expressway, archaeologists excavated portions of the town to the north and east of the museum, finding extensive remains from the Classic period (1100–1450 CE). At about the same time, the Pueblo Grande Museum published a synthesis of a century of research at the site, gleaned from archived field notes and unpublished reports.

One wonders, of course, why Pueblo Grande and other Hohokam sites were abandoned. Various reasons have been proposed: one is environmental problems including drought; another, a breakdown of the regional system; and a third, canal destruction from floods. The Akimel O'odham (Pima Indians), who live nearby, have oral traditions relating to Pueblo Grande. One story says that long ago the *Sivanyi* (Hohokam) offended their hero, Elder Brother, and even tried to kill him. In retaliation, Akimel and Tohono O'odham people made war upon the Sivanyi and destroyed their villages. Perhaps archaeological findings will someday be able to substantiate the legend.

Archaeologist Doug Mitchell excavating ceramic dog figurines at Pueblo Grande.

While in Phoenix, you will find the Heard Museum worth a visit, as well as Mesa Grande and Sears Kay Ruin (p. 54).

Suggested Reading: *Desert Farmers at the River's Edge: The Hohokam and Pueblo Grande,* by John P. Andrews and Todd W. Bostwick, City of Phoenix, Arizona, 1997.

SITES IN MESA, ARIZONA

Mesa Grande Cultural Park

Mesa Grande, located at 10th and North Date Streets, in Mesa, Arizona, is open limited hours from Thursday through Sunday. For current information on the hours, call (480) 644-3075 or go to www.azmnh.org/arch/mesagrande.aspx. Admission fee.

Like Phoenix, Mesa overlies many Hohokam archaeological sites—temple mounds, villages, field houses, irrigation canals, and agricultural plots. To its credit, the city has preserved two important ones within densely populated urban areas.

When you visit the Mesa Grande platform mound, you'll find a visitor center with a fine selection of exhibits and a trail that passes by nine interpretive stations and leads around and over the platform mound. Audio tours are being developed to provide more information.

The mound, which is larger than an American football field and 27 feet high, dates to between around 1100 and 1450. Like the big house at Casa Grande, its builders used local dirt, which has a high content of clay and caliche. The hardness of these materials has helped preserve it from erosion for centuries. Also, like Pueblo Grande (p. 48), this mound had houses on top and a wall around it and it was the focal point of a populous Hohokam farming community. Built atop the basic structure was a second-tier mound from which community leaders could look over the surrounding village and canals. These elite individuals were responsible for managing what archaeologist Jerry Howard estimates were 27,000 acres of irrigated fields. One canal that Mesa Grande supervised was 15 feet deep, 45 feet wide, and 16 to 18 miles long.

Fortunately, with thanks to preservationists, volunteers, the Arizona Museum of Natural History, the Salt River Pima-Maricopa Indian Community, and the city of Mesa, the huge Mesa Grande platform mound has survived the forces of urban growth and been developed into an interesting and educational archaeological park.

In 1927, to preserve it, archaeologist Frank J. Midvale purchased Mesa Grande from Ann Madora Barker, who had acquired it with her husband a decade earlier. Midvale had previously conducted excavations at La Ciudad, another platform mound in Mesa that was later destroyed by urban development. Still another person instrumental in the mound's preservation was Acquanetta Ross, an actress of Native American heritage whom publicists dubbed the Venezuelan Volcano. (She starred in *Tarzan and the Leopard Woman* with Johnny Weissmuller.) Her efforts and support helped the city acquire the site in the 1980s.

It is no coincidence that people resettle places where people lived before; we are drawn to areas where resources such as water, fertile soil, and food resources are available. And we all are fascinated when archaeologists find the layers of one culture or civilization resting on top of a previous one, and sometimes a third below that. Like Phoenix, the city of Mesa overlies Hohokam sites.

Park of the Canals

Park of the Canals is at 1710 N. Horne Street, between East McKellips and East Brown Roads. www.mesaaz.gov/parksrec/parks/ParkofCanals.aspx.

The Hohokam were masters of irrigation agriculture who dug extensive canal systems that splayed out from rivers such as the Salt and Gila. They built their settlements and tilled their fields along the canals, raising corn, beans, squash, and cotton.

Canal building began between 600 and 700 CE and reached its greatest extent between 1100 and 1450 when as many as 500 miles of canals existed in the Salt River Valley alone. Jerry Howard, who has researched the Salt River canal networks, estimates the Hohokam may have supported enough agriculture to sustain a population of between 50,000 and 80,000 people. It is interesting to note that in the nineteenth and twentieth centuries, some of the ancient canals were restored and modified for reuse by Euro-American farmers.

Typically, primary Hohokam canals were wide at the river intake to allow a large volume of water to enter the irrigation system. As the system extended and water was diverted into fields, the canals narrowed to maintain constant speed flow of water. It was also diverted into ditches, the smallest probably being no more than the width of a shovel. They were designed to have a 1- to 2-foot drop in elevation per mile. Today, due to the Roosevelt Reservoir upstream, the Salt River is bone dry most of the time. But before the dam was built, its flow fluctuated, sometimes dramatically. Even so, the Hohokam were able to control the amount of water diverted into the canals. To accomplish such a water-delivery network, they acquired sophisticated engineering knowledge and developed effective social management skills.

In this park, you'll see canals from three time periods. From the parking area, a footbridge leads over a Hohokam canal, which was rehabilitated in the 1870s by Mormon pioneers. Just west of the botanical garden, you will find a historic canal constructed in 1891 by Dr. Chandler to bring water to his new community, which now bears his name. Still another is modern and remains operational. When you see the ancient canals, remember that the Indians excavated them with only wooden digging sticks (used like crowbars) and stone hoes. They carried off the dirt in baskets and dumped it along the border to form a berm.

While you are in Mesa, don't miss the Arizona Museum of Natural History. To see another similar platform mound, a visit to Pueblo Grande is worthwhile.

Suggested Reading: www.azmnh.org/arch/treasure.aspx. *Hohokam Legacy: Desert Canals*, by Jerry B. Howard, Pueblo Grande Museum Profiles No. 12. Go to: www .waterhistory.org/histories/hohokam2/.

SOUTH MOUNTAIN PARK ROCK ART

South Mountain Park is in Phoenix, Arizona. The main park entrance is at 10919 South Central Avenue. The Pima Canyon entrance is at 9904 South 48th Street. Information: (602) 262-7393; phoenix.gov/parks/trails/locations/south/. For hiking information, click on "View hiking maps and trail descriptions."

————————

Phoenicians love South Mountain Park. This 17,000-acre municipal park is a fine place to escape the traffic and noise of the city, relax, picnic, and explore some 50 miles of hiking and horseback trails, some of which originated long ago. The South Mountains are an area where people spent time for many centuries before Phoenix came into being, and today, we can find evidence of their presence in a multitude of petroglyph panels containing thousands of images.

Sun symbol petroglyph in South Mountain Park.

The first Native Americans to live in the Phoenix Basin were Western Archaic hunter-gatherers who left their markings, though only a few, on South Mountain rocks. Their petroglyphs, like Archaic-period rock art in other parts of the Southwest, often are abstract and geometric designs (meandering lines, clusters of circles, rakes) but sometimes include depictions of atlatls, or spear-throwers. Some rock art in the park, on the other hand, was created much later by Indians such as the Akimel and Tohono O'odham, whom Spanish explorers met in the late 1600s and whose descendants still live in southern Arizona. The style of their petroglyphs is markedly different and even includes depictions of European-looking heads.

By far the greatest quantity of the rock art in the park, according to archaeologist Todd W. Bostwick, author of the book cited below, is Hohokam and it can be found extensively throughout this mountain range. The Hohokam, most archaeologists today think, descended from previous peoples living in the region—foragers and hunters who eventually adopted agriculture. Certain aspects of Hohokam culture—architecture, ball courts, and religion, for example—probably came into Arizona from peoples in West Mexico. Some Hohokam rock art iconography, such as pipettes, also probably is of Mesoamerican origin, but much likely derives from the Western Archaic tradition.

The Hohokam depicted a range of life forms including, most frequently, animals, human-like figures, and abstract or geometric designs, especially circles. There are also insects, birds, reptiles, and even celestial designs. In the 1990s, Bostwick and photographer Peter Krocek, after thoroughly surveying the park, identified fifty-three especially rich localities. For readers interested in seeing South Mountain rock art, seven places with especially high concentrations are Box Canyon, 32nd Street, Hieroglyphic Canyon, 36th Street, 28th Place, 48th Street, and Upper Pima Canyon. Bostwick and Krocek noticed that on some panels glyphs had been added over a long period of time, as shown by differences in patina and figures superimposed over other figures. Pottery they found also suggested that Hohokam petroglyph making took place over many centuries.

Phoenix has a wealth of Hohokam sites but most are buried beneath buildings and streets. One important and easily accessible site you can go to is Pueblo Grande (p. 48). You can also learn much about Arizona's Native American cultures at the Heard Museum.

Suggested Reading: *Landscape of the Spirits*, by Todd W. Bostwick and Peter Krocek, University of Arizona Press, Tucson, 2002.

SEARS KAY RUIN

Sears Kay Ruin is in Carefree, Arizona, north of Phoenix. In Carefree, follow Cave Creek Road east and after you pass Bartlett Dam Road, continue 2.5 miles farther to the parking area and trailhead. Note that upon entering Tonto National Forest, Cave Creek Road becomes Seven Springs Road (Forest Road 24).

Sears Kay Ruin, a fortified settlement in the foothills north of Phoenix, is an impressive Hohokam site on a hilltop. From the parking lot, a rough mile-long loop trail takes you up a ridge to a commanding view over the surrounding landscape. Far below, you can see a ranch located along a spring-fed wash, a source of water. As at so many settlements in the Southwest, you may wonder why build here, and perhaps you think defense. Sears Kay, in fact, is one of a string of foothill villages situated in defensible locations with strong protective stone-masonry walls. What was going on to motivate such construction? Certainly, conflict and competition must have been important factors; at present, however, since excavations have not been conducted at Sears Kay, archaeologists can only theorize about who was fighting whom and why.

This Hohokam settlement, or fort, which thrived between about 1070 and 1200 CE, is organized as a series of five separate residential compounds containing a total of forty rooms. A trail with informative signs leads through the site and its courtyards, which originally had ramadas to provide shade. The largest plaza area was built up and reinforced by a stone-masonry retaining wall. As you follow the path, note the impressive size of the building stones. According to archaeologist Scott Wood of Tonto National Forest, some of the largest ones were brought to the site from an area about three miles away while others, used to outline doorways, came from even farther. Fifteen-foot timbers were required to span some rooms and these, too, were transported from distant locations. How the Hohokam did this and the human labor required boggles the mind.

A portion of the Sears Kay site.

The inhabitants of Sears Kay raised corn, squash, and beans in fields below the ridge as well as agave on the slopes. They also harvested food and fiber from native wild plants such as saguaro, cholla, prickly pear, and mesquite, and hunted deer, bighorn sheep, and rabbits.

Euro-Americans first discovered the Sears Kay Ruin in 1867 when nearby Camp McDowell was active and patrols were being sent out. It is named for J. M. Sears, whose Sears-Kay Ranch also was in the vicinity. Although the village has not been scientifically excavated, many walls have been stabilized; that is, building stones were restacked to help visitors better appreciate the architectural layout.

Other archaeological sites around Phoenix include Pueblo Grande (p. 48), Mesa Grande (p. 50), and Hieroglyphic Canyon. Visits to the Heard Museum and the Musical Instruments Museum also are recommended.

HIEROGLYPHIC CANYON

Hieroglyphic Canyon is just east of Apache Junction, Arizona. On US 60, between mileposts 202 and 203, turn onto King's Ranch Road. After 2.7 miles, turn right on Baseline Road. Go 0.3 miles and turn left on Mohican Road. After 0.3 miles, turn left on Valley View Road, which becomes Whitetail Road. When you come to Cloudview Avenue, turn right and proceed 0.5 miles to a parking area. The trail is signed as the Lost Goldmine Trail, but after about five minutes, Hieroglyphic Trail branches off to the left.

———————

The trail gradually angles up the lower slopes of the Superstition Mountains until, after about an hour of leisurely to moderate walking, you will come to the petroglyphs. They are contained in a series of panels above two spring-fed pools (if they have water) in Hieroglyphic Canyon. This is a very pleasant walk but should be done, in the summer months, early or late in the day to avoid intense heat. As you can easily spend an hour relaxing by the pools and absorbing the rock art, you should allow about three hours for the excursion. Don't forget to bring water with you.

About a third of the way along the trail, you will pass through a gate and enter Tonto National Forest land. Farther along, when you pass a large boulder on the left with seven deep man-made holes, you'll know that you are nearing the rock art site. Anthropologist Polly Schaafsma has written that pits similar to these, though usually more shallow, are commonly found in association with Hohokam rock art sites and one can only speculate as to their function. A likely possibility is that they were mortars used to pound seeds; however, grinding paint pigments in them also has been suggested. Still another suggestion is that they were filled with sand to hold prayer sticks: the pools and petroglyphs must have been a very sacred place to the Hohokam. When you hike back along the trail, you'll enjoy wide vistas of the Phoenix Basin and distant mountains.

The first panel you will see in the mouth of the canyon includes about a dozen antlered animals, probably deer, which seem to look over one of the pools.

Petroglyphs of animals, Hieroglyphic Canyon.

Another panel further up shows more animals, these resembling antelope. The presence of game-animal pictures suggests that this was a place to hunt. There is a "pipette," an abstract figure with rectangular segments and "eyes." It is commonly depicted in Hohokam rock art and some scholars think it is an abstract representation of the Mesoamerican rain god, Tlaloc. One very striking petroglyph on the cliff above the upper pool shows a tall, slender, vertical figure with stacked rounded segments and antennae on top. The longer you stay here and look around, the more images you will spot.

To see more Hohokam rock art, you may wish to explore some of the hiking trails in Phoenix's South Mountain Park (p. 52).

CASA GRANDE RUINS NATIONAL MONUMENT

The entrance to Casa Grande is 1 mile north of Coolidge on Arizona 87, just off Arizona 287, 58 miles south of Phoenix. Information: (526) 723-3172; www.nps .gov/cagr/index.htm. Entrance fee.

So tall and massive are the remains of Casa Grande that early missionaries and explorers from Spain and the United States could spot the building from far across the surrounding expanse of desert. It is a truly stunning architectural and archaeological monument. When you come here, you'll find, in addition to a visitor center and museum, a short, flat, easy interpretive trail that loops around the ruins. The centerpiece, of course, is the big house, built of earth, but you will also see the remains of roomblocks, an encircling wall, and a cactus garden. Also in the monument are the remains of a ball court next to a compound containing two platform mounds. These sites can be viewed from a nearby platform. Also, ground tours are offered during Arizona's Archaeology Week each spring. A mile to the east, outside the monument, is the Grewe site, another large and archaeologically important Hohokam community whose occupation predates that of Casa Grande. It is closed to the public.

The big house has survived so well because its walls are thick (four feet at the base tapering to two at full height) and made of caliche-adobe. Caliche is a desert soil containing calcium carbonate and adobe is clay-rich soil. When mixed with water to a stiff consistency, laid up in walls, and dried in the sun, this material becomes brick-hard and resistant to the forces of erosion. The two-foot-high construction courses in the walls are plainly visible. The building also had hundreds of pine and fir roof beams that were brought in—hand carried or possibly floated in the Gila River—from distant sources. Smaller wood members were of juniper. Ceiling beams were overlaid with a decking of sticks, such as saguaro cactus ribs, which were covered with grass and reeds. Caliche mud served as a final sealer.

The ancestral people who built this three-story mansion in the early 1300s were farmers who irrigated their fields from the Gila River. The structure is oriented

The big house at Casa Grande Ruins National Monument.

to the cardinal directions. While technically four stories in height, the first story is actually a 5-foot-high base, which serves only to elevate the building. A lord or high priest living here would have commanded a view over residential compounds surrounding the big house, and hundreds of mud and stick huts beyond. The view over the canal system, whose intake was 20 miles up the river, was probably an important factor, as well.

What was the *casa grande*? The literature is replete with theories: a chief's residence, grain warehouse, temple, administrative center, and astronomical observatory. Most scholars think a person of power and status lived here. The presence of numerous wall slots and portholes that align to key events in the annual cycle of the sun and 18.6-year cycle of the moon is intriguing and suggests that the building probably also had a calendrical and/or religious purpose.

The first European to lay eyes on Casa Grande, in 1694, was the Jesuit missionary Eusebio Francisco Kino. Father Kino is renowned for the missions he built in southern Arizona and Sonora, Mexico. The ruin soon became a well-known landmark for explorers, travelers, soldiers, and pioneers. By 1880, travelers on the Southern Pacific Railroad, which had a station only 20 miles away, were making side trips to the site and, predictably, carrying off artifacts and relics.

National interest to protect this desert monument began to crystallize following the 1887–1888 Hemenway Southwestern Expedition. This research team included such anthropological luminaries as Frank H. Cushing, J. Walter Fewkes, Adolph F. Bandelier, and Frederick Webb Hodge. Four years later, Congress set aside 480 acres for the protection of the ruins, and in 1903, a roof was erected over the big house.

Like all Classic-period (1100–1450 CE) Hohokam communities, Casa Grande's population experienced decline later in the 1300s and by the mid-1400s, the place was vacant. Theories abound regarding the end of Hohokam culture. Archaeologists wonder about crop failures due to waterlogged or salt-impregnated soils, or destructive floods that destroyed canal systems, and the O'odham people tell of warfare. Whatever crises befell the society, Casa Grande represents the pinnacle of Hohokam architecture and village planning.

Food and lodging are available in both Florence and Coolidge and there are campgrounds nearby, although not in the monument itself.

Suggested Reading: *Casa Grande Ruins National Monument*, by Rose Houk, Western National Parks Association, Tucson, Arizona, 1996.

GATLIN SITE

The Gatlin site is in Gila Bend, Arizona. To reach it, follow Pima Street east and turn north on Old Highway 80. After a short distance, bear left on Stout Road. The site is 3 miles farther on the left.

Most of the remains of this large Hohokam village are owned by the town of Gila Bend. In 2014, the town was developing a trail, house replicas, and an interpretive program preliminary to opening the site to the public. Until the plan is accomplished, the site can only be visited by special arrangement by calling (928) 683-2255.

The most prominent prehistoric feature at Gatlin is its platform mound, the first one to be excavated in Arizona. It is small in scale compared to some others in the Hohokam region, and one might think, at first glance, that it is a low oval hill rather than a man-made structure. Indeed, before putting shovel to it, William W. Wasley, the Arizona State Museum archaeologist who excavated it in 1958–1959, wondered if the feature was a large trash mound. With excavation, however, it became clear that it was structural and overlooked an extensive surrounding residential complex and agricultural fields along the south side of the Gila River.

Hohokam Indians lived here between around 900 and 1200 CE. The site is half a mile long by a quarter of a mile wide, covering about 300 acres. In addition to the platform mound, there are many house remains, two ball courts, a plaza, trash mounds, a 5-mile-long irrigation canal, and cemeteries. The Hohokam cremated their dead so concentrations of ash mark burial areas. Not all these features can be seen and others are hard to see as you walk along the trail. Some were covered by dirt to protect them, others were plowed under in the past by farmers, and still more were vandalized and looted.

A private citizen tracked down and recorded some of the lost artifacts, including many carved marine shells imported from the Gulf of California and sixty to eighty copper bells acquired through trade with Mexico. The Gila River was a natural corridor for travel, and many trails, both prehistoric and historic, marked this region of Arizona.

Archaeology is a dynamic scientific discipline, which is to say that as knowledge grows and broadens and research methods become more refined, archaeologists' interpretations change. Wasley, in 1960, did not recognize the full extent of the Gatlin site, and based on the presence of the platform mound and ball courts, he thought it was a ceremonial center with very few residents, "a northern extension into the Hohokam area of the pyramid idea found in many of the prehistoric cultures in Mexico" (*American Antiquity* 26). Subsequent researchers, including David E. Doyel, who worked after Wasley, agree that Gatlin was a ceremonial place but recognize it as a regular Hohokam village of its time, where people lived for many generations carrying on all the normal activities of life that characterized their culture.

As this region is arid, Gatlin's inhabitants depended on the Gila River, which, besides water, supplied them with many edible native plants, animals, and fish. They located their village where the river made a wide loop or bend. Today, alas, the Gila is a dry riverbed; upstream dams and irrigation systems long since took away its water with the inevitable outcome that a once fertile riparian habitat disappeared.

The town of Gila Bend hopes the Gatlin site will become an interesting, well-interpreted, educational park drawing visitors to learn about the area's history. When you are in the area, don't miss the petroglyphs at Painted Rock and Sears Point, which are some of the best in the region and easily accessible to the public.

Suggested Reading: "Vacant Ceremonial Centers Revisited," by David E. Doyel, *Kiva* 64, no. 2 (Winter 1998), pp. 225–44, a publication of the Arizona Archaeological and Historical Society.

PAINTED ROCK AND SEARS POINT PETROGLYPH SITES

Painted Rock Petroglyphs

Painted Rock Petroglyph Site, near Gila Bend, Arizona, is about 90 miles southwest of Phoenix. From Gila Bend, drive 12.5 miles west on Interstate 8, exit at Painted Rock Dam Road (exit 102), go 11 miles north, then turn west on Rocky Point Road. The parking area is half a mile farther. Information: (623) 580-5500; www.blm.gov/az/st/en/prog/recreation/camping/dev_camps/painted_rock.html. Admission fee.

This dense concentration of petroglyphs (they're not painted) was made on smooth-surfaced basalt boulders on the side of a hill. From the parking area, a

Hohokam petroglyphs at Painted Rock.

wheelchair-accessible path leads by them. Interpretive information designed by the Bureau of Land Management helps place them in cultural and historical context. To avoid high desert temperatures, it is best to visit this site and Sears Point from October through April.

The boulders are covered by an astounding array of pictures, seemingly randomly placed. Human-like figures are common as are animals (dogs, deer, antelope, lizards, snakes), sun symbols, hands, and abstract designs. The rock art here probably has much time depth. Although patterns such as grids, rakes, ladders, and clusters of circles were commonly made by Western Archaic foragers, these are mostly Hohokam, in the Gila Petroglyph Style, and include wavy lines, meanders, spirals, and mazes. In addition, a few figures mounted on horseback show that glyph making was going on after the arrival of Spaniards in the region. Early Spanish travelers called this place *Piedras Pintadas*; it has been reported that some pecked images were also painted but there is no evidence of that now.

Why did Native Americans choose this place to make petroglyphs? The outcropping of basalt rocks is a singular landmark in the flat desert terrain and is situated along one or more trade routes that were well traveled in both ancient and historic times, some even evolving into modern highways. It is probably safe to surmise that Indians attached stories and myths to this hill, and it may have been a shrine where people from the region came for periodic gatherings.

So much time has passed since these petroglyphs were made that it is difficult now to decipher or reconstruct their meaning. This site is at the western edge of the Hohokam and eastern edge of the Patayan (ancestral Yuman) regions and some markings are Patayan. Finally, ancestors of the Akimel and Tohono O'odham Indians, who still live in southern Arizona, were responsible for some of the petroglyphs on the hill. These peoples either followed or directly descended from the Hohokam.

In 1980, University of Arizona students recorded 758 glyphs, most of which were on the southern and eastern sides of the outcrop even though suitable boulders existed on all sides. In years past, thieves carried off numerous boulders but, thankfully, that activity has not been occurring recently. The site, which is administered by the Bureau of Land Management, has picnicking and camping areas and vault toilets but no potable water. A ramada is provided for group activities.

Sears Point Petroglyphs

Near Painted Rocks is Sears Point, which also has extensive petroglyphs. To reach it, continue west on Interstate 8 for about 24 miles (75 miles east from Yuma) and exit at Spot Road. Go 1 mile east on the frontage road, turn north on Avenue 76 1/2 E, and continue for 7 miles to the site and parking area. Since this rough unpaved road becomes muddy in wet weather, a high-clearance vehicle may be needed. The site is remote, there are no facilities, and you should be careful not to disturb honeybee hives. Information: (928) 317-3200; www.blm.gov/az/st/en/prog/cultural/sears/petro.html.

Patayan petroglyphs at Sears Point. Photo by and courtesy of Henry D. Wallace.

A visit to the Sears Point petroglyphs is for the more adventurous. Although there are excellent examples of rock art near the parking area, many more can be found by exploring unimproved trails along nearby basalt cliffs. The varied imagery that can be observed here reflects the long period of time during which the glyphs were made by several ancient cultural groups.

Like Painted Rock and the Gatlin site, Sears Point is near the now-dry Gila River and along both prehistoric and historic travel routes. Today, due to dams and water diversion, the Gila River no longer exists and its riparian environment has vanished. Before the river died, however, it supported a variety of plants, animals, birds, and fish, as well as humans, and played a vital role supporting life in an otherwise harsh desert. When the Gila was alive, travelers crossed it here on their way to Agua Caliente hot springs. Anthropologist and rock art scholar Henry D. Wallace thinks that it was likely an important waypoint in pre-Hispanic times, as well.

Sears Point is on the eastern edge of the Patayan cultural region, the western edge of lands once occupied by the Hohokam, and in an area previously used by nomadic foragers and hunters. The petroglyphs reflect all three cultural groups, as well as some later markings from post-European contact times. Between 2008 and 2012, Rupestrian CyberServices and Plateau Mountain Desert Research documented more than 2,000 petroglyph panels here, including nearly 10,000 individual glyphs, and recorded 87 archaeological features and 19 miles of ancient trails and trail segments. They also found several geoglyphs (large man-made designs on the ground), one resembling a serpent and another interpreted as a possible racetrack. In their report, which is published online, they write that Sears Point was a "major gathering place and hunting area, where surrounding people came together to collect food resources, hunt, and participate in ceremonies."

While in this area, you may wish to visit the nearby Gatlin site (p. 59) and Casa Grande Ruins National Monument (p. 57) in Coolidge. Gila Bend has plenty of travel services.

Suggested Reading: *Sears Point Rock Art Recording Project Arizona, USA*, by Evelyn Billo, Robert Mark, and Donald E. Weaver Jr. This online report can be read at: www.rupestrian.com/Sears_Point_IFRAO2013.pdf. "Hohokam, Patayan, or ?: Rock Art at Two Sites Near Gila Bend, Arizona," by Richard J. Martynec, in *Rock Art Papers*, vol. 6, edited by Ken Hodges, San Diego Museum Papers No. 24, San Diego, California, 1989.

ROMERO RUIN

The Romero Ruin is in Catalina State Park along Hwy. 77 (Oracle Road), 10 miles north of Tucson, Arizona. The park's entrance is at milepost marker 81. Information: (520) 628-5798. Entrance fee.

————————

Given the thousands of Hohokam archaeological sites in southern Arizona, relatively few are open to the public; and so we're grateful that several agencies and organizations collaborated to make the Romero site available and built an interpretive trail. Like most Hohokam ruins—Casa Grande being an exception—the features of this one are subtle.

There are many sites in the foothills and along the drainages of the Santa Catalina Mountains—Archaic-period camps, Hohokam house remains, and petroglyphs. The Romero Ruin, which covers 15 acres along a ridge between two stream beds, is the largest. Along the trail, you will see some remnants of the village, which was founded around 500 CE. Its population reached a peak around three hundred people between 850 and 1000, then went into decline until the last families moved away about 1450. This long period of continuous occupation was made possible by the availability of water in Sutherland Wash, below the site, and an abundance of food resources ranging from native plants to animals and birds, such as deer, rabbits, rodents, and quail.

Between 1987 and 1993, archaeologists from the Center for Desert Archaeology (now Archaeology Southwest) spent three field seasons surveying, mapping, and conducting excavations at this site. They collected 11,500 artifacts from the surface of the ground. They also dug two test pits in the site's seventeen trash mounds, finding stone and ceramic artifacts and the remains of food that people consumed. The latter included corn, squash, mesquite pods, agave, and paloverde

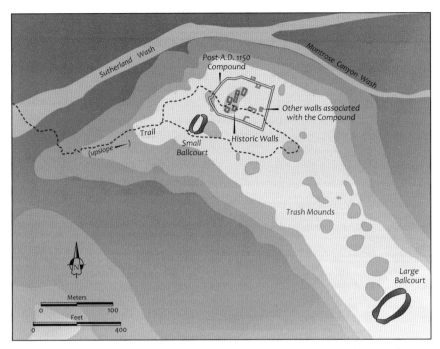

Map of the Romero site showing archaeological features. Map by Catherine Gilman, courtesy of Archaeology Southwest.

seeds; bones of jackrabbits and other animals; and bracelets made of glycymeris shells from the Gulf of California, hundreds of miles away.

The Romero villagers built two ball courts—they now appear as shallow depressions—that served as places to hold ceremonial games. Neither has been excavated. Around 1150, in the middle of their village, the residents built a high rock wall whose function is uncertain. They also developed extensive farming fields extending for about a mile from the southern edge of the ridge toward the mountains. In this area, archaeologists have found the remains of cobble-masonry field houses, rock piles, and terraces.

In 1949, a hunter hiking through the foothills four miles from the Romero Ruin made a remarkable discovery. When his foot sank into a soft spot on the ground, he investigated and found a ceramic jar filled with some 100,000 stone and shell beads plus thirty copper bells. There were many petroglyphs nearby. It was a spectacular find, but what the trove represents is a mystery.

A ¾-mile loop trail with interpretive signs leads through the Romero Ruin. In addition to the prehistoric remains, you will see the remains of a historic ranch house that belonged to Francisco and Victoriana Romero in the late 1800s. They built their residence and outbuildings on top of the Hohokam site, probably recycling some of the building stones.

It seems inevitable that myths and legends develop around historic sites like this one. Some people speculated that the Romero ranch compound was the long lost Spanish Mission of Ciru, and yes, they wondered if it contained buried treasure. Efforts to find it, of course, proved fruitless.

Catalina State Park is near Tucson, where you will find a visit to the Arizona State Museum on the University of Arizona campus most rewarding. It has permanent and changing exhibits about the Indian cultures, ancient and living, of southern Arizona.

Suggested Reading: *In the Mountain Shadows*, by William H. Doelle and Deborah L. Swartz, Archaeology Southwest, Tucson, 2013. This is volume 27, number 1 of *Archaeology Southwest* magazine.

The Salado

⊃|⊂

A center of Salado culture was the Tonto Basin in southeastern Arizona near
the present-day towns of Globe and Miami. The Salado region also extended
southward along the upper San Pedro River and eastward along the Gila River
into southwestern New Mexico. The Tonto Basin is a high-desert region through
which flows the Rio Salado, or the Salt River, the largest tributary of the Gila
River. The Salt was dammed in 1911 to form Roosevelt Reservoir, which provides
year-round water to the ever growing Phoenix metropolitan area as well as to
extensive agricultural lands. To the detriment of archaeological research, the lake
inundated many Salado sites. However, a decision to raise the reservoir's pool
level resulted in much archaeology being done in the 1990s.

For a long time, archaeologists have discussed and debated the origins and
even the identity of the Salado, some even questioning whether this culture existed, distinct and separate from that of neighboring peoples. Debates also have
arisen over whether the Salado people were indigenous to the Tonto Basin or immigrants from other regions. Were they Hohokam expanding eastward or locals
emulating their Hohokam neighbors? And later on, did ancestral Kayenta Pueblo
people immigrate here? Artifacts uncovered in archaeological sites around Roosevelt Lake have been variously interpreted. Of course, these are not necessarily
either/or questions and some researchers think that after around 1300, immigration accounted for about 25 percent of the basin's large population. Two points
to remember is that in the late thirteenth century, much of the Southwest was
experiencing severe drought and people were on the move and resettling in new
territories with more water. In that regard, the Tonto Basin would have been a
draw bringing together diverse groups into what one researcher has called "co-
alescent communities."

A Salado polychrome bowl. Courtesy of Robert A. Ellison Jr.

The Salado time period, using Salado polychrome pottery as the cultural marker, began in the 1100s and ended in the mid-1400s. The best known type is Gila polychrome, which was produced between around 1275 and 1425. This beautiful form of pottery is noted for its black-and-white designs on a red base.

The Salado raised corn, beans, squash, amaranth, and cotton and built platform mounds and pueblos and cliff dwellings that resembled those of the Puebloans to the north. They wove baskets, beautiful cotton textiles, and sandals of yucca fiber. Although archaeologists have debated their identity, the Salado certainly knew who they were and what to call themselves.

It was the legendary explorer-anthropologist Adolph F. Bandelier, for whom a national monument is named (p. 205), who first noted Salado sites around Globe in 1883. Some forty years later, Eric Schmidt from the American Museum of Natural History and Harold and Winifred Gladwin conducted research in the area. The Gladwins also established a research center in Globe known as Gila Pueblo. In the 1990s, the Roosevelt Lake Project gave archaeologists more opportunities to conduct excavations in the Tonto Basin. More recently, a great deal of Salado research has been done by Archaeology Southwest, an organization based in Tucson.

Suggested Reading: "The 1976 Salado Conference," edited by David E. Doyel and Emil W. Haury, *The Kiva* 42, no. 1, Arizona Archaeological and Historical Society,

Tucson, Arizona, 1976. "A Complicated Pattern: Pursuing the Meaning of Salado in Southwestern New Mexico," *Archaeology Southwest* 26, nos. 3/4, Archaeology Southwest, Tucson, Arizona, 2012.

SHOOFLY VILLAGE

Shoofly Village is 5 miles north of Payson, Arizona, in the Tonto National Forest. From the junction of Arizona 260 and 87, follow 87 north to Houston Mesa Road and turn east. The entrance to the site and parking area is about 3 miles farther, past the Mesa del Caballo subdivision, on the right.

Even today, from whatever direction you approach Payson, you will find yourself passing through vast forested regions of sparsely inhabited central Arizona. These pueblo remains lie in the shadow of a major topographical feature—the Mogollon Rim, a 200-mile east–west escarpment that separates the Colorado Plateau from lower elevations to the south.

When you visit Shoofly Village, you will follow a quarter-mile trail through the ruins along which the Forest Service has placed informative signs describing the site's architectural features and other relevant subjects. When you reach the north side of the site, a beautiful view of the Mogollon Rim and intervening landscape awaits you. Plan at least half an hour to explore this site.

A room in Shoofly Village.

Beginning with Archaic-period hunters and foragers, people have traveled through or lived in the Payson Valley for a very long time. Shoofly Village is one of several large sites in the Payson Valley that were established when, around 1000 CE, population was on the rise and people living in the region's many homesteads and hamlets found it to their advantage to form larger villages. As time passed, the settlement slowly expanded to cover some four acres and include three distinct residential centers containing eighty-seven rooms. These walled compounds seem to represent sequential time periods when the population grew. At its peak, Shoofly housed an estimated 250 people who constructed a massive stone wall that surrounds the site; its remains are still visible today.

They made their living by farming and hunting, as well as gathering native plant foods. Houston Mesa, on which Shoofly is situated, had many resources: water, wood for construction and fuel, and stone for building and tool making, not to mention strategically advantageous views. In the late 1200s, when Shoofly's population was at its greatest, everyone left. In fact, between 1275 and 1300, during what archaeologists call the Great Drought in the Southwest, the entire Payson area was abandoned. Many of those people appear to have moved south into the Tonto Basin where the rivers were still flowing.

Shoofly Village has some characteristics that have intrigued researchers. One is the variety of architectural styles they found during their excavations. Earlier masonry rooms, for example, are oval in shape while those built later are rectangular. There is free-standing adobe construction and there are jacal rooms; these had thatched walls plastered with mud. What does this variety signify? One interpretation is that groups of people moved into Shoofly at different times from other regions, where they were used to different building traditions. Another is that the village's social organization rapidly evolved and, as the interpretive brochure states, "the range of architectural types . . . mirrors these changes."

There is another interesting question: who were these people? Archaeologists like to put ancient peoples into cultural categories: Puebloan, Hohokam, Fremont, and so forth. If those who lived in Shoofly Village need a designation, it might be "Northern Salado." However, their village was situated between the Northern Sinagua to the north, the Mogollon to the east, the Southern Sinagua to the west, and the Salado and Hohokam to the south. It is reasonable to think that this geographically central position allowed them to benefit from all the customs and products of their neighbors, as well as opportunities to intermarry. Probably, they represent a cultural mix and this contributed to the variety of architectural styles found in their village.

From Shoofly Village, it is an easy drive to Cline Terrace Platform Mound (p. 71) and Tonto National Monument (p. 73). You will find gas, food, and lodging in Payson.

Suggested Reading: *People of the Tonto Rim: Archaeological Discovery in Prehistoric Arizona*, by Charles L. Redman, Smithsonian Institution Press, Washington, D.C., 1993.

CLINE TERRACE PLATFORM MOUND

Cline Terrace Platform Mound, in the Tonto Basin, is between Punkin Center and Roosevelt, Arizona, east of Highway 188. A few miles south of Punkin Center, turn east on A+ Road (A-Cross Road), cross Tonto Creek, and bear right at the Y. After crossing three cattle guards, look to the right for a brush-covered platform mound on the flat river terrace. An unpaved road leads to it off the main road. There is a parking area and interpretive sign. (Do not drive around on other informal roads and jeep trails.) Information: (602) 225-5200; www.fs.usda.gov/tonto/.

———————————

If you have visited the platform mounds at Pueblo Grande (p. 48), near the Phoenix airport, and Mesa Grande, in downtown Mesa (p. 50), you'll experience something quite different at the seldom-visited Cline Terrace. This Salado mound is in the countryside, covered with grasses and bushes, and overlooking Tonto Creek at the north end of Roosevelt Reservoir. The drive to it from Highway 188 takes about ten minutes and you'll want about forty-five minutes to walk around the site.

Although it looks pristine, this platform mound was almost completely excavated by archaeologists from Arizona State University between 1991 and 1993 as part of the extensive Roosevelt Platform Mound Study. Plans to raise the maximum pool level of the reservoir necessitated the study. Of the dozen mounds in the Basin, four are usually underwater. At the time of this writing, however, with an ongoing dry spell in the region, the lake was not even in sight. More than a

Cline Terrace platform mound.

century before, the intrepid anthropological explorer Adolph F. Bandelier surveyed and mapped Cline Terrace. Today, it is managed and protected by Tonto National Forest.

The platform mound consists of a broad first-level terrace, which is surrounded by a boxed-rampart compound wall, a rare feature in Southwestern architectural engineering. According to Tonto National Forest archaeologist Scott Wood, it is made of interior and exterior stone walls, five feet apart, with the space between them filled with compacted dirt and stones. The outside wall reached high enough to serve as a defensive palisade, and the rampart between the walls was paved with slabs of gypsum. Open areas on the first terrace served mainly as public spaces where communal functions took place that probably involved residents from all the smaller settlements that made up the surrounding Cline Terrace community. The two upper terraces held houses where residents slept, prepared and cooked food, and did craft work, such as making pottery, stone tools, and shell ornaments including bracelets, rings, tinklers, and beads. Some shells (glycymeris, conus, olivella) were imported from the Gulf of California.

ASU archaeologist David Jacobs concluded that construction of the terraced mound began about 1320 and the site's principal function was as a residential settlement for between eighty and a hundred people. In the late 1300s, the mound was expanded to more than twice its previous size. The builders made some of the new walls of fine gypsum slabs instead of rounded river cobbles set in mud. This huge construction effort would have required the participation of many workers beyond those living at the site. The mound then became a public gathering place and served an important social, ceremonial, and integrative function for the larger community.

Scott Wood thinks that Cline Terrace and other platform mounds housed a leadership class whose role was civil administration and the adjudication of the irrigation system, which brought water to agricultural fields. They may also

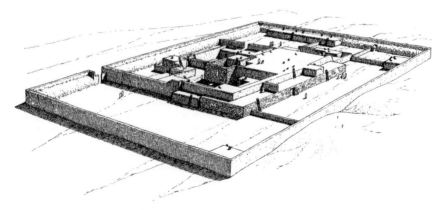

Artist's reconstruction of Cline Terrace in the late fourteenth century. Courtesy of Arizona State University.

have served as central markets. About 1400, fire destroyed all the houses on the mound, an event that occurred at the time everyone left, or shortly thereafter.

Cline Terrace's inhabitants were farmers who raised corn, squash, beans, cotton, agave, and a little barley. They also collected a wide variety of native foods from cacti and other plants and hunted deer, pronghorn, and small game. They produced an abundance of plain ceramics for utilitarian use and beautifully decorated Salado polychrome vessels for storage and other purposes. Only a short drive south of Cline Terrace are the cliff dwellings of Tonto National Monument, and further south, in Globe, is the reconstructed pueblo known as Besh Ba Gowah (p. 75).

Suggested Reading: *A Salado Platform Mound on Tonto Creek: Report on the Cline Terrace Mound, Cline Terrace Complex*, by David Jacobs, Arizona State University, Office of Cultural Resource Management, Department of Anthropology, Tempe, 1997.

TONTO NATIONAL MONUMENT

Tonto National Monument is in Roosevelt, Arizona. From Phoenix, take Arizona 60 (Superstition Freeway) east to Globe/Miami (75 miles); turn left on Arizona 188 and continue 25 miles to the monument. The drive takes about two hours. An alternate slower route is on the Apache Trail (Arizona 188). Information: (928) 467-2241; www.nps.gov/tont/index.htm. Entrance fee.

―――――――――

Although Roosevelt Lake now dominates the landscape, seven centuries ago the Salado Indians living in what is now Tonto National Monument enjoyed a breathtaking view over the Salt River as it meandered through the Tonto Basin. When you visit this monument, you can hike to the Lower and Upper ruins and a site called the Annex. To reach the Lower Ruin and the Annex, you walk uphill half a mile to a twenty-room cliff dwelling. Plan about an hour to do this and see the cliff dwelling, which also can be viewed at a distance from the visitor center. To see the larger Upper Ruin, you'll join a three-hour tour led by a ranger for which advance reservations are recommended.

The Tonto Basin's first permanent settlers built pithouse villages and grew crops in the floodplain long before any cliff dwellings appeared. The architecture and pottery found at their sites show they had close ties with the Hohokam of the lower Salt River Valley. Some researchers think they may indeed have been Hohokam who moved up. Artifacts found from a later time period show these folk were developing their own Tonto Basin, or *Salado*, identity. Their key cultural marker is Salado polychrome pottery. In the Hohokam tradition (p. 45), they built platform mounds, though not ball courts. Archaeologists are not in agreement whether, in the late thirteenth century, visible changes in the archaeological record reflect purely local developments, the arrival of immigrants from the north, or a combination.

The occupants of Lower and Upper Ruins enjoyed a comfortable climate and a long growing season during which they cultivated corn, pumpkins, squash, gourds, several varieties of beans, cotton, and grain amaranth. Between the basin and the hills, they also harvested a wide variety of native plants, including cactus fruit, pinyon nuts and acorns, mesquite beans, wild grapes, and various seeds. Still other plants provided medicinal herbs, fiber for clothing, and wood for building houses. Little wonder that recovered skeletal remains show the Salado to have been a strong, healthy people.

In the late 1200s, many basin dwellers moved to higher elevations where they built fortified cliff dwellings such as those in this monument. One wonders what pressures motivated them to live so far from their croplands. Dry caves—the Lower Ruin cave is 48 feet deep—provide excellent shelter and archaeological preservation (if the artifacts aren't pilfered). Ethnobotanist Vorsila Bohrer was impressed by the excellent condition of plant remains excavated in the Lower and Upper Ruins. "Dried beans," she wrote, "look like ones that might have come in a cellophane package on the grocery shelf" (*Archaeological Studies at Tonto National Monument*, 1957).

The caves also contained fine examples of cotton textiles, yucca, and hair, as well as some plaited yucca sandals, baskets, matting, and cordage. In addition, archaeologists found a 30-inch bow of netleaf hackberry (a tough bending wood), arrows, clubs, and such household items as fire-making equipment, fiber pot rests, brushes, torches, stirring sticks, tattoo needles, gums and adhesives, and spinning and weaving implements. Ceremonial items included prayer sticks, charms, paint daubers, reed cigarettes, dice, and a bow. The recovery of so many intact artifacts has helped reconstruct their owners' way of life.

In 1907, due to ongoing vandalism, President Theodore Roosevelt created Tonto National Monument and placed it under the protection of the National Forest Service. Archaeological research began after 1933 when the National Park Service took over responsibility for the sites.

Food and lodging are available in Roosevelt and Globe and there are camping places nearby. An additional attraction is the scenic drive on Arizona 88 from Apache Junction to Roosevelt. This tortuous road, which is unpaved in some sections, offers stunning desert and mountain views. Be warned, however, that some sections are closed to vehicles more than 30 feet in length and driving is slow. While here, don't miss Besh Ba Gowah, in Globe.

BESH BA GOWAH ARCHAEOLOGICAL PARK

Besh Ba Gowah is in Globe, Arizona, 87 miles east of Phoenix. From US 60, take the Broad Street exit, turn right on Jesse Hayes Road, and follow signs to the park. Information: (928) 425-0320; toll free (800) 804-5623. Entrance fee.

———————

There are only a few Salado sites that are open to and interpreted for the public so if you are in the Globe-Miami area, a stop to see Besh Ba Gowah certainly is

Lower Ruin in Tonto National Monument.

worthwhile. This region has copper mines, and local Apaches gave it the name Besh Ba Gowah, meaning "place of metal" or "metal camp," which also was given to the ancient Salado village site. It sits on a ridge overlooking Pinal Creek, a tributary of the Salt River, and is surrounded by the Pinal Mountains and the Apache Mountains to the southwest and north, respectively. The presence of water and the variety of plant and animal resources drew many people to this region in pre-Hispanic times.

Besh Ba Gowah was a large village with more than two hundred first- and second-story rooms and a few more above those. Taking into account that modern developments destroyed significant portions of the site, the total room count must have been greater. Archaeologists uncovered the remains of Hohokam dwellings beneath those of the Salado and have dated that earlier occupation to between around 900 and 1100 CE. The Salado began construction of their pueblo in the early 1200s and lived here until the early 1400s. Unlike the Hohokam, whose houses of brush, poles, and mud were short-lasting, the Salado built these structures of unshaped granite cobbles set in thick clay mortar.

The many small lower-story rooms are thought to have been used for storage, whereas the larger upper-story ones, averaging 225 square feet, were residential. There were workrooms, too, and some that were used for ceremonies. Researchers recovered beans and corn, as well as stone hoes and other implements: clues

Besh Ba Gowah Archaeological Park.

that the people were farming along Pinal Creek. They were also fine makers of jewelry and pottery and traded with local communities and as far away as Mexico and the Pacific Coast.

It was the noted archaeologist, historian, and explorer Adolph F. Bandelier who first mapped Besh Ba Gowah while he was waiting in Globe for Apache hostilities to subside. He noted the Salado characteristics of ceramics he found. Irene S. Vickery conducted formal archaeological investigations here in the mid-1930s as a Federal Emergency Relief Administration project. She unearthed more than a hundred rooms and recovered 350 Salado burials. Sadly, she died before being able to publish the results of her work. For many years thereafter, the ruins lay unattended and little appreciated.

In 1948, to accommodate the needs of a national jamboree to be held at Besh Ba Gowah by the Boy Scouts of America, the Army Corps of Engineers bulldozed and leveled a portion of the ruins. The city of Globe subsequently developed this flattened area into a park and leveled more of the site to make room for recreational facilities.

In 1984, with the area's mining economy in decline, the city began redeveloping the site and park complex to draw tourists. To carry out the plan, they engaged the services of professional archaeologists. Under the direction of John H. Hohmann, archaeologists mapped, excavated, stabilized, and partially reconstructed the pueblo. Other additions are a modern museum and an interpretive trail.

The trail leads through a once-covered entrance corridor to the pueblo's central plaza. One notable feature along the trail is a large square subterranean room, with benches along the wall that the inhabitants apparently used for religious ceremonies. It had an altar and a sipapu (a symbolic entrance into the underworld), which was filled with ground turquoise and sealed with a large quartz crystal.

Along the way, you will be able to climb a ladder into rebuilt second-story rooms, an experience offering a sense of what the village originally was like. Besh Ba Gowah's museum contains a reconstructed model of the pueblo, numerous fine examples of Gila polychrome and other types of regional pottery, and an array of prehistoric tools and implements.

The transformation of this site from overgrown looted mounds to an interpreted archaeological park reflects the growing public interest and pride in America's rich aboriginal heritage. Today, this site, which is managed by the city of Globe, is a rewarding place to visit, where you can learn much about the little-known Salado culture. While here, you may wish also to make a side trip to Tonto National Monument (p. 73).

Suggested Reading: "Besh Ba Gowah," by Irene S. Vickery, *The Kiva* 4, no. 5, 1939.

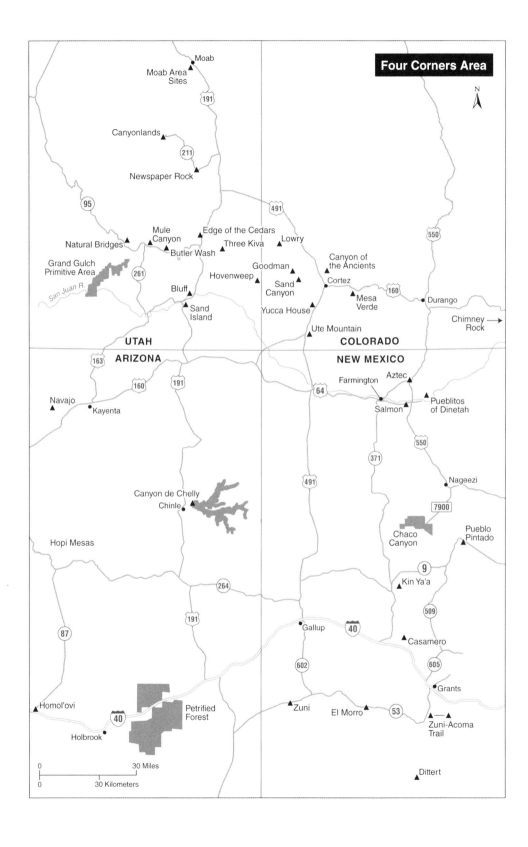

Four Corners Area

N

Moab
Moab Area
Sites
191

Canyonlands
211
Newspaper Rock

95

491
550

Mule
Canyon   Edge of the Cedars
Natural Bridges   Three Kiva   Lowry
Butler Wash
Grand Gulch   Canyon of
Primitive Area   Goodman   the Ancients
261   Hovenweep   Cortez
San Juan R.   Sand   160
Bluff   Canyon   Mesa
Sand   Yucca House   Verde   Durango
Island   Chimney
UTAH   Ute Mountain   Rock →

COLORADO

163
ARIZONA   NEW MEXICO
160   Aztec
191   Farmington
Navajo   64   Pueblitos
Kayenta   Salmon   of Dinetah

550

371
Nageezi

Canyon de Chelly   7900
Chinle   Pueblo
Pintado
Hopi Mesas   Chaco
Canyon
9
264   Kin Ya'a

191   509

87
Gallup   40   Casamero
602   605
Grants
Homol'ovi   40   Petrified
Forest   Zuni   El Morro   53
Holbrook   Zuni-Acoma
Trail
0   30 Miles
0   30 Kilometers   Dittert

The Mesa Verde Region

Archaeologists, like all scientists, organize their data into logical and understandable categories. The data, by their very nature, consist of material objects—potsherds, baskets, buildings—but refer to human beings and their culture. The people, it follows, are categorized by the things they made, especially pottery since it lasts and is abundant at sites. Nonmaterial aspects of culture, such as language, are not (or only minimally) revealed when excavating sites; therefore, the cultural categories created by archaeologists should not be regarded in broad contexts for they are archaeological constructs.

Richard Wetherill, one of the first archaeological investigators (amateur, to be sure) in the Four Corners region, identified a culture he observed on Mesa Verde and other places as the "Cliff Dwellers." After more than a century of experience and accumulated information, we now know these folks also lived in farmsteads, hamlets, and pueblos on the open mesas and plains.

Archaeologists today recognize commonalities of material culture and settlement patterns among ancestral Pueblo people living across a wide area in what is now referred to as the "Mesa Verde" or "Northern San Juan" region. Covering some 10,000 square miles on the Colorado Plateau, it is bordered by the Colorado River in the west, the Piedra River in the east, and the San Juan River in the south. A wavy line drawn from north of Monticello, Utah, to Durango, Colorado, would indicate the northern edge. (The map here shows only the central part of the region.) The dotted lines on maps that indicate prehistoric cultural subdivisions do not signify "territories" or "borders"; nor do they suggest that everyone living within belonged to a certain "tribe." Within these archaeologically defined regions, considerable diversity existed and very likely different languages were spoken.

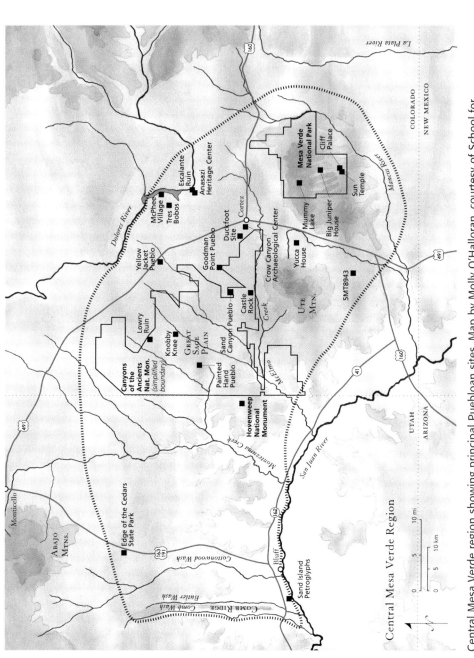

Central Mesa Verde region showing principal Puebloan sites. Map by Molly O'Halloran, courtesy of School for Advanced Research.

Pueblo people, of course, have their own words for their ancestors in their various languages. The Hopi, for example, refer to Southwestern hunter-gatherers as *Motisinom* and later agricultural people as *Hisat'sinom*. English-language terms for Native American groups, past and present, sometimes change in consideration of Native American sensitivities; for example, "Anasazi," which comes from a Navajo word signifying something like "enemy ancestors," has been largely dropped in favor of ancestral Pueblo or Ancestral Puebloan.

The Mesa Verde region is famous for its large stone-built villages and visually stunning cliff dwellings, which generally date to the thirteenth century. Mesa Verde National Park (p. 82), a World Heritage Site visited by thousands of people every year, is considered the jewel among these sites, but the Montezuma Valley and Great Sage Plain to the north and west contain the remains of many impressive open-site pueblos. For a century prior to being vacated, this central area, which was blessed by favorable climatic conditions and fertile soil, was densely populated. The western and eastern areas, however, due to poorer farming conditions and mountains, supported fewer inhabitants.

The region's deep history saw the presence of nomadic hunter-gatherers. They were followed by Basketmakers, who lived in rock shelters and pithouse settlements and began practicing horticulture. After the turn of the millennium, the bow and arrow replaced the atlatl as the weapon of choice, people depended increasingly on the cultivation of corn, and there was a transition to a more sedentary way of life. Agriculture became the economic base and society grew more complex. Although agriculture was the economic base, people continued to forage and hunt; however, at least in good farming years, these activities were secondary.

Between around 1075 and 1125, large masonry buildings—Chacoan great houses—were constructed in some forty Mesa Verdean communities, usually on a high place overlooking, and seeming to dominate, the surrounding community. Lowry (p. 91), Escalante (p. 89), and Bluff (p. 110) great houses are examples. Some scholars think that people from Chaco Canyon came up into this northern San Juan country to exert their influence; others believe that local headmen built them to express their status by emulating the monumental buildings in Chaco Canyon.

As a general pattern, though it fluctuated along the way, population was on a rising track in the central Mesa Verde region until the 1270s. Beginning in 1275, however, an extended period of drought caused malnutrition, sickness, starvation, declining birth rate, social turmoil, and inter-Puebloan conflict. After the mid-1280s, those who survived the hard times began to leave, migrating southward and eastward to found new settlements or join existing communities.

Popular literature about the Four Corners region often has emphasized the mystery of the vanished Anasazi or the "lost civilization." Vacant villages do seem mysterious and we all enjoy mysteries. But human beings act in fairly predictable ways in the face of environmental difficulties and those of the Four Corners region were no exception: they gathered up what they could carry and moved to places with better prospects. Today, their descendants live on reservations in New Mexico and Arizona and in towns and cities around the country.

The Mesa Verde region contains a wealth of archaeological sites, not a few of which, to our good fortune, are well cared for and open to the public. In two days, you can visit some of the major ones, and with more time, you will be able to go to other places that are a bit off the beaten track. The experience will give you insights to the region's fascinating culture and history.

MESA VERDE NATIONAL PARK

The entrance to Mesa Verde National Park is along US 160 midway between Cortez and Mancos in southwestern Colorado. Here, too, is the visitor center, where tour reservations are made. From here, the road leads up and across the mesa to various archaeological sites and the Chapin Mesa Museum, which is 20 miles away. Information: (970) 529-4465; www.nps.gov/meve/index.htm. Entrance fee.

———————————

"A little city of stone asleep . . . still as sculpture . . . looking down into the canyon with the calmness of eternity," is how Willa Cather described a Mesa Verde cliff dwelling in her novel *The Professor's House*. More recently, others have referred to this park as the Disneyland of American archaeology. Some truth lies in both descriptions. The many ancestral Pueblo dwellings tucked in cliff alcoves and under rocky overhangs certainly do have romantic appeal, which draws thousands of tourists from around the world to see them.

Classic black-on-white kiva jar, in the Chapin Mesa Museum. The jar was excavated by Jesse L. Nusbaum in 1929 from a site on Wetherill Mesa.

Access to Mesa Verde National Park's cliff dwellings varies according to the time of year, and reservations for guided tours are required to visit most sites. Your first stop, therefore, should be the Far View Visitor Center, 15 miles into the park, where tour information is available. Tours are led by knowledgeable park staff, who will guide you through Cliff Palace, Balcony House (which involves a 32-foot ladder and tunnel), and sites on Wetherill Mesa.

On your own, you may walk to Spruce Tree House from the Chapin Mesa Museum. You also can drive the 12-mile Ruins Road, which passes by a series of scenic canyon and cliff-dwelling overlooks. From the Cliff Palace trailhead, you can gaze down on this two-hundred-room village, one of the largest cliff dwellings in the Southwest. The Balcony House tour, when it is being offered, offers a unique trail experience to a well-preserved cliff house.

Spruce Tree House.

In a single day, you can sample a few of the park's archaeological highlights and the museums. Two days will allow you a fuller experience and time to take the petroglyph trail. In summer, various activities are offered including campfire talks and nature walks for children.

In 1888, while rounding up stray cows on Chapin Mesa in December, Richard Wetherill and Charlie Mason, Mancos Valley ranchers, caught sight of a large multistory cliff dwelling and named it "The Cliff Palace." Although they were the first Euro-Americans to see this place, local Ute Indians had long known about it and many other cliff houses scattered among the canyons of Mesa Verde.

In the days and months following the discovery, Wetherill became fascinated by the ruins and began digging in them and collecting artifacts. In 1891, a young scientifically trained Swedish visitor named Gustav Nordenskiold arrived in Mancos and gave him lessons on how to excavate scientifically and take notes. With this encouragement, Wetherill gave up ranching to focus on finding and excavating ruins here and in Grand Gulch (p. 105), Chaco Canyon (p. 121), and other places.

Mesa Verde was first settled around 600 CE by Basketmaker people, who lived in pithouse dwellings in hamlets and practiced farming along with hunting and foraging. Within a century and a half, their descendants were building aboveground houses of wattle and daub, which consisted of upright posts woven through with slender branches to form walls that were then mud-plastered. These airy structures afforded comfort in summer but less than adequate warmth and protection in Mesa Verde's frigid snowy winters. Eventually, these structures developed into the more permanent stone-masonry homes whose remains have survived for centuries. One is Badger House on Wetherill Mesa.

People were drawn to Mesa Verde by its fertile soils, its abundant timber for construction and fuel, and the fact that its elevation (between 6,000 and 8,500 feet) and abundant precipitation made it ideal for farming. Other favorable attributes were springs, wild game, nutritious and medicinal native plants, and quarries for obtaining stone to make tools and utensils.

In the popular view, the inhabitants of Mesa Verde were cliff dwellers; however, beginning around 800 and continuing well into the 1200s, most settlements were situated on the open mesas. A good example, located just off the main road, is Far View Ruin, which was occupied beginning around 900 CE and by 1100 had some five hundred residents.

There are more than six hundred buildings in alcoves in Mesa Verde National Park, ranging from small storage rooms to villages with 150 rooms. Cliff dwellings, some of which were used seasonally, became popular in the 1200s, a time when many people were moving into the central Mesa Verde region from its fringes. Although population pressure may well have encouraged people to build in alcoves and caves, concerns about defense and protection from the elements probably played a role, too. Most cliff dwellings face south and benefit from passive solar heating in the cold season.

Square Tower House.

Many isolated cliff dwellings were connected by a network of trails, which made it easier for the residents of scattered communities to have communications and contacts with each other, especially at ceremonial times. Cliff dwellings were at their highest use between the early and late 1200s.

Emigration began in the early 1280s, and by the end of the century Mesa Verde's pueblos and cliff dwellings were vacant, never to be reoccupied. What initiated the exodus, archaeologists generally agree, was an extended drought. This led to malnutrition and starvation, decreasing birth rate, violence and conflict, and perhaps even loss of faith in the religious practices designed to bring rain and fertility. A probable additional factor was that the food and fuel resources people needed became used up.

Mesa Verde has been well researched by archaeologists ever since Edgar L. Hewett, author of the Antiquities Act of 1906, turned Harvard student Alfred Vincent Kidder loose on the mesa to map its cliff dwellings. Accompanying him with a camera was twenty-year-old Jesse Nusbaum, who later became the park's superintendent. Nusbaum stabilized many sites and obtained funding to build the stone-and-timber headquarters, staff residences, and museum on Chapin Mesa. Another early archaeologist, who conducted excavations at Spruce Tree House, Sun Temple, Far View Ruin, and other sites, was Jesse Walter Fewkes of the Bureau of American Ethnology. Later, James A. Lancaster, a local farmer who learned the archaeologist's trade, devoted much of his life to excavating and stabilizing ruins on Mesa Verde. The Wetherill Mesa Archaeological Project, which began in 1958 and continued for seven years under the supervision of Douglas Osborne, had a year-round crew of fifteen and hired as many as fifty during the summer seasons.

There is a campground and Far View Lodge is open from about May 1 to mid-October. Other conveniences include a gas station, general store, self-service laundry, restaurant, and snack bar. More travel and tourist facilities are available in Cortez, Mancos, and Durango.

Mesa Verde, a World Heritage Site, is a true natural and archaeological wonder. Remember, however, that while more sites are open in summer, you will be contending with large numbers of visitors. To see the park in a quieter atmosphere, visit it off-season. Other sites in the area include Ute Mountain Tribal Park, Yucca House (p. 95), and Canyon of the Ancients National Monument (p. 89).

Suggested Reading: *The Mesa Verde World: Explorations in Ancestral Pueblo Archaeology*, edited by David Grant Noble, School for Advanced Research Press, Santa Fe, New Mexico, 2006.

UTE MOUNTAIN TRIBAL PARK

Ute Mountain Tribal Park is located near Towaoc, Colorado, and adjacent to Mesa Verde National Park. Guided half-day, full-day, and backcountry tours are offered by

Eagle Nest, a fortress-like cliff dwelling in Ute Mountain Tribal Park.

the Ute Mountain Ute Tribe between March/April (depending on road conditions) and the end of October. They begin at the Visitor Center/Museum, 20 miles south of Cortez at the junction of highways 160 and 491. For current information on tour departure times and to make reservations, call (970) 565-9653; www.utemountain tribalpark.info/; umtp@utemountain.org. Tour fee.

In 1776, when the first Spanish traders and explorers arrived in the Mesa Verde region of southwestern Colorado, they found it inhabited by Ute Indians. Today, the descendants of the people they met, members of the Ute Mountain Ute Tribe, still live here on a reservation of more than half a million acres. They manage a 125,000-acre natural and cultural preserve containing many ancestral Pueblo ruins and rock art panels located on Mesa Verde and in Mancos River Canyon.

It is a privilege to tour ancient sites with a Native American guide, which is what you'll experience when you join a Ute Mountain Tribal Park tour. The ancestral places in this preserve are markedly less developed than in nearby Mesa Verde National Park; there are no crowds, traffic congestion, or commercial concessions here. The tours will take you along footpaths to see pristine cliff dwellings, surface ruins, panels of petroglyphs and pictographs, and captivating scenery. To join a tour, it is best to call ahead to reserve space.

Since the ancestral Pueblo history here parallels that of Mesa Verde National Park (p. 82), readers are referred to the previous section for this information. The three-hour morning tour is limited to sites in and around Mancos River Canyon, whereas the full-day version goes to more distant sites up on the mesa. In Lion Canyon, you will follow a mile-and-a-half rustic cliffside trail to Tree House, Lion House, Morris V, and finally the high-perched Eagle Nest cliff house. Along the way, you'll have time to enjoy the canyon panoramas, walk in and around rooms, pick up (and put down) artifacts, converse with your guide, and, of course, take pictures. The hike does involve some climbing and use of ladders. The long ladder climb to Eagle Nest, however, is optional.

Mancos Canyon was first surveyed in 1874 by a small offshoot party of the exploring expedition in the southern Rockies led by Ferdinand V. Hayden. Heading it was William Henry Jackson, the noted photographer. While outfitting in Denver, Jackson heard a tale about abandoned cliff dwellings in the rugged canyon country north of the San Juan River in southwestern Colorado. His imagination piqued, he decided to investigate. One evening after a long day's ride, he and his cohorts were camped in the lower Mancos Canyon, discouraged that their arduous travels had not yet confirmed the story. Just then, one member of the group spotted what looked like a house above them. The following day, they investigated, and lugging his heavy view camera and glass plates, Jackson made the first photograph of a Mesa Verde cliff dwelling.

Along the Mancos Canyon road, you will pass several impressive rock art sites, including Ute pictographs showing human figures and horses with riders. One site is near the former dwelling of Chief Jack House, the last traditional chief of the Ute Mountain Utes, who died in 1971 at the age of eighty-six. Since his death, the tribe has been governed by an elected chairman and council.

In joining a tour, you will have the option of driving your own vehicle or, for an extra charge, riding in a van. The full-day tour involves about 80 miles of driving on dirt roads. Bring drinking water and food for the day. For the more adventurous, special backcountry tours can be arranged in advance.

Cortez offers many travel services, and the tribal park has a campground as well as unfurnished cabins for rent. There is such a wealth of archaeological sites and parks in this Four Corners area that in a stay of several days you'll find plenty to do.

Suggested Reading: *The Ute Indians of Utah, Colorado, and New Mexico*, by Virginia McConnell Simmons, University Press of Colorado, Boulder, 2000.

CANYON OF THE ANCIENTS NATIONAL MONUMENT

The visitor center of Canyon of the Ancients National Monument is at the Anasazi Heritage Center, 27501 Highway 184, 3 miles west of Dolores, Colorado. It is 10 miles north of Cortez and 17 miles north of the entrance to Mesa Verde National Park. Information for all sites described below: (970) 882-5600; www.blm.gov/co/en/fo/ahc.html. Admission fee charged from March to October.

———————

Canyon of the Ancients was proclaimed a national monument by President Bill Clinton in 2000 following years of efforts by preservation organizations. The 176,000-acre monument safeguards thousands of archaeological sites across its rugged, scenic, canyon-riven landscape in the Montezuma Valley and Great Sage Plain. Among them are five areas that the public is invited to visit: the Anasazi Heritage Center, Lowry Pueblo, Painted Hands Pueblo, Sand Canyon Pueblo, and the McElmo-Sand Canyon Trail. Stop first at the heritage center for an introduction to the ancient cultures of the region and to obtain information about specific places to go.

Anasazi Heritage Center

This excellent small museum focuses on the cultural history of southwestern Colorado and archaeological methods. It has permanent and special exhibits and hands-on displays that both children and adults will find interesting. It also maintains a research library, laboratory, and archaeological repository and has a theater, conference rooms, and a gift and book shop. The entire facility is an outgrowth of one of the biggest archaeological projects ever conducted in the United States. The Dolores Archaeological Program began in 1978 under the direction of David A. Breternitz and continued until 1983. It employed 550 people and spent just under $10 million just on archaeological research. These years of scientific investigations preceded the building of the Dolores Dam and Reservoir.

At the heritage center, you can visit two twelfth-century sites—the Dominguez and Escalante pueblos—whose names recognize the Franciscan priests who camped here while trying to find a route from Santa Fe, New Mexico, to Spain's missions in California in 1776. The twenty-room Escalante Pueblo sits on a hill above the museum overlooking the Dolores Reservoir. To the south, the low dark ridge line on the horizon is Mesa Verde.

View to the west from the Escalante great house.

The pueblo was built around 1129 CE and occupied, except for two short periods of vacancy, until the early 1200s. Its dominating hilltop position, large rectangular preplanned roomblock enclosing a central kiva, and walls of dressed exterior stones with rubble and mud cores signal that it was a Chacoan great house, one of forty in the Mesa Verde region. The actual builders were either from Chaco Canyon (p. 121) or local folk who were familiar with and inspired by Chaco. The presence of Mesa Verde–style pottery at the site suggests the latter to be more probable. Another possibility is that elites or engineers from Chaco came up and directed the work of local residents.

The small Dominguez Ruin, next to the parking lot, is Mesa Verdean, not Chacoan, and probably housed a single family. In the course of excavating this site, archaeologists made a rare discovery—the remains of a thirty-five-year-old woman who had been interred with a large collection of artifacts and jewelry, including 6,900 beads. She must have had special status in the community.

The Dolores valley had, and still has, favorable conditions for farming as well as hunting deer, elk, antelope, and bighorn sheep. A trade route passed through here linking Dolores settlements with near and far neighbors.

Suggested Reading: "The Mesa Verde Region during Chaco Times," by William D. Lipe, in *The Mesa Verde World: Explorations in Ancestral Pueblo Archaeology*, edited by David Grant Noble, School for Advanced Research Press, Santa Fe, New Mexico, 2006.

Lowry Pueblo

Lowry Pueblo is located 27 miles northwest of Cortez, Colorado. From Cortez, take Highway 491 to Pleasant View and turn west on County Road CC. The site is 10 miles ahead. It is also easily reachable from Hovenweep National Monument.

Lowry great house.

Like Escalante, Lowry Pueblo is a Chaco-style great house built on an eminence. Its great distance from Chaco Canyon—about 125 miles as the crow flies—shows the extent of Chaco's reach in the late eleventh century. The great house had fifty or more rooms, some two stories high, and close by there is an excavated great kiva. Archaeologists have located the faint remains of prehistoric roadways. Built in five phases, the main one being from 1085 to 1090, Lowry was one of eight population centers that thrived in the region. The largest, Yellow Jacket (now a preserve of the Archaeological Conservancy), had a population that has been estimated at around 2,500 people.

The Lowry great house overlooks a community of more than a hundred recorded sites. Most prominent is the Pigg site, located just to the east. It was excavated in the 1990s by archaeology students from Fort Lewis College under the tutelage of W. James Judge, who had previously directed the Chaco Project. The Lowry community includes great houses, small pueblos, field houses, shrines, storage structures, roads, and a water-control system that included reservoirs.

The Dominguez-Escalante Expedition missed seeing Lowry in 1776 and the site was missed again after the Civil War by the Hayden Expedition. Subsequent settlers gave it little notice, and it was not recorded until 1919, when it was named for George Lowry, an early homesteader. Paul Martin, from the Chicago Field Museum of Natural History, conducted excavations in the great house between 1930 and 1934. (Photographs from his project can be viewed on the Field Museum's website.)

There are picnic tables and a restroom here and brochures to help guide you along the interpretive trail.

Suggested Viewing: *People of the Past: The Ancient Puebloan Farmers of Southwest Colorado*, a CD-ROM available at the Anasazi Heritage Center.

Painted Hands Pueblo

Drive north from Cortez, Colorado, on Highway 491, then west on County Road BB. In 6 miles, turn left on County Road 10 and continue 11.3 miles. Turn left onto an unpaved road marked 4531 and go 1 mile to the Painted Hands parking area. This rough section of road becomes muddy in wet weather. If you are approaching from Hovenweep National Monument, follow County Road 10 north for about 10 miles and you will come to the same turnoff.

———————

Painted Hands Pueblo is near Lowry Pueblo and Hovenweep National Monument (p. 97). If you are staying in Cortez, an interesting day tour would be: Anasazi Heritage Center, Lowry Pueblo, Painted Hands, and Hovenweep. A map showing back roads is useful. Painted Hands is relatively unknown and the chances are good you will have the place to yourself. The round-trip hike to the pueblo is less than a mile in length but rough in places and involves some up-and-down climbing. Plan an hour or so to do it. The main feature along the way is a lovely stone tower perched on a large boulder. General information in the Hovenweep section in this book pertains equally to this site.

In the early 2000s, Ruth Van Dyke, with colleagues and students from Colorado College, conducted a complete survey of 80 acres surrounding the main Painted Hands tower. Their report, published in 2004 for Canyon of the Ancients National Monument, describes four towers of which Painted Hands is the most prominent and best preserved. From it, you will enjoy a view of Sleeping Ute Mountain.

On the basis of survey results, the towers are dated to between 1150 and 1300 CE. The walls of Painted Hands are made of shaped sandstone cobbles and stand nearly 15 feet high. Beneath the boulder supporting the tower, you will find an alcove room and five faint hands painted in white in the back. Surrounding rubble is from the tower and collapsed pueblo rooms. An enclosed plaza and two kivas were downslope of the tower. The survey found evidence of Late Archaic sites and Puebloan habitations dating to between 1000 and 1150. One unexpected site the archaeologists recorded was an apparent looters' camp from the early 1900s. In it were a fire ring, tin and tobacco cans, and glass sherds. They found similar metal and glass artifacts in a couple of looted prehistoric sites.

On the way back along the loop trail, you will see the remains of other towers and alcove rooms. Travel services are abundant in Monticello and Cortez.

Sand Canyon Pueblo

Sand Canyon Pueblo is near Cortez, Colorado. From the intersection with Highway 491 and 160 in Cortez, drive 4.8 miles north on 491, then turn west on County Road P and N. It is 9.5 miles to the site. A detailed map can be obtained at the Anasazi Heritage Center.

Sand Canyon is one of the eight large prehistoric pueblos in the Great Sage Plain and Montezuma Valley area. Between 1984 and 1993, Crow Canyon Archaeological Center conducted excavations here. This research was done as part of its educational public-archaeology program under the direction of professional archaeologists. To preserve the excavated rooms and kivas, they were backfilled with dirt. Detailed reports on the results of the project are available on Crow Canyon's website (see reference below).

Sand Canyon was a horseshoe-shaped village surrounding a spring at the head of a side canyon, which is part of the McElmo drainage that flows to the San Juan River. The pueblo's occupants began construction about 1250 and stayed only until about 1280. In that short span of occupation, they built 420 rooms, 80 kivas, 14 towers, a great kiva, a D-shaped bi-wall building, a plaza, and an encircling wall. Kivas are usually circular rooms built partially underground: this village

Artist's reconstruction of Sand Canyon Pueblo around 1250. Painting by Glenn Felch, courtesy of Crow Canyon Archaeological Center.

had a lot of them. In modern pueblos kivas are used in connection with religious ceremonies and this interpretation used to be applied to ancient ones. However, archaeologists have shifted their thinking about kivas and see them as living rooms in which ritual activities sometimes were carried out. Today, archaeological reports often refer to kivas simply as "circular structures."

Sand Canyon's architectural features—especially the encircling wall and watch towers—suggest that the builders were concerned with defense. In the mid- to late thirteenth century, the population of the central Mesa Verde region grew rapidly; then came drought, environmental degradation, and food shortages. The Sand Canyon people depended heavily on corn and domestic turkeys, both requiring large quantities of water. Conditions hit them hard and it is apparent in the archaeological record that both corn and turkey declined dramatically as nutritional sources. Soon after 1277, the inhabitants of the pueblo experienced a violent attack by an outside Puebloan group. Many of the inhabitants were killed, their bodies left in place or thrown down hatches. Soon afterward, Sand Canyon was a ghost pueblo.

A 6.5-mile trail between Sand Canyon Pueblo to McElmo Canyon has become popular with hikers, horseback riders, and bicyclists. The lower part of the trail passes several cliff dwellings and Castle Rock Pueblo, which is near the McElmo

Canyon trailhead. To reach this trailhead from Cortez, go south on Highway 491, then turn west on County Road G at the sign for the airport. The trailhead is 12 miles ahead on the right.

The central Mesa Verde region has many archaeological sites to see. Goodman Point Pueblo (p. 99) and Yucca House are nearby, as is Mesa Verde National Park (p. 82). Cortez has an abundance of tourist services.

Suggested Reading: *The Archaeology of Sand Canyon Pueblo*, edited by Kristin A. Kuckelman, Crow Canyon Archaeological Center, Cortez, Colorado. This online report is accessible at www.crowcanyon.org/publications/sand_canyon_pueblo.asp.

YUCCA HOUSE NATIONAL MONUMENT

To reach Yucca House from Cortez, Colorado, drive 8 miles south on Highway 491 and turn right on MC Road B, a dirt road 1 mile south of MC Road C. Drive 0.8 miles, crossing a paved road, and take the next dirt road on the right, before the farmhouse on the left. Follow this road for 1.4 miles, heading toward a white ranch house with a red roof to the west. The road may not be passable in wet weather. Be sure to close all gates behind you. On the left side of the ranch house driveway, you will see the entrance gate and trail to the Yucca House ruins. Please remember that the ranch itself is private property and Yucca House is open only during daylight hours. Mesa Verde National Park manages this site, and it may be wise to call the park to make sure it continues to be open to public visitation. Information: (970) 529-4465; www.nps.gov/yuho/index.htm.

With Sleeping Ute Mountain as a dramatic backdrop to the west and the Montezuma Valley stretched eastward toward Mesa Verde, Yucca House is truly a site with a view. It's interesting archaeologically, too. This is not an excavated and neatly cleaned-up ruin with stabilized walls like the ones in Mesa Verde National Park. Its walls, built of locally quarried sandstone and limestone, plus some cobbles from Ute Mountain, collapsed over time to form brush- and grass-covered rubble mounds. Once multistory roomblocks, the mounds still rise high above ground level.

In the past, looters dug out some important features in the site. As for archaeologists, they have mapped it, conducted test excavations, and stabilized some walls but conducted no major excavation. The place has much potential for future research and appears pristine to visitors.

The site has two components: West Complex and Lower House. West Complex contains hundreds of rooms and kivas, a great kiva, several towers, and a massive compound-walled structure. It is referred to as Upper House and deemed a Chaco-style great house. There are many similar Chacoan outliers in the Mesa Verde region. The size of the West Complex testifies to this community's once considerable population. Note that the buildings surround a spring; it seems that during the extended drought in the late thirteenth century, people here were protecting their source of water.

Aerial photograph with Yucca House reconstruction superimposed. Courtesy of Adriel Heisey, photographer, and Dennis Holloway, architect.

Below West Complex to the east are the mounds of a square-shaped construction made up of an L-shaped suite of rooms and a masonry wall. They enclose a plaza with a second great kiva and, in the southeast corner, a possible reservoir.

William Henry Jackson and W. H. Holmes recorded Yucca House in the 1870s as part of the Hayden Geological Survey. When Jesse Walter Fewkes studied these ruins in 1919, he learned that the Tewa Pueblo Indians of the northern Rio Grande Valley call Sleeping Ute Mountain *Papin*, which means Yucca Mountain in their language. This reinforces theories and traditions that the ancestors of today's Tewa Pueblo Indians in New Mexico once lived in this region.

In 2000, Crow Canyon Archaeological Center and Mesa Verde National Park, which manages the monument, conducted noninvasive investigations at Yucca House. Donna Glowacki, who directed the project (and made her unpublished findings available to the author), mapped the site and interpreted its chronology. Her findings show evidence of Yucca House having been occupied in the 1200s and especially during the latter half of that century. Future excavations, however, could turn up evidence at deeper levels of an earlier occupation. As elsewhere in the region, everyone left in the late 1200s.

In July 1919, Henry Van Kleeck, who owned the land on which Yucca House sits, donated the site to the federal government. Five months later, President Woodrow Wilson employed the Antiquities Act of 1906 to proclaim it a national monument. In the late 1990s, to further protect the site, Hallie Ismay donated an additional 24 acres to the National Park Service, thereby protecting some nearby sites and more than doubling the monument's size. More surrounding land may be added in the future.

There are no facilities or travel services here, the nearest being in Cortez and Towaoc. This region boasts a wealth of archaeological sites and museums. Foremost among them are Mesa Verde National Park, the Anasazi Heritage Center (p. 89), and Hovenweep National Monument.

Suggested Reading: *Visitor Guide: Yucca House National Monument*, National Park Service, Department of the Interior. This brochure is available at the site and at the website indicated above.

HOVENWEEP NATIONAL MONUMENT

Hovenweep National Monument straddles the Colorado-Utah border 42 miles west of Cortez, Colorado. From south of Cortez on US 491, turn west on County Road G (McElmo Canyon Road). After 30 miles, turn right on 401 for 4 miles, then right on 413/213 for 6 miles to the monument entrance. From US 191 in Utah, take Utah 262 for 8 miles, then turn left on 401 for 16 miles (passing Hatch Trading Post) and then left at the Hovenweep sign. Continue 6 miles to the park entrance. The Park Service recommends not using a GPS to find Hovenweep. Information: (970) 562-4282, ext. 10; www.nps.gov/hove/index.htm.

———————

The poetic resonance of the word Hovenweep, which means "deserted valley" in the Ute language, evokes the remoteness of this region's mesas and canyons. Today, this landscape in the Great Sage Plain barely supports a few range cattle

Cajon Ruin, Hovenweep National Monument.

and scattered Navajo homesteads. One wonders how it could have sustained a vigorous population of farmers in ancient times.

The Hovenweep visitor center is at Little Ruin Canyon, where you can walk the Rim Trail Loop past a series of stone towers and habitations. The scenery here is outstanding. The monument includes six groups of outlying ruins, such as Hackberry, Holly, Cajon, and Cutthroat Castle, which are most rewarding to see, weather permitting. Monument staff will give you directions to them and advise you about road conditions.

Recent studies of the region's past climate, precipitation, and soil fertility have shown that the Hovenweep area (Cajon Mesa) saw extended periods when farming could produce enough corn and other crops to feed a lot of people. There were bad times, too, of course, during which families suffered severely from malnutrition and, if they survived, were obliged to relocate. The worst bad time came between 1275 and 1299, the so-called Great Drought, when many ancestral Pueblo people starved and experienced violence and conflict. By 1300, Hovenweep's population was gone.

As in so many places, this region saw the presence of semi-nomadic foragers and hunters for thousands of years. After about 500 CE, some people settled on the mesas, built pithouse hamlets, and began farming. Within a couple of centuries, the population began to swell and settlements tripled in number. This growth continued, with a few dips, around Hovenweep and across the Great Sage Plain with most people still living and farming on the open mesas.

After 1150 CE, these settlers moved to the heads of canyons where they were closer to more permanent water sources such as springs and seeps. Access to water seems to have been a high priority. They built check dams and terraced garden plots along the canyons and raised corn, beans, and squash. They also semi-cultivated native plants such as beeweed, ground cherry, sedges, milkweed, cattail, and wolfberry and built stone pueblos, towers, and granaries around the canyon heads and on the canyon bottoms. Best constructed were the towers, some of which have endured to the present day and are impressive to see. They are famously enigmatic as regards their purpose and function. Some are alone, some in groups, some on rims, some on the mesas, and some in the canyons. Theories about their use include defense, communication, habitations, and ceremonial sites. Probably they served multiple functions. These Hovenweep communities thrived from around 1150 to 1300 when this area and the entire Four Corners region became depopulated.

Hovenweep National Monument is an exceptionally beautiful place. The beginning of the Rim Trail is wheelchair-accessible and goes to a scenic viewpoint over Little Ruins Canyon. Then it continues around the canyon. From the visitor center, there is also a longer trail going to some distant ruins. You will find picnic tables by the parking lot and a campground nearby. Travel services are available in Bluff, Blanding, and Cortez, which is a central place from which to visit numerous other archaeological sites described herein.

Suggested Reading: *The Towers of Hovenweep* by Ian Thompson, Canyonlands Natural History Association, Moab, Utah, 2004.

GOODMAN POINT PUEBLO

To reach Goodman Point, take Highway 491 northwest out of Cortez about 4.5 miles to County Road P. Go west on this road about 4 miles to a T in the road, turn left (south) and follow the curve in the road; after curving to the west, the road will become County Road P again. Continue west for about ¾ mile to a small graveled parking lot on the south side of the road. The trail to the site begins here.

———————

A walk through Chaco Canyon's Pueblo Bonito or Mesa Verde's Balcony House will give you a sense of the past's immediacy. The extraordinary architecture of such sites makes you feel as if the former inhabitants of these buildings just packed up and left. Goodman Point Pueblo offers quite a different experience. The remains of this village have lain on an open plain exposed to rain, snow, and wind for more than seven centuries. Natural erosion has collapsed roofs and walls; winds have blown dust and sand to fill room cavities; and vegetation has overgrown the rubble mounds. Here you will sense how much time has passed and wonder about the people who once lived here and what happened to them.

Although Goodman Point Pueblo has a low public profile, it was one of the first two archaeological sites in the country to be set aside for protection by the federal government. That happened in 1889, seventeen years before Congress passed the Antiquities Act and established Mesa Verde as a National Park. The ruins, which cover 143 acres, include many other small sites within the overall community. When you come here, you will find an easy pathway that winds through the site. The round trip is about a mile long.

Goodman Point is one of about eight major prehistoric villages scattered across the Montezuma Valley and Great Sage Plain near Cortez, Colorado. Most of these sites—including the largest, Yellow Jacket Pueblo—are owned and protected by

Aerial photograph with reconstruction of Goodman Point Pueblo superimposed. Courtesy of Adriel Heisey, photographer, and Dennis Holloway, architect.

the Archaeological Conservancy or the National Park Service. Goodman Point is in the latter category and is the easternmost unit of Hovenweep National Monument (p. 97).

For four summers beginning in 2005, Crow Canyon Archaeological Center, in partnership with the National Park Service, conducted intensive investigations here. Under the direction of Kristin Kuckelman, professional archaeologists aided by students and members of the public made extensive test excavations and recovered a wide sampling of material to be analyzed. This included Black-on-white pottery, stone implements and weapons, bone tools such as awls and deer antlers (used for flaking projectile points), pendants, and many other items. Food remains they found included wild game (especially cottontail rabbits); domesticated turkeys; corn, beans, and squash; and a variety of wild edible plants. During times of normal precipitation, these ancestral Pueblo people successfully made their living as farmers, hunters, and foragers.

Kuckelman and her colleagues think Goodman Point's inhabitants built their village between 1260 and 1275. This was a time when people living in the greater Mesa Verde region were in flux and many in the hinterlands were pulling up stakes and relocating to form large defensible communities in the central Mesa Verde region. Densely populated villages like this one offered strength in numbers and were better equipped to protect their precious farm fields and water sources. Two springs at Goodman Point indeed are surrounded by rooms in the pueblo.

At its peak, this pueblo is thought to have housed between 570 and 800 people. In only a fifteen-year time span, they built 13 roomblocks (with an estimated 450 rooms, some two-story) and at least 114 kivas, which were primarily residential rooms. In addition, they constructed an unroofed great kiva, a defensive village-enclosing wall, and several double-walled rooms, called "bi-wall structures," whose function is uncertain. After such an intensive spate of building, it seems surprising that they vacated the place about 1280. Why did this happen? Evidence shows conclusively that a severe drought beginning around 1275 brought on famine and internecine conflict. When the quality of life became unbearable, the survivors departed to seek a better existence elsewhere. It was a pattern that repeated itself throughout the Four Corners region.

Another nearby site you may wish to see is Sand Canyon Pueblo (p. 93). Its time period, general layout, and history are similar to Goodman Point.

Suggested Reading: www.crowcanyon.org/publications/goodman_point_pueblo .asp.

THREE KIVA PUEBLO

Three Kiva Pueblo is located along Montezuma Creek east of Blanding and south of Monticello, Utah. From Blanding, go 2 miles south on Utah 191 and turn east on 219. Just over a mile, turn south (right) on 206 (Perkins Road), continue for 18 miles and turn north (left) on Montezuma Canyon Road (146). The site is 7 miles farther on the left. From Monticello, go 5.5 miles south on Utah 191, turn east on 146, and continue 27 miles to the site. A brochure with map is available at the offices of the BLM or the U.S. Forest Service in Monticello and at the Blanding Visitor Center. Information: (435) 587-1500; www.blm.gov/ut/st/en/fo/monticello/recreation/places/Montezuma_Canyon/Three_Kiva.html.

————————

This is a beautiful, unpopulated area whose scenic charm lies in contrasts between spare, rugged mesas, canyons, and cottonwood-shaded arroyos. When driving the back roads to reach this site, be sure to have a spare tire, plenty of gas, and water, and be alert for poor conditions.

In Montezuma Canyon, you will be following in the footsteps of William Henry Jackson, the noted American explorer and photographer who conducted an archaeological reconnaissance here in 1886. Nearby is Alkali Ridge, where groundbreaking archaeological investigations were carried out in 1908 and in the

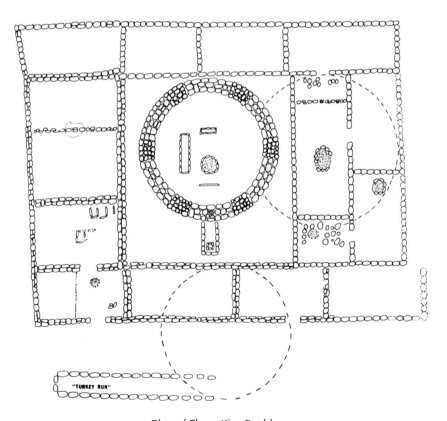

Plan of Three Kiva Pueblo.

1930s. An article in the April 2013 issue of the *Journal of Archaeological Science* reported that researchers found traces of *Theobroma cacao* in ceramic vessels at an Alkali Ridge site dating to the eighth century. This is the oldest evidence to date of Southwestern Indians trading for chocolate with Mesoamericans.

In the summers between 1969 and 1972, the Brigham Young University Field School of Archaeology excavated Three Kiva Pueblo. Their conclusions were that ancestral Pueblo Indians of the Kayenta Branch (p. 143) began construction here in the 800s CE, subsequently adding to the pueblo in three building phases. The main occupation here, however, was between 1000 and 1300 when the inhabitants maintained close ties with Mesa Verdean communities to the east.

This site, named for its three kivas, is a fourteen-room pueblo laid out in a square. Windblown fill on a kiva floor under its collapsed roof measured more than two feet deep—a clue that the kiva survived intact for a long time after the villagers left. Just south of the pueblo is an interesting 2-by-20-foot masonry room; the abundance of turkey bones found here indicates it was a turkey run. Domesticated turkeys were an important source of food, not just here but also in many other communities. The Indians also wove blankets of turkey feathers and made whistles and flutes from the birds' leg bones.

In the course of excavations, diggers found two abalone-shell pendants, evidence that a trade network existed to the Pacific Coast. Predictably, they also turned up many stone tools: knives, scrapers, drills, spear and arrow points, hammer stones, hoes, axes, mauls, and grinding stones. Artifacts such as these help reconstruct a picture of daily life in the pueblo a millennium ago.

The Bureau of Land Management curates this site and reconstructed one of its kivas, which can be entered by ladder. If you hike down the canyon a short distance, you will come upon Ute petroglyphs along the east-facing walls. The images include cranes, abstract forms, and a panel depicting horseback riders hunting bison.

You will find gas, restaurants, and lodgings in Bluff, Blanding, and Monticello.

EDGE OF THE CEDARS STATE PARK

Edge of the Cedars State Park is in the southeastern Utah town of Blanding on US 163 between Bluff and Monticello. From the main intersection in the town, go west and follow signs to the park at 660 West 400 North. Information: (435) 678-2238; www.stateparks.utah.gov/park/edge-of-the-cedars-state-park-museum. Admission fee.

———————

Chaco Canyon's influence reached far to the north into the Mesa Verde, or Northern San Juan, region. The effect of Chaco is most visible in the existence of some forty "great houses." Some examples described in this book are Escalante, Bluff, Yucca House, Lowry, and Far View. Still another can be seen at Edge of the Cedars.

This park has an anthropological museum, which features an exceptional collection of prehistoric art and artifacts. Its display cases include Archaic-period atlatls (spear throwers), spear and arrow points, stone tools, textiles, ornaments, items of wood, and one of the best pottery collections in the region. Perhaps the best known object in the collections, discovered in a cave in the vicinity, is a beautiful sash woven of scarlet macaw feathers. Another interesting item is a copper bell, excavated from the ruins; it came all the way from Mexico. The museum has a gallery of rotating art and ethnographic exhibits.

From the museum, follow the trail to the archaeological site where you can climb down a ladder into a restored kiva. The most prominent part of the site, however, which was excavated and restored, is known as Complex 4, the great house. It dates to the late eleventh and early twelfth centuries, with a major construction period between 1109 and 1117. This building was two stories high and had approximately twelve ground-floor rectangular rooms, two enclosed kivas, and a contiguous great kiva (now a circular depression). Archaeologist Winston Hurst has written that the inhabitants of Edge of the Cedars actively participated in the widespread Chacoan communication and ideational system. The inhabitants knew about Chaco and tried to emulate its style. The villagers remodeled part of Complex 4 around 1215, indicating that the building was being used long after the Chaco system collapsed in the early 1100s.

Several rubble mounds near this structure represent roomblocks occupied earlier than the great house, and buried beneath them are the remains of even

The great house at Edge of the Cedars State Park.

older habitations dating to the Pueblo I period (700–900 CE). The site has a refuse mound on the east side but there is no enclosing berm. The original village probably extended beyond the present park boundaries; however, when early American settlers plowed fields here, they obliterated archaeological traces.

Field schools from Weber State College and Brigham Young University conducted excavations at this site from 1969 to 1973. Regrettably, the work was poorly documented, no report was written, and no systematic analysis of the collection was ever done. The quality of this scientific work contrasts to that conducted at nearby Bluff Great House (p. 110).

Blanding is a quiet town with several cafés, gas stations, and motels. From here, you can easily make a trip to Hovenweep National Monument (p. 97).

NATURAL BRIDGES NATIONAL MONUMENT

Natural Bridges is at the end of Highway 275, which branches off Utah 95, 35 miles west of Blanding, Utah. It is 26 miles east of Fry Canyon along the same route. Information: (435) 692-1234, ext. 16; www.nps.gov/nabr/index.htm. Admission fee.

––––––––––––

Natural Bridges' main attraction, of course, is its three wondrous bridge formations, but when you're visiting this monument, you may wish also to know about and see evidence of its rich prehistory. This can be done by hiking the canyon trails that pass by ruins and rock art. They can be accessed from the main bridge overlooks.

Archaeological surveys have recorded nearly five hundred prehistoric sites within the park's boundaries. They range from scatters of potsherds and stone flakes to small collapsed or buried structures on the sage- and juniper-covered mesa, to granaries, rock art panels, and multi-component pueblos. Archaic-period sites are scarce; however, the presence of spear points dating to as long ago as 7000 BCE shows that early hunter-gatherers came through the area in small numbers and probably only for short visits. Basketmaker people were here, too, and beginning to practice agriculture.

Ancestral Puebloans moved to the canyons and mesas of what is now the park around 700 CE and lived here off and on for six centuries. The archaeological sites they left show cultural links with the Mesa Verdeans to the east; however, connections also are evident with Kayenta people south of the San Juan River. House building in the area ceased around 1250, and by the end of that century everyone was gone. This was part of the thirteenth-century exodus from the Four Corners region. Later, Navajos arrived and, in the latter part of the nineteenth century, Euro-Americans.

Only a few of the park's many sites are readily accessible and visible to the public; ask about them at the visitor center. One of the best is Horsecollar Ruin, a well-preserved cliff dwelling, and near Kachina Bridge you will find ruins and rock art. Seeing these sites adds an interesting cultural-historical dimension to the beautiful landscape and spectacular views of the natural bridges.

Natural Bridges became a national monument in 1908, only two years after passage of the Antiquities Act by Congress. You can drive the 9-mile loop, stopping at bridge overlooks, and attend interpretive programs offered by NPS rangers. The park has a campground but the nearest places to find gas, food, supplies, and lodging are in Blanding and Fry Canyon. Grand Gulch is only a few miles south on Highway 261, and Mule Canyon Ruins (p. 109) are about 16 miles east on the way to Blanding.

GRAND GULCH

Grand Gulch is a wilderness study area on Cedar Mesa in southeastern Utah. The main trailhead is adjacent to the Kane Gulch Ranger Station along Utah 261, 4 miles south of its junction with Utah 95. Another trail access is about 13.5 miles south of Utah 95 at Bullet Canyon. A permit from the Bureau of Land Management is required to enter this area. Day-use permits may be obtained at the Kane Gulch Ranger Station or at trailheads. During the spring and fall, overnight backpacking permits are only available at the ranger station and must be obtained on the morning of the trip. They may be reserved up to ninety days in advance by calling (435) 587-1510. During other seasons, these permits may be obtained from the Monticello Field Office. Information: (435) 587-1500; www.blm.gov/ut/st/en/fo/monticello/recreation/places/grand_gulch.html.

A pictograph panel in Grand Gulch.

Grand Gulch is a 60-mile-long canyon that meanders through Cedar Mesa to join the San Juan River shortly before it flows into the still waters of Lake Powell. Snowmelt, seasonal rains, and springs sustain lush undergrowth along the canyon bottom, above which sandstone cliffs rise precipitously to the surrounding tableland. This is a beautiful place with some well-preserved ruins and rock art sites. Since the canyon is accessible only to people traveling by foot or horseback, a visit—whether day hiking or overnight camping—requires careful planning. Be prepared for rough trails and changeable weather. Be sure to carry sufficient water and food, bring a map and water filter, and be equipped with appropriate footwear and clothing.

By 200 CE or so, Cedar Mesa, including Grand Gulch, was inhabited by the Colorado Plateau's earliest agriculturalists, known as Basketmakers. Most of their inner-gulch sites are found under rock overhangs, sometimes underneath later Puebloan structures. The Basketmaker culture eventually was replaced by ancestral Pueblo farmers, who began living in the gulch sometime after 1000 and thrived there for three centuries. They built extended-family-size cliff houses with storage granaries and farmed on the canyon bottom and up on Cedar Mesa. Some of their dwellings have survived in good condition with roofs intact and fingerprints still visible in the mud plaster of the walls.

Numerous amateur and professional archaeologists have worked in the Grand Gulch area. In 1893–1894, Richard Wetherill, known for his "discovery" of Mesa Verde's cliff dwellings, led a relic-collecting expedition here and amassed large quantities of artifacts, which were packed out and later given to the American Museum of Natural History. Although Wetherill has been criticized for his methods, to his credit, he recognized in Grand Gulch that in some sites Basketmaker material underlay and predated the overlying Puebloan ruins. Thus, he contributed to our understanding of the cultural chronology of the region. Some eight decades later, William D. Lipe, a leading Southwestern archaeological scholar and teacher, conducted professional research on Cedar Mesa, which resulted in numerous scientific reports.

Hiking through Grand Gulch is a memorable experience. Some major sites you will see are Junction Ruin, Turkey Pen Ruin, Split Level Ruin, Big Man Rock Art Panel, Bannister Ruin, and Perfect Kiva Ruin. The petroglyph and pictograph panels are outstanding. To help orient yourself and find ruins and rock art, obtain a large-scale map of the canyon. Please remember that the privilege of visiting well-preserved but fragile sites such as these involves responsibilities: do not remove any artifacts, disturb sites, climb on walls, or touch rock art.

Nearby archaeological sites include Butler Wash Ruins, Mule Canyon Archaeological Ruins (p. 109), and Edge of the Cedars State Park (p. 102).

Suggested Reading: *Cowboys & Cave Dwellers: Basketmaker Archaeology in Utah's Grand Gulch*, by Fred M. Blackburn and Ray A. Williamson, School for Advanced Research Press, Santa Fe, New Mexico, 1997.

BUTLER WASH RUINS

This site is a cliff dwelling 14 miles west of Blanding, Utah. Drive 3 miles south of Blanding, then 11 miles west on Utah 95 to the parking area. Information: (435) 587-1500.

———————

Travelers along Highway 95 should take a driving break to see this small crumbling but picturesque cliff dwelling. From the highway rest area, a half-mile walk takes you across the desert terrain and slickrock to an excellent viewpoint. On the slickrock, the trail is marked by stone cairns. Binoculars are helpful, as is a telephoto lens for picture taking.

This thirteenth-century pueblo in a deep cliff alcove has living and storage rooms and four kivas. A second large alcove beneath it would have discouraged an assault by enemies coming up the canyon. The site's access was by means of a still-visible but eroded hand-and-toehold trail chipped into the rock face on the left side. Due to drought, the late 1200s were challenging times for Puebloan folk in this region and many communities felt threatened by their neighbors; thus, defensively sited homes like this one became common.

Notice how the cliff dwelling has a southern orientation, which allowed the benefits of solar warming in winter, when the sun's rays penetrated deep into the cave. In the summer months, by contrast, the cliff's overhang provided shade to the inhabitants. Note, too, the water stains over the cliff edge directly above the pueblo, made by runoff from rains and snowmelt. This convenient drainage provided fresh water—a kind of natural off-and-on plumbing system—to the inhabitants. Runoff would also have been channeled to down-canyon garden plots of corn, beans, and squash. Food and other items were stored in back rooms and separate small masonry rooms tucked under rock ledges. One of these granaries is visible from the overlook to the left of the main cliff dwelling.

Along the trail to the overlook, you'll pass a variety of desert plants, some of which the Indians found useful. They harvested the fruit of the prickly pear cactus in late summer, for example, and in fall collected nuts of the pinyon pine, which are highly nutritious and keep for several years under good storage conditions. The Pueblo people also used fibers from the yucca plant to make sandals, baskets, and rope, and shredded cliff rose bark to fashion mats and other fabrics. Juniper berries, with which we flavor gin, were used as a food seasoning.

Butler Wash flows along the east side of Comb Ridge, a 90-mile hogback along which many ancient habitations and rock art panels can be found. This geologic feature, through which the highway makes a dramatic cut just west of Butler Wash near Bluff, was formed seventy million years ago.

A short distance east of the Butler Wash Ruins parking area is another longer trail, which leads up Butler Wash to several more cliff dwellings. The well-developed Mule Canyon Ruin (p. 109) is a few miles farther west along Highway 95, as is Natural Bridges National Monument (p. 104).

There is only a restroom at this site and the nearest travel services are in Blanding.

MULE CANYON ARCHAEOLOGICAL RUINS

The Mule Canyon ruins are located along Utah 95, 16 miles east of Natural Bridges National Monument and 20 miles west of the intersection of Utah 95 and US 191. Information: (435) 587-1532; www.blm.gov/ut/st/en/prog/more/cultural/archae ology/places_to_visit/mule_canyon.html.

———————

Like the Butler Wash cliff dwelling, this site makes an easily accessible and interesting stop along Utah 95. It includes the remains of a twelve-room stone-masonry pueblo, kiva, and tower. Crawlways, which now are sealed, lead from the kiva to both the pueblo and tower. Several rooms, the kiva, and the base of the tower have been restored for public viewing. The kiva is open for viewing but was originally roofed with timbers. To protect it from the elements, a protective cover has been constructed. From the edge, you can look down and see the tunnel openings as well as the hearth, air vent, and surrounding bench.

This pueblo is on Cedar Mesa, a large forested tableland cut by a series of canyons. The area had a significant pre-Columbian Indian population off and on from Archaic times through the Basketmaker and Pueblo periods. However, like the Four Corners region in general, it was empty of people by 1300 CE. In the winter of 1879–1880, the famous Hole-in-the-Wall expedition of Mormon pioneers made their way across Cedar Mesa en route to establishing a settlement in Bluff.

Although Mule Canyon's first settlers came around 750 (Pueblo I period), the pueblo's main occupation was between 1000 and 1150. Artifacts unearthed here show that the inhabitants had links with Mesa Verdean communities to the east and also the Kayenta to the south. We associate stone towers with Hovenweep National Monument, but they were commonly built in this area as well. Archaeologists have suggested numerous possible functions for these impressive structures, from storage to defensive habitations to astronomical observatories to signaling stations. They may well have been multipurpose. This one has a line-of-sight connection to others about a mile to the east.

It is unusual, though not rare, for tunnels to be incorporated in the design of a site like Mule Canyon. No one is sure why they were built, but one possibility may simply have been convenience, especially in winter. On the other hand, in the event of an attack, people could have moved from one building to another without exposing themselves. Then, too, there is the common fallback interpretation that they served a ritual function.

The University of Utah conducted excavations here in 1973 after which the Bureau of Land Management stabilized and interpreted the site for the enjoyment

Butler Wash cliff dwelling.

Mule Canyon pueblo.

and education of Highway 95 travelers. Construction of this road, a major project funded by bicentennial grants, was not without controversy, traversing as it did a large pristine wilderness region. Conflicts between pro- and anti-development factions inspired Edward Abbey's popular novel *The Monkey Wrench Gang*.

Nearby places of archaeological interest are Butler Wash Ruins (p. 107) and Grand Gulch (p. 105). The towns of Blanding and Bluff have travel services.

BLUFF GREAT HOUSE

Bluff Great House is in the town of Bluff, in southeastern Utah. From downtown, go up the cemetery road and you will see the great-house mound on the left. Parking is on the right next to the information kiosk. An informal pathway leads around the site.

———————

If you are visiting Bluff or driving along US 191, Bluff Great House is a short, easy detour off the highway. The site's principal feature is the remains of a large building, one of many in southeastern Utah and southwestern Colorado that were related to Chaco Canyon. This one is on a hill, and parts of it reached three and possibly four stories in height. It has four interior kivas—not all being in use at the same time—and its occupants built some of the walls in the core-and-veneer masonry style characteristic of buildings in Chaco Canyon. The site complex also includes a great kiva, "road" segments, a built platform, and several substantial berms.

The designation of this building as an outlying Chacoan great house does not imply that migrants from Chaco Canyon actually came here and built it, though that possibility is not entirely discounted. More likely, local people who knew about Chaco—some may even have traveled there to see its impressive architecture—wished to emulate its style. Doing so may have signaled higher social status.

Dr. Catherine Cameron, who co-directed research at Bluff Great House, reported that among the 50,000 artifacts recovered, most were locally made and only a very few originated in Chaco Canyon, which is some 125 miles away. She regards the site "as connected to Chaco Canyon politically and ritually, but without strong economic ties." This kind of association characterizes many other great houses in the Mesa Verde region.

Bluff Great House overlooks the present town and the San Juan River Valley. Numerous other contemporaneous pueblos lie within a few minutes' to a couple of hours' walk away. Archaeologists, therefore, see this great house as having been the focal point of a much larger community whose members probably came here frequently to trade, participate in religious ceremonies, and join social functions. Supporting this view is the existence of a network of road segments that connect more than half a dozen pueblos. From the top of the great house, one of these roads can still be seen on the east side of the great house heading north.

The great house was constructed between 1075 and 1150 CE; however, researchers found evidence that Basketmaker III people lived here some seven centuries earlier. After around 1150, when most of the great houses in Chaco Canyon were vacated (p. 124), Bluff Great House continued in use for another hundred years. This, too, was a pattern in the northern San Juan region. During its long occupation, the building saw much remodeling (in the Mesa Verdean style) and the addition of rooms and kivas.

The trail leads about 30 yards southwest of the great-house mound to a great kiva, which archaeologists tested but did not thoroughly excavate. Its masonry-lined interior is about 43 feet in diameter and surrounded by a bench. It has a vault in the floor and antechambers built in the cardinal directions. The north antechamber probably was the entryway while the others may have served as storage and dressing rooms for participants in ceremonies.

Several earthen berms surround the great house, one of them being cut by the present-day paved road. They are made up of household trash, construction and demolition debris, and dirt. How they were used isn't clear. On the north side of the great house, you will notice a flat expanse with less vegetation. The ancestral Pueblo inhabitants placed 3,200 cubic yards of dirt here to form a platform. Not having been excavated, its function, too, is uncertain, though an educated guess might be as a dance plaza. Together, all these features make up a thoughtfully built landscape surrounding the main building.

The Southwest Heritage Foundation owns Bluff Great House. For six summer seasons between 1996 and 2004, archaeologists Catherine Cameron and Stephen H. Lekson directed University of Colorado Archaeological Field School excavations at the site.

Suggested Reading: *Chaco and After in the Northern San Juan: Excavations at the Bluff Great House*, by Catherine M. Cameron, University of Arizona Press, Tucson, 2009.

SAN JUAN RIVER

The San Juan River rises in the southern Rockies, flows through the Four Corners region, and empties into Lake Powell, its waters eventually joining the Colorado River. This section addresses the stretch of river between Montezuma Creek and Mexican Hat, Utah. These sites are best seen while on a float trip.

_____

As a major drainage of the Colorado Plateau, the San Juan River and some of its tributaries were a cradle of ancestral Pueblo culture. Today, the river serves as an important water source for Navajos, Utes, and Euro-Americans. As one might

Sixteen-Room House along the San Juan River.

expect, there are many archaeological sites along or close to this waterway. Some can be reached by land, remembering that private land owners and the Navajo Nation require permission, but the best plan is to travel the river by raft, canoe, or kayak. If you go on your own, you will need a permit from the Bureau of Land Management. Several commercial rafting companies, on the other hand, offer single- or multiday float trips with professional guides who take care of travel logistics, prepare meals, and share information about geology and human and natural history. Choose a company that specializes in educational raft trips and has well-informed guides.

How many archaeological sites you are able to see depends on how much time you have and knowing where they are. Having a knowledgeable guide along is very helpful. Several of the main sites are indicated in the book *San Juan River Guide: Sand Island to Clay Hills*. These include Sand Island Petroglyphs (p. 115) near the BLM boat ramp; Lower Butler Wash petroglyphs, between miles 4 and 5; and River House, a cliff dwelling near mile 6. (Mileage numbering begins at the Sand Island boat ramp.) The book's map also shows two historic sites: Barton's Trading Post and San Juan Hill, where Mormon pioneers built a dugway (road up a cliff) for their wagons while journeying to Bluff in 1880.

The Butler Wash Site is an extensive petroglyph panel most remarkable for its impressive human-like figures from the early Basketmaker period (1000 BCE to 500 CE). It is the type site of the San Juan Anthropomorphic Style, and its figures appear in many rock art books. Scholars generally agree that the imagery reflects visions experienced by shamans while in a trance state. In addition to these stunning figures, the panel includes hundreds of animal and plant forms and abstract designs.

River House, a cliff dwelling with fourteen rooms and two kivas, is beautifully situated in an alcove about a ten-minute walk from the river's edge. On the wall above the dwelling, you will see painted handprints, a serpent, and horizontal wavy lines. In their oral traditions, certain Hopi clans tell of their ancestors having lived here and they call the place Snake House. Clues found in River House indicate that people were here in Basketmaker III times; however, the building itself is from a later time period, between around 1150 and 1300. Intense visitation from river runners and others has necessitated its being repeatedly stabilized by the BLM. Please treat it with respect and consideration and do not climb on walls. A walk along the ledge west of the cliff house will lead you to some petroglyphs and a well-preserved granary built in a crevice.

There are more cliff dwellings, surface pueblos, and rock-art panels along the San Juan River upstream and downstream of Sand Island: the Citadel, Sixteen-Room House, Moki Steps, and Floating House are a few examples. Archaeology aside, a San Juan float trip is an experience you won't quickly forget. The scenery, especially as you enter the canyons, is spectacular and people come from all over the world to see and study the geologic formations. The chances are good, too, of seeing ducks, geese, herons, lizards, beaver, and desert bighorn sheep. In the spring, you will enjoy an array of wildflowers and at night you will be amazed at the brilliance of the stars and planets.

The Moki Steps, an ancient, possibly Chacoan, staircase along the river.

Not far away, you can visit Hovenweep National Monument (p. 97) and in Blanding, Edge of the Cedars Museum has an excellent collection of artifacts. Bluff has motels and restaurants but plan to do grocery shopping in a larger town.

Suggested Reading: *San Juan River Guide*, by Lisa Kearsley, Shiva Press, Flagstaff, Arizona, 2002.

SAND ISLAND PETROGLYPHS

The Sand Island Petroglyphs are located along a sandstone cliff bordering the San Juan River 4 miles west of Bluff in southeastern Utah. From Bluff, drive west on US 163 and turn left at the Sand Island sign. There are two petroglyph areas: to see the downstream one, turn right at the bottom of the hill and go several hundred yards to a pull-off and sign. The trail to the upstream panels begins at the east end of the camping area. It is about a ten-minute walk to the petroglyphs.

Although ancient Indian rock art can be found in thousands of locations throughout the Southwest, there are certain places that contain especially high concentrations of images. Sand Island is one. Its varied images were made over a long span of time. Unlike many rock-art sites, which are remote, these are easily accessible.

The earliest images, usually higher on the cliffs, are armless anthropomorphic stick-figures with horizontal or vertical stripes in their torsos and horns or

A detail of the Lower Sand Island petroglyph panel.

antennae on their heads. These petroglyphs, in the Glen Canyon Linear Style, date to the late Archaic period, at least 2,000 years ago. Some animal figures and abstract designs also are this old.

Early Basketmaker imagery (later than the Archaic) is visible in both upstream and downstream panels. You will recognize these by the human-like forms with broad-shouldered trapezoidal bodies and weak dangling arms and legs. Also from this period are abstract designs, such as wavy lines, and what textbooks refer to as "lobed circles," which resemble doughnuts with a handle. The Sand Island panels also include later Basketmaker and Pueblo-era figures of bighorn sheep and other animals, snakes, and humped-back flute players.

Of more recent making are horse and riders and several long-nosed caricatures of European faces in profile. Navajo and/or Ute Indians made these, probably in the late nineteenth and early twentieth centuries. One of the upstream panels contains what some observers argue to be a rendition of a mammoth superimposed by an Archaic-period bison. If that is so, it dates to Paleoindian times. A key factor in the ongoing mammoth-or-not controversy is whether the "tusks" were naturally formed or man-made.

You may wonder how some of the high-up petroglyphs were made. Notice where the cliffs are lighter near its base; at one time, when the river followed a different course, sand dunes were piled high against the cliff. To attain even greater heights, glyph makers used ladders or built scaffolding.

Since many of the pecked images in the Sand Island rock-art panels are of extreme age, their patina has darkened to that of the background rock, making

Historic-period Ute or Navajo petroglyphs, Upper Sand Island panel.

them faint and hard to see. Binoculars help. The cliffs have glare when the sun is striking them directly. The rock art is easier to see and photograph in the early morning and late afternoon.

The Bluff area is rich in ancient sites, most of which are best explored with an informed guide. Another way is by taking a river-rafting trip (single-or multi-day); raft trips are offered by several commercial companies.

Sand Island has a lovely campground along the river, and in Bluff, you will find lodgings, restaurants, a trailer park, and other travel services. Easy day trips can be made to Monument Valley, Goosenecks State Park, Hovenweep National Monument (p. 97), and Edge of the Cedars State Park (p. 102).

NEWSPAPER ROCK STATE MONUMENT

Newspaper Rock, in southeastern Utah, is on the north side of Utah 211, 13 miles west of its intersection with US 191, north of Monticello and south of Moab. The site is along the road to the Needles District of Canyonlands National Park. Information: (435) 587-1500. Free admission.

———————

Of the thousands of rock-art panels scattered throughout the American Southwest, this densely packed panel is the most accessible. On a highly patinated slab of Wingate sandstone along Indian Creek, Native Americans made petroglyphs of horned anthropomorphs, bison, deer, bighorn sheep, human and animal footprints, horses and riders, stretched pelts, and abstract designs. There's even a

Detail of Newspaper Rock.

wagon wheel. The different motifs and styles suggest that several cultural groups made images here. Some have an ancestral Pueblo look, some are Fremont, and others are Ute. It has been suggested that Ute Indians pecked imitations of other styles they had seen; thus, where to place the site in this book is problematic. The important thing is to see this fascinating collection of varied imagery.

Several dating methods can be used in this panel. One is how fresh or faint the petroglyphs appear or, to put it another way, the degree to which patina or desert varnish has built up on some as opposed to others. Since patination happens over time, the darker the glyph, the older it is.

Distinctive artistic styles point to particular cultural groups. Here, the chunky human-like figures with square heads and horns suggest Fremont, whose culture thrived to the north between around 300 and 1300 CE. Some images contain historical references; horses and riders, for example, were done after European contact in 1540 and probably after the Pueblo Revolt of 1680 when many captured horses were traded out of the Rio Grande Valley.

Regardless of culture and chronology, petroglyphs such as those at Newspaper Rock are enjoyable simply on their own visual merits. Some images seem clear in meaning, some obscure; some are carefully executed, others sloppily scrawled; some seem to tell a story, others are just designs. While this panel was not a "newspaper," it surely was meant to communicate at some level. Although you can peruse this panel in a few minutes, you'll probably want to inspect it longer, pondering all the fascinating details.

Nearby Shay Canyon also has rock art that includes a variety of human and animal figures and abstract designs. To reach it, continue west on Route 211 for 2 miles to an informal pullout. Here a rough trail leads down an embankment, across a streambed and flat area, and climbs up a short talus slope to some cliffs where the glyphs are visible. The walk is about 300 yards from the highway. Remember that touching petroglyphs accelerates their deterioration.

There are picnic tables across the road from Newspaper Rock, and travel services are available in Monticello and Moab.

Suggested Reading: *Petroglyphs and Pictographs of Utah*, by Kenneth B. Castleton, M.D., Utah Museum of Natural History, Salt Lake City, 1987.

The Chaco World

⋛⊁⊱

In 1878, the noted anthropologist Lewis Henry Morgan visited Aztec Ruins (p. 126) and remarked on the similarity of the architecture there to sites he had seen in Chaco Canyon. Succeeding generations of Southwestern archaeologists have noticed the similarity, not just at Aztec but at many other sites in the region, some more than a hundred miles away.

Artists' reconstruction of Kin Hocho'I, an outlying great house, as a procession approaches on a wide roadway. Local folk watch dancers in the plaza from a surrounding berm. Painting by and courtesy of Robert and Karen Turner.

119

At a conference in 1972, Cynthia Irwin-Williams, who was directing excavations at Salmon Ruins (p. 129), coined the term "Chaco phenomenon," which was immediately incorporated into the archaeological lexicon. Eventually, other terms came to be used: "the Chaco system," for example, and "the Chaco world." All refer to the fact that the architectural design and construction details of many ruins around the San Juan Basin and beyond resemble the huge buildings in Chaco Canyon.

These structures are known as *great houses* and *great kivas.* In Chaco Canyon, Pueblo Bonito, with some eight hundred rooms, is the largest and best known, but there are eleven others in the canyon as well and scores more (called *outlying great houses* or *outliers*) have been recorded around the San Juan Basin, north into Utah, west to near Flagstaff, Arizona, and far to the south. Many are associated with puzzling alignments, referred to as "roads." Now the database contains some two hundred great houses and possible great houses.

The ones in Chaco Canyon are massive, multistory masonry structures that usually have a formal symmetrical layout. The rooms are more spacious than ordinary pueblos of the period, have thick masonry walls with beautifully crafted exteriors of hand-shaped tabular-sandstone veneer, and attain three, four, and even five stories. Circular rooms (*kivas*) are found within the great houses and in open public spaces. Sometimes the plazas are built-up platforms, and earthen berms often partially surround the buildings. Before the late 800s, the ancestral Pueblo people had never built structures like these, nor would they again, with a few possible exceptions, after they left Chaco Canyon in the first half of the twelfth century CE. It was, indeed, a phenomenon.

An example of Chacoan stonework.

John Kantner and Nancy M. Mahoney, contemporary Chaco scholars, have written that Chaco Canyon's great houses "still stand several stories tall almost in defiance of our ability to explain why they were constructed and the activities that occurred within them" (*Great House Communities Across the Chacoan Landscape*, 2000). Explanations have been suggested, of course: they were residential villages; they were warehouses used to store and redistribute corn; they were religious and ritual centers and destinations for pilgrims; they were palaces for ruling elites. Or, at different times, all of the above.

Stephen H. Lekson, another Chaco archaeologist, wrote in *The Chaco Meridian*:

What was Chaco? For twenty years I've weaseled out of a direct answer to that question. . . . If Chaco is the *bête noire* of the Southwest, Bonito is the black hole. It sucks in astonishing amounts of interest, energy, and resources, like some giant space vortex. It emits almost nothing: only the faint clipped signal of Pepper's field notes or Judd's decaying reminiscences.

A focus of research has been how the outlying great houses, especially the distant ones, related to Chaco Canyon. As a general rule, the farther away from the canyon they are located, the smaller and less Chacoan they are. Most scholars think local community headmen wanted to emulate Chaco Canyon in how they built. Perhaps showing the connection communicated their special status. As puzzling as the Chaco phenomenon is, it's clear that communities across thousands of square miles were linked in some way to Chaco Canyon.

Many of the outliers continued to be inhabited or used after Chaco Canyon's fall. The Dittert site (p. 138) was built in the 1200s, for example, and Aztec experienced dramatic growth and development around the time that people were leaving Chaco Canyon. Some believe, therefore, that Aztec replaced Chaco as the regional power center. A wide, straight, constructed roadway—the North Road—leads from Chaco Canyon toward Aztec, a seeming physical and metaphorical link between these two important centers. There are other long roads, too. One heads south past Kin Kletzin to Kin Ya'a (p. 133). Another goes to the west. Most outliers have short road segments leading to them that probably served as approaches for processions at ceremonial times.

This chapter of the book discusses Chaco Canyon and some outlying great houses. The chapter on the Mesa Verde Region includes more outliers. When you visit these places, think about the Chaco phenomenon and how they were linked to Chaco Canyon; generations of professionally trained archaeologists have done so and the field remains open to creative thought, reason, and speculation.

CHACO CULTURE NATIONAL HISTORICAL PARK

Chaco Culture National Historical Park is in northwestern New Mexico between Bloomfield and Grants. From the north, turn off US 550 at CR 7900 (3 miles east of Nageezi and 50 miles west of Cuba). From there, the 21-mile route to the park, which includes 13 miles of unpaved road, is well marked. From Hwy 9 to the south (which runs between Crownpoint and Cuba), you can take either Hwy 57 or Navajo 46 and then CR 7900 and CR 7950. All roads to Chaco have unpaved sections that can become impassable in inclement weather. Information: (505) 786-7014; www .nps.gov/chcu/. Entrance fee.

———————

Since much more has been written about Chaco and the "Chaco phenomenon" than can be summarized in a guidebook, this chapter will touch on some basic, widely accepted information and offer suggestions on how to manage your time when you visit the park.

On approaching Chaco Canyon, you'll be struck by the desolate, arid landscape of the San Juan Basin and you may wonder how this remote area in the desert could once have been an important cultural center. This question has puzzled scholars, too, and no quick, clear answer has been found. A basic decision to be made is whether you want to spend a single day in the canyon or longer.

Stephen H. Lekson, a leading Chaco archaeologist and thinker, once wrote, "Architecture is the central matter of Chaco Canyon" (*In Search of Chaco*, 2004) and indeed it is, and it is worth driving miles of dusty roads to see at least a few of the dozen buildings known as "great houses." They are multistory, massive, and built of stone. Before them, the American Southwest had seen no structures of such scale. Conveniently, a few of them, in what has been called "Downtown Chaco," are short walks from parking lots. The two most impressive are Pueblo Bonito and Chettro Kettle, both of which have been excavated. To reach some of the others, be ready to hike between 3 and 7 miles round-trip.

As a canyon, Chaco is 15 or so miles long, shallow, and wide and in places, the Chaco Wash, which flows sporadically, is deeply downcut. Archaic people hunted and foraged here, and later, sedentary farmers (Basketmakers) lived in pithouse communities, such as Shabik'eshchee Village. But it is what happened later that has gained Chaco Canyon fame and for which it was designated a World Heritage Site by the United Nations.

After around 850 CE, Puebloan migrants, probably arriving from the Mesa Verde region to the north, moved into the canyon and began construction of three great houses: Pueblo Bonito, Una Vida, and Penasco Blanco. Afterward, more such buildings began to appear, all well engineered and with similar elements of design and layout. They were beautiful, too, with large living and storage rooms, walls of meticulously hewn stone facing, and spacious courts in which to hold public events and ceremonies.

The canyon has "small houses," too—standard-size residential pueblos. They are clustered across the canyon from the great houses. One of these south-side communities has a great kiva, Casa Rinconada, excavated in the 1930s. It is a highlight of any visit.

View of Chaco Canyon from Hungo Pavi, looking toward Fajada Butte.

So what does all this mean? For more than a century, this question has been at the root of all discussions about Chaco. A currently prevailing theory holds that families of an elite class lived in the north-side great houses while the small houses were lived in by common folk. Chaco Canyon, as the architecture alone demonstrates, was a place of differentiated socioeconomic classes: some rich and powerful families, and working-class folk. Clues in the archaeological record have led to differing interpretations of the makeup of Chaco's society; thus, many papers, books, and debates. As you walk around the ruins, consider possible parallels you are familiar with in the modern world and you may come to your own conclusions.

Chaco Canyon received most of its resources—wood construction timbers, pottery, grinding stones, some corn, and special goods such as macaw feathers, copper bells, and chocolate—from elsewhere. To obtain these goods, what did Chaco exchange? This is a puzzle. Some scholars, however, think they traded something of a nonmaterial nature, such as religious rituals performed by priests in the great houses to bring harmony and balance in the world—and rain. Indeed, Chaco may have been a religious center to which people from the region came periodically to participate in ceremonies that were necessary to attain the favor of the spirit beings who send moisture and fertility and make it possible to survive in a challenging environment.

Archaeological research began here in May 1877 when William Henry Jackson mapped the major ruins. In the late 1890s, the Hyde Exploring Expedition carried out excavations in Pueblo Bonito. Since then, institutions that have sponsored research in the canyon have included the University of New Mexico, the National Geographic Society, the Smithsonian, and the National Park Service. Much data are held in archives.

Archaeologists have recorded as many as two hundred buildings beyond Chaco Canyon that resemble, though on a smaller scale, the great houses of the canyon. These outlying Chaco great houses, often referred to as "outliers," can be found from a few miles to well over a hundred miles away. Clearly, Chaco's influence, particularly between 1050 and 1140, spread far and wide. Exactly what the relationship was between the far-flung outliers and Chaco central is a focus of ongoing investigation.

Another subject of research is the so-called Chaco roads, of which the North Road and the South Road are the best known. These two reach out from the canyon for many miles and are 30 feet wide in places. Some roads had formal borders and climbed over mesas by means of ramps and stairs. Most, however, extended only a short distance from outlying great-house complexes. It is speculated that they were used for ceremonial processions, perhaps not unlike those that occur around Roman Catholic churches and cathedrals during religious holidays.

Around 1140 CE, during a drought, the Chaco phenomenon ceased. Most Chaco Canyon residents left, and the great houses began the slow process of crumbling to mounds. The exodus appears to have been methodical, not motivated by warfare. Coincidentally, Aztec (p. 126) experienced a building boom.

Some scholars think, therefore, that the Chacoans went north and made Aztec, along the Animas River, their new capital. It's a credible theory.

However long you spend in Chaco Canyon, be sure to see Pueblo Bonito and Chettro Kettle and the great kiva at Casa Rinconada. If you can, take the trail up the north side of the canyon to Pueblo Alto or up South Mesa to Tzin Kletzin. For a longer hike, passing by petroglyphs, follow the trail to Penasco Blanco. Remember that regulations do not allow straying off designated trails and, of course, artifact collecting is strictly forbidden.

Pueblo Bonito.

The park's visitor center has a small museum, library, bookshop, and film showings. There are picnic tables there and a campground nearby. If you camp, you should bring in food, water, and supplies. The roads into Chaco Canyon can be washboard and slick in wet weather. The nearest lodgings, restaurants, grocery stores, and gas stations are at least 25 miles away.

Suggested Reading: *In Search of Chaco: New Approaches to an Archaeological Enigma*, edited by David Grant Noble, School for Advanced Research Press, Santa Fe, New Mexico, 2004.

AZTEC RUINS NATIONAL MONUMENT

Aztec Ruins National Monument is on Ruins Road (Road 2900), half a mile north of NM 516 in Aztec, New Mexico. US 550 leads to Aztec from the north and south. The monument is 14 miles east of Farmington on NM 516. Information: (505) 334-6174; azru_information@nps.gov; www.nps.gov/azru/index.htm. Admission fee.

It is the nature of archaeology that interpretations of sites and their history shift as more research is done and more data are recovered. This has happened at Salmon Ruins (p. 129), Chaco Culture National Historical Park (p. 121), and certainly at Aztec Ruins.

Aztec lies along the Animas River, one of two major tributaries of the San Juan River near present-day Farmington, the other being the La Plata River. This area is often referred to as the Totah, a Navajo term meaning where three rivers come together. Like Salmon Ruins, Aztec Pueblo is believed to have been conceived, planned, and designed by a group of colonists who moved north from Chaco Canyon. The Chacoans recruited workers from the thriving and populous Totah community to procure building materials and supply the labor to construct Aztec West, the centerpiece of a visit to the monument. It was a pattern repeated at nearby Salmon Ruins along the San Juan River.

With more than four hundred rooms, Aztec West is the largest of the many great houses that were built beyond Chaco Canyon between around 1075 and 1125. It experienced three building spurts between 1100 and 1130; this was an astonishingly short period of time to accomplish so much construction.

In its heyday, the Aztec complex included much more than the stunning Aztec West great house and great kiva. Aztec East, another great house, lies only a short distance away and beside it, the Earl Morris Ruin; both have been only minimally excavated. The National Park Service gives special reservation-only tours of these sites a couple of times a year. There are also three tri-wall structures, whose functions are not known. And there's more still: in the late 1980s, John R. Stein and Peter J. McKenna conducted a reconnaissance on the mesa just above the monument's north boundary and recorded thirty residential sites, four of which were

Interior of a roomblock, Aztec Ruins.

"of great house proportions," as well as several road segments and other features. These Aztec North sites date to between about 1050 and 1130.

It was Earl Morris's opinion, which was generally accepted for some sixty years, that Aztec's history had three phases: (1) built and lived in by people from Chaco Canyon; (2) left vacant for a couple of generations; (3) reoccupied by immigrants from the Mesa Verde region. After much new research and reanalysis of data, today's scholars view Aztec's history differently: they see one continuous occupation by both Chacoans and locals—of course, with shifts in social makeup and leadership through time. They do not see Aztec as a satellite of Chaco Canyon or Mesa Verde, but rather as an important regional center in its own right exerting considerable influence over its Puebloan neighbors.

By the time Morris began his work in Aztec West in 1916 under the auspices of the American Museum of Natural History, the site had been repeatedly looted and many of its artifacts given away, sold, lost, or destroyed. Even so, it still contained a trove of valuable cultural material, much of it in the lower-story rooms, which were well sealed off from the impacts of looters and weather.

In 1947, Sherman S. Howe, an elderly resident of Aztec, recorded his recollections of breaking into Aztec West when he was a child in school in the 1880s. His account conveys the irresistible attraction to dig into a ruin in search of treasures. After the adults he was with had dug down to a ground-floor room, he vividly describes what happened (*Aztec Ruins National Monument*, 1962).

We broke a hole through the wall and entered the room to the northeast, and there we really did see things! I got into that room and stood, trying my best to take it all in and see everything I could, while that excited crowd were rummaging it, scattering and turning everything into a mess. There were thirteen skeletons ranging from infants to adults. . . . There were several baskets, some of the best that I have ever seen, all well preserved. There were a lot of sandals, some very good, others showing considerable wear. There was a large quantity of pottery. . . . There were a great many beads and ornaments . . . [and] quite a lot of turquoise.

When we had finished this work, the stuff was taken out and carried off by different members of the party, but where is it now? Nobody knows. . . . it is gone. I, being only a small kid, did not get my choice of artifacts. I had to take what was left, which made a nice little collection, at that. But it, too, is about all gone.

Sealed tombs and buried treasure have romance and mystery and have lit a fire under both pot hunters and archaeologists. Earl Morris, who devoted much of his professional life to excavating and restoring Aztec Ruins, remembered digging up his first pot at age three and a half, "the clinching event that was to make me an ardent pot hunter, who, later on was to acquire the more creditable, and I hope earned, classification as an archaeologist" (*Aztec Ruins National Monument*, 1962).

One highlight of a visit to Aztec Ruins is walking through a long series of well-preserved rooms with intact doorways and ceilings on a self-guided or ranger-guided tour. Another is the reconstructed great kiva. In the visitor center, don't miss the new video about the site and new exhibits in the museum.

Aztec's reconstructed great kiva.

The Aztec-Farmington area has a large choice of lodgings and eating places. Visits to Salmon Ruins and Chaco Culture National Historical Park will expand your understanding of this region's prehistory.

Suggested Reading: "Animas Anamnesis: Aztec Ruins or Anasazi Capital?" by Gary M. Brown, Thomas C. Windes, and Peter J. McKenna in *Chaco's Northern Prodigies: Salmon, Aztec, and the Ascendancy of the Middle San Juan Region after AD 1100,* edited by Paul F. Reed, University of Utah Press, Salt Lake City, 2008.

SALMON RUINS

The Salmon Ruins and museum are at 6131 Highway 64 about 2 miles west of Bloomfield, New Mexico. Information: (505) 632-2013; www.salmonruins.com. Entrance fee.

———————————

The San Juan River, which rises in southern Colorado, flows through the Four Corners region and empties into Lake Powell where it mingles with the waters of the Colorado River. The remains of Salmon Pueblo are situated on an alluvial terrace above the river's floodplain about equidistant between Mesa Verde (p. 82) and Chaco Canyon (p. 121). Salmon Ruins, a major outlying Chacoan great house, was purchased in 1968 by San Juan County to save it from being mined for antiquarian souvenirs. Archaeological research began at the site two years later under the direction of Cynthia Irwin Williams (1936–1990) and in partnership with the county.

The tower kiva at Salmon Ruins looking south toward the great kiva.

Highlights of a visit here include walking around the extensive archaeological site; viewing the museum, which has very interesting displays; and seeing the rustic homestead of the Salmon family, who were nineteenth-century pioneers in this area.

Scholars agree that colonists from Chaco Canyon planned, built, and occupied this pueblo. Chacoan architects laid out its rooms, tower kiva, and great kiva in a design very similar to that of Hungo Pavi in Chaco Canyon. Construction was accomplished in a remarkably short and intense building episode beginning in 1088–1090. (A few rooms in the east wing were built several years before, possibly to house architects and workmen while they planned the construction, prepared the site, and procured building materials.) When finished, the great house had 275 rooms, an elevated or tower kiva, and a great kiva in its plaza. Its first occupants stayed here until around 1125 when, it seems, a transition occurred. As currently interpreted, Puebloan people living in the vicinity modified the great house, building 25 kivas in roomblocks. Then they moved in and stayed for another century and a half.

Black-on-white mug, Salmon Ruins Museum. Courtesy of the Salmon Ruins Museum, Salmon Ruins Collection, FS#32831. Photo by David Grant Noble.

Salmon's two phases of occupation are sometimes referred to as the Chacoan and San Juan or Mesa Verde. Although people from Salmon and Mesa Verde, which is about 45 straight-line miles to the north, certainly were acquainted and traded with each other, there is no evidence, as once was thought, of a migration here from the Mesa Verde region in the 1120s. Life at Salmon Pueblo ended abruptly in the 1280s or 1290s when a catastrophic fire consumed the pueblo. It is unclear how the fire started, but it happened at a time when the Four Corners region was being generally depopulated and thousands of Puebloan people were moving to other regions of the Southwest.

During their investigations of Salmon, archaeologists made a disturbing discovery: twenty-two burned corpses in the tower kiva, most of whom were young children or infants. In past years, various interpretations have been suggested in attempts to reconstruct what happened; however, after careful research of the site where this occurred and of the human remains, no definitive answers have come forth. It does appear, however, that all the children did not die at the same time.

When you walk around Salmon Ruins, remember that in its short construction period some 7,500 to 9,500 trees were felled and carried here for the roof timbers and door and window lintels, and the ponderosas and firs came from many miles away. That alone was an amazing and laborious feat. The cutting of thousands of juniper trees must have transformed the local landscape for generations. The human labor recruited to accomplish these tasks and build the great house was tremendous and those who took responsibility for the planning and management of such an operation had expertise, experience, and power.

To gain a fuller perspective of ancient life in this area, you will find it rewarding also to visit Aztec Ruins National Monument (p. 126), which is 12 miles away, and Chaco Canyon (p. 119), which is 65 miles distant. You will find travel services in Bloomfield, Aztec, and Farmington.

Suggested Reading: *Chaco's Northern Prodigies: Salmon, Aztec, and the Ascendancy of the Middle San Juan River Region after AD 1100*, edited by Paul F. Reed, University of Utah Press, Salt Lake City, 2008.

CASAMERO PUEBLO

To reach Casamero Pueblo, take the Prewett exit from Interstate 40 (19 miles west of Grants, New Mexico) and turn right on Old Route 66. After a few hundred yards, turn north on County Road 19 and continue 4 miles to a small parking area with a Bureau of Land Management sign on the left. From there, it is only a short walk to the site. Information: (505) 761-8700; www.blm.gov/nm/st/en/prog/recreation/rio_puerco/casamero.html.

———————

In the eleventh and early twelfth centuries, Chaco Canyon's influence spread far beyond the canyon itself. This influence is most visible in the existence of outlying great houses whose architecture and masonry style have a distinctly

Chacoan look. Casamero, which is only a ten-minute drive from I-40, is a good example. From where you park, the walk to the site is easy and the BLM, which administers the ruin as a Chaco Culture Archaeological Protection Site, has placed interpretive signs.

The ruin is situated on a slope with a grand view over the Red Mesa Valley and the cliffs of Tecolote Mesa as a backdrop. It has twenty-two ground-level and six second-story rooms and a built-in kiva. Excavated between 1966 and 1975 and subsequently stabilized by the BLM, it is the main feature to see on a visit here. Researchers date Casamero's occupation to between the early 1000s and early 1100s. This coincides with the period when the Chaco phenomenon was beginning to expand and then reached its peak. It has been called "Chaco's Golden Century." People from Chaco Canyon, 50 miles to the north, may actually have come here and constructed the building. On the other hand, local Red Mesa Valley inhabitants possibly went to Chaco and consulted architectural engineers and masons about how to build a great house.

A plaza area in front of the great house, which is barely noticeable today, probably served as a space where people worked and held social activities and religious ceremonies. Two hundred feet to the southeast, a shallow circular depression is what remains of a great kiva; it has never been excavated. With a 70-foot diameter, it is among the largest in existence, twice the size of the great kiva at Aztec Ruins (p. 126). A prehistoric roadway, which is difficult to see from ground level, approached Casamero from the southeast and led to the Andrews Ranch site, which was contemporaneous.

Casamero Pueblo.

In addition to the great house, there were more than thirty other associated sites in the Casamero community. These dwellings have only been surveyed and there is little specific information about them. However, a pithouse found beneath the great house dates to 715 CE, indicating that Puebloan people were living here long before the building of Casamero Pueblo. Archaeologists estimate the entire population at around 154 people.

The Casamero community was not alone: eight other similar ones nearby thrived during roughly the same time period. (None are open to the public.) Andrews Ranch, which is the closest, lies about 2 miles to the southeast, and another, with the romantic name Coyote Sings Here, is a little farther to the northwest. Clearly, for a century, the Red Mesa Valley was the place to be.

In the 1970s, archaeologists from the School for Advanced Research in Santa Fe carried out extensive investigations near Casamero Pueblo, especially in the vicinity of the coal-fired electrical generating plant that you'll see along the way from Thoreau. They identified more than 140 archaeological sites in the area, ranging from early Basketmaker pithouses to Puebloan structures to early-twentieth-century Navajo homesteads.

Grants and Gallup have abundant travel services. To more fully appreciate Casamero, a visit to Chaco Canyon (p. 121) is recommended.

Suggested Reading: *Great House Communities across the Chacoan Landscape,* edited by John Kantner and Nancy M. Mahoney, University of Arizona Press, Tucson, 2000.

KIN YA'A

Kin Ya'a Pueblo is located east of New Mexico 371 just outside Crownpoint, New Mexico. As you approach the town from the south, turn right at the Ikard-Newson Propane site (Kin Ya'a Road). You will need to open and close a gate. Soon the ruins will be visible in the distance. Follow this braided, often rutted dirt road about 1 mile to the site. A high-clearance vehicle is recommended. Information: (505) 786-7061, ext. 221; www.nps.gov/chcu/plan yourvisit/outliers.htm.

Kin Ya'a is a unit of Chaco Culture National Historical Park and has been open to visitors for many years. However, as this book goes to press, it is temporarily closed due to a land claim issue, but will reopen when the problem is resolved. Contact park headquarters before going here to check accessibility.

Kin Ya'a, a Chacoan great house located 25 miles south of Chaco Canyon, is particularly noted for its tower kiva, parts of which still stand four stories high. Originally, the tower reached nearly 40 feet above ground level. Tower kivas are not common, and for one still to have a portion intact is rare. To support such weight and height, its builders made the base of its walls 5 feet thick, tapering to 2 feet at the top. The tower shows signs of having been burned but whether this was intentional or accidental is uncertain.

Kin Ya'a.

The terraced building beneath the tower has twenty-six ground-floor rooms, nine second-story rooms, and three enclosed kivas, all with core-and-veneer masonry. In addition, a great kiva sits on a nearby low hill and a prehistoric roadway—its swale is 18 to 27 feet wide and 3 feet deep—heads northeast to Chaco Canyon. Another branch points northeast, headed toward Pueblo Pintado (p. 139). The road also leads southwest to a topographic landmark called Hosta Butte. All these features—architecture, massive stone walls, great kiva, roads—are classically Chacoan in design.

Even after decades of study, just what connected outliers like Kin Ya'a to Chaco Canyon has stumped archaeologists, though theories abound. In the vicinity of Kin Ya'a (off the monument on Navajo reservation land), archaeologists have found many sites and dwellings. They range from potsherd scatters to an irrigation ditch and check dam, to small houses, to a fifty-room pueblo. Tree-ring dating places the building of the Kin Ya'a great house to the early 1100s. Many surrounding sites date to between 950 and the 1100s and some go back to the Basketmaker III and Pueblo I periods several centuries earlier.

Residents of this community could easily walk to Kin Ya'a but had a longer trek to Chaco Canyon if they wished to attend ceremonies or were required to contribute their labor to build the great houses there. Since Chaco Canyon's farm fields were limited, they would probably have carried food supplies with them. The land surrounding this site was well suited to growing crops.

In a 1917 report, the archaeologist Jesse Walter Fewkes wrote, "It must be remembered that the ceremonial room or kiva, in modern mythology, represents the underworld out of which the early races of men emerged." He went on to speculate that the Kin Ya'a tower "may have been four kivas, one above the other, to represent the underworlds in which the ancestors of the human race lived in succession before emerging into that in which we now dwell." Although archaeologists date Kin Ya'a to the ancestral Puebloan culture, in Navajo oral traditions, it is the home of the *Kin yaa'aanii* (Towering House People) clan. Past trade relations, intermarriage, and sharing of cultural traditions between the Pueblo Indians and the Navajos may account for some Navajo clans having stories relating to the Chacoan culture.

Other nearby Chacoan great houses are Casamero (p. 131) and Pueblo Pintado. You can find travel services and lodging in Crownpoint and Gallup.

Suggested Reading: *Anasazi Communities of the San Juan Basin* (pp. 201–6), by Michael P. Marshall et al., Public Service Company of New Mexico, Albuquerque, and New Mexico Historic Preservation Bureau, Santa Fe, 1979.

CHIMNEY ROCK NATIONAL MONUMENT

To reach Chimney Rock from Pagosa Springs, Colorado, drive 16 miles west on US 160, then 3 miles south on Colorado 151. From Durango, drive 44 miles east on 160 to its intersection with 151, then 3 miles south. The visitor center is half a mile from the entrance gate. Guided tours are conducted daily from May 15 to September 30. Information and tour schedule: (970) 883-5359 in-season and (970) 731-7133 off-season; www.chimneyrockco.org/. Admission fee.

––––––––––––––

In 2012, President Barack Obama proclaimed the Chimney Rock archaeological area a national monument, signaling its value and significance to the nation. Indeed, this is one of the most dramatic and scenic archaeological and natural places in the Southwest.

For the most informative experience, guided walking tours are recommended. One tour (guided or self-guided) goes to a great kiva and pueblo ruins. It is one-third mile and ADA accessible. Along the way, you'll see a curious circular hole carefully hand-carved in the bedrock. Another one, which is guided only, follows a rough steep trail up to the main attraction, Chimney Rock Pueblo. This is an outlying Chacoan great house perched on a narrow mesa in the shadow of two rock spires and has a spectacular view over the wooded foothills of the southern Rockies.

Special group or personal tours can be arranged, as well. Off-season, the gate is closed but visitors are permitted to walk, ski, or ride horseback in and out: 6 miles round-trip. The monument also offers special events, such as moonlight walks. For details, visit the monument's informative website.

Archaeological surveys in the area surrounding Chimney Rock have turned up hundreds of sites located in the valleys and on the mesas and spanning a time from the late 800s to the mid-1100s. Some people lived in isolated houses, others in distinct residential clusters or hamlets. People arriving here in the tenth century probably came up the Piedra River, a tributary of the San Juan, to settle this rugged, hilly terrain. The short growing season would have made farming tenuous at best; however, these Puebloans also hunted deer and elk, foraged for wild plants, and probably fished in the creeks. Another available resource was timber, which they may have lumbered and traded to lowland communities, transportation being provided by rivers during high water in spring. The ability of the inhabitants of this area to cope successfully with high-altitude subsistence; long, cold winters; and deep snows was remarkable.

Chimney Rock great house is the highlight of a visit here. To reach it, be prepared to climb up a steep slope (there are stairs) and traverse a narrow causeway to an elevation of 7,600 feet. The ancient occupants of the great house could gaze down on the surrounding community of farmers and far off in the direction of Chaco Canyon. Whether it was people from Chaco who built the great house or supervised the construction is uncertain. Possibly, like other great houses north of the San Juan River, it was simply Chaco-inspired. The building has fifty-five rooms and two kivas and some sections attained two stories. The formal planned layout of rooms is characteristically Chacoan, as are the core-and-veneer style of masonry and other features.

A single timber cutting date of 1076 hints at the initial building date. Many more wood samples show a cutting date of 1093. Researchers have noted that both years coincide with major lunar standstills, an 18.6-year cyclical celestial occurrence during which the moon, when observed from the great house, rises between the spires. University of Colorado astrophysicist J. McKim Malville has proposed—and many other researchers are in accord—that ancestral Pueblo sky-watchers noticed this pattern and built Chimney Rock Pueblo as an astronomical observatory. Between 2005 and 2007, the Chimney Rock Interpretive Association, which manages the monument in concert with the U.S. Forest Service, offered programs to the public to watch the moon rises, which were especially impressive when full at night. The association plans to do so again in 2022. This site may have religious significance, as well, considering that some Pueblo Indian groups today regard Chimney Rock and Companion Rock as topographical manifestations of the Twin War Gods, who are important in their mythology.

Archaeological studies in the Chimney Rock district began in 1921 when J. A. Jeançon and Frank H. H. Roberts Jr. conducted surveys and excavations under the auspices of the Colorado State Historical Society and other organizations.

Chimney Rock great house.

Between 1970 and 1972, more research was carried out by Frank W. Eddy of the University of Colorado. He recorded more than ninety sites and excavated four to prepare for public tours. In 2007, Stephen H. Lekson, also of the University of Colorado, carried out additional excavation. Malville began studying solar and lunar alignments in the 1980s. His and his colleagues' findings have been widely published.

In addition to seeing the beautiful landscape and learning about archaeology, you may be lucky enough to see peregrine falcons flying around the spires, where they nest. Many travel accommodations and services are to be found in Pagosa Springs and Durango.

Suggested Reading: *In the Shadow of the Rocks: Archaeology of the Chimney Rock District, Southern Colorado*, by Florence C. Lister (author) and Elizabeth A. Green (editor), Durango Herald Small Press, Colorado, 2011. *A Guide to Prehistoric Astronomy in the Southwest*, by J. McKim Malville, Johnson Books, Boulder, Colorado, 2012.

DITTERT SITE

From Interstate 40 east of Grants, New Mexico, take State Road 117 south and proceed 26 miles to County Road 41. Turn left here and go 3.5 miles. Across from the York Ranch headquarters entrance, head east past the Armijo Canyon sign on a sandy two-track. Drivers with low-clearance, two-wheel-drive cars should take care on this road. Go 1.3 miles to the wilderness boundary fence and park. The Dittert site is visible about 400 yards away. Directions also can be obtained at the El Malpais Ranger Station along Highway 117. Information: (505) 876-2783.

———————

At the Dittert site, you will find a small pueblo consisting of a substantial mound and low room walls of hand-formed sandstone blocks. If you are a confirmed archaeology buff, you'll enjoy finding and walking around it, but if you're on the hunt for dramatic photographs of ancient ruins, you might leave this one off your itinerary. The site is named for the late archaeologist Alfred E. Dittert, who excavated eight rooms and a kiva here in the late 1940s.

The pueblo has an L-shaped house block containing about thirty ground-floor rooms, a dozen or more second-story rooms, and a large interior kiva. The plaza was in front. There are some sixty nearby small pueblos and farmsteads, suggesting that Dittert was the focus of a considerable community.

Ancestral Pueblo people were drawn to this place, near the base of Cebolleta Mesa, by its good hunting and foraging and because waters flowing from Armijo Canyon and other drainages offered the potential to farm. Two miles up the canyon, there is a spring that the locals must have counted on in dry spells, and more resources were to be found in *el malpais* (the badlands), not far to the west. Also, a corridor between the badlands and Cebolleta Mesa would have served as a natural travel and trade route to connect the pueblos in the community.

Tree-ring samples produced dates between 1226 and 1267; however, the pueblo's residents built their home on an earlier mound. Dittert Pueblo has some Chacoan characteristics: larger-than-ordinary rooms, strong compound walls of pecked sandstone, a blocked-in kiva, and two road segments. There is also a possible great kiva nearby. Interestingly, however, the pueblo postdates the depopulation of Chaco Canyon by nearly a century. This shows how strong and long-lasting Chaco's influence was—that people living several generations later wanted to emulate its style. As an analogy, think how Classical Greek architecture is reflected in so many American civic buildings. Visual links to the past convey status and importance.

Be careful when you go to the Dittert site for it is remote and unpaved roads can be tricky in wet weather. Be sure to leave all artifacts you see at the site in place and do nothing that might compromise future archaeological study here.

The nearest travel services are in Grants and Quemado. Nearby El Malpais National Monument is a geologically fascinating and scenic place to explore, and if you are energetic and well prepared, consider hiking the Zuni-Acoma Trail (p. 242). You may also visit Acoma Pueblo, whose residents probably have ancestral links to the people who lived in the Dittert site.

PUEBLO PINTADO

Pueblo Pintado can be reached from the north or south. From Cuba, New Mexico, which is along US 550, follow 197 south to Torreon and continue on Route 9 to the small Navajo community of Pueblo Pintado. Here, a graded unpaved road leads north 1 mile to the ruins. From Milan, along Interstate 40, take NM 605 north and after 13 miles bear left on Highway 509. At the end of 509, turn right on Route 9 to Pueblo Pintado.

———————

Pueblo Pintado is located along the Chaco River 16 miles east of Chaco Canyon's visitor center. This large outlying great house has been surveyed and mapped but not excavated and only minimally damaged by looters. Situated far from major travel routes, it receives little visitation and the chances are you will have the place to yourself and will appreciate its quietness and natural, unrestored character. There is an interpretive sign at the entrance to the site but no formal trail. This is a large impressive ruin with standing walls, and you will probably want half an hour or more to walk around.

Pueblo Pintado has long been known by Pueblo and Navajo Indians, but it was the American military officer Lt. James Simpson who first reported it in 1849. Following the Mexican War, General Stephen W. Kearny assigned Simpson to lead a reconnaissance expedition into Navajo Country. He had Navajo and Mexican guides from whom he learned that the building was known by various names: Pueblo de Ratones (village of rats), Pueblo Grande, Kin Kale (great house), and Pueblo de Montezuma. The last was from a story that the Aztec king once lived

Pueblo Pintado.

here. It also appears in various Navajo legends. A Navajo elder told Marietta Wetherill that his people used it as a stronghold in their wars. This very likely happened during the period when Spanish settlers were pushing westward from the Rio Grande Valley and encroaching into Navajo territory.

According to reports, the eastern wing of the great house was used as a trading post with residence in 1901, the ancient rooms having been restored for this purpose. Twelve years earlier, another merchant set up a store at the site where he traded horses, saddles, silver ornaments, and whiskey (a bottle for a sheep).

Work on the great house began in the early 900s, but the big building whose ruins we see today was constructed in the mid-1000s, coincidental with a building boom in Chaco Canyon. Where the pueblo's first residents came from is unclear, but the presence of potsherds (McElmo black-on-white) shows that people were living here as late as the 1250s.

Pueblo Pintado was a tall building built on a rise; thus it was (and still is) visible from a considerable distance and had visual linkages with nearby sites and shrines. It had ninety ground-floor rooms, forty in the second story, and several more in a third story. There also were four kivas in the great house, more in the plaza, and a great kiva a short distance to the southeast. A road heads northwest from just south of the building's long back wall. Potsherds found along it date to the early 900s. It goes for 2 miles and then drops into Chaco Canyon by means of a staircase cut in sandstone. Another road leads southwest to a quarry.

At the same time that Pueblo Pintado was inhabited, a community of Puebloan people were living in small houses a mile to the west, and another community existed 3½ miles beyond. No doubt, the great house was a focal point for these people.

Researchers with the Solstice Project (www.solsticeproject.org) have determined that the layout of this building is on lines that correspond to the bearings of the lunar minor standstill—the rising of the southern minor standstill moon—which occurs every 18.6 years.

The nearest tourist facilities are in the town of Cuba. Chaco Canyon itself is only about an hour's drive away. To get there from Pueblo Pintado, follow County Roads 7900 and 7950.

The Kayenta Culture

><|<

Archaeologists have traditionally recognized three main prehistoric cultural regions ancestral to the Pueblo Indians: Chaco, Mesa Verde, and Kayenta. These oversimplified cultural categories are based on the styles of artifacts found, architecture and ceramics being the most prolific and visible. Other factors such as settlement patterns also matter. This short section introduces the Kayenta branch of the ancestral Pueblo or Anasazi culture. As has been mentioned elsewhere, researchers don't know how the people identified themselves or what language(s) they spoke and only have indirect clues to their belief system—all key aspects of culture. What is known are the material objects they left behind that did not disintegrate or decompose over the centuries.

The Chaco phenomenon thrived from around 850 to 1150 CE, with some outlying Chacoan great houses still being used into the 1200s. The Mesa Verdean subculture, first identifiable in the early centuries CE, continued until the late 1200s, when the Four Corners region was vacated.

The area the Kayenta people inhabited was mainly in the northeastern part of Arizona. It reached south to the Hopi Mesas and beyond, west to the Colorado River, and north to the San Juan River. In this region, early Basketmaker people began cultivating corn around 1000 BCE. Later, innovations such as ceramics and the bow and arrow came into use. But the Kayentans lagged somewhat behind their neighbors to the north and east in some of the developments we think of as Puebloan: aboveground masonry architecture, sizable villages and communities, and social complexity.

Residences built after around 1000 CE consist of suites of aboveground masonry and *jacal* living and storage rooms. (A jacal wall is made of upright poles interwoven with thin branches, such as willow, and plastered with mud. They are strong and effective but not long-lasting.) These hamlets were small, however, the

View of Kayenta country from a once-inhabited high mesa and the author.

largest having no more than thirty rooms, and scattered across a broad landscape. Between 900 and 1100 (the Pueblo II period), weather patterns and precipitation were favorable to farming and the Kayentans fared well.

After 1150, those living on the peripheries of the region began moving to the core where they formed larger, more compact interdependent communities focused around a central pueblo facing a plaza. Interestingly, some villages still consisted of pithouses. Naturally, they favored well-watered locales with arable soil.

After 1250 (the Tsegi Phase) this trend continued with some plaza pueblos attaining considerable size—the cliff dwelling Kiet Siel, for example, has 150 rooms. Population growth and density led to competition for water and farmland and, apparently, to tensions between communities. During the final half century of Kayenta occupation in the region, defense appears to have been on the minds of these communities, many pueblos being sited on remarkably hard-to-access mesas and ridges with line-of-sight links to neighbors.

By the end of the century, a general exodus had occurred. Deteriorating environmental factors undoubtedly were the main cause. Another factor probably was social disruption. Also, people probably were drawn away by better conditions elsewhere and new religious developments in other areas. Many migrants went south to the middle Little Colorado River Valley and even farther into southern Arizona.

Suggested Reading: "Before the Great Departure: The Kayenta in Their Homeland," in *Archaeology Southwest* 27, no. 3, edited by Jeffrey S. Dean and Jeffery J. Clark, Tucson, Arizona, 2013.

NAVAJO NATIONAL MONUMENT

Navajo National Monument is located in northeastern Arizona. From Kayenta, take US 160 southwest for 22 miles to Arizona 564, which leads 9 miles to the visitor center. From Tuba City, the 564 turnoff is 50 miles along Route 160. Information: (928) 672-2700; www.nps.gov/nava/index.htm.

———————————

Viewed from a distance, the large, well-preserved cliff dwellings of Kiet Siel and Betatakin in Navajo National Monument appear small and fragile within the vaulted rock alcoves that shelter them. But they are two of the largest cliff villages in the Southwest.

From the visitor center, you can follow two short scenic trails, one leading to a view of Betatakin. To see this site close-up, however, involves joining one of two offered ranger-led hikes of 3 or 5 miles round-trip and some strenuous hiking. The trail to Kiet Siel is about 16 miles round-trip and can be done in one long day or two if you camp there overnight. Call the monument for schedule, reservation, and backcountry permit information. The hiking season at these sites is restricted to between late May and early September.

The inhabitants of Betatakin and Kiet Siel were of the Kayenta branch (p. 143) of the ancient Pueblo culture and like related peoples in the Mesa Verde and Chaco regions, they were experienced farmers, expert builders, and skilled at making crafts. They built cliff dwellings mostly in the last half of the thirteenth century, during the Tsegi (*say-ghee*) Phase of Kayenta culture. At this time, many

Kiet Siel.

Puebloans, here and in the Mesa Verde region, consolidated their scattered settlements in large, protected, defensive villages. Often they built cliff dwellings in the shelter of cliff alcoves close to a source of water, but some pueblos, sacrificing such convenience, are situated in the open atop steep-sided, hard-to-reach mesas, often with line-of-sight connections to neighbors (see first photo in this chapter). All the sites are within or on the edge of a canyon system through which travel is slow and arduous.

Defensive considerations seem to have been paramount during this time when rainfall and food were scarce and farm fields were eroding. Archaeologists have mostly found evidence of preparations for conflict, rather than of actual warfare; under stress, communities must have felt threatened. In the late 1200s, everyone seems to have recognized that the best strategy was to leave. Many went south to the Little Colorado River and Hopi country. Others traveled even farther; archaeologists at Point of Pines, an eight-hundred-room pueblo in southeastern Arizona, for example, documented the appearance at this time of a large enclave of Kayenta immigrants.

Betatakin, which means "ledge house" in Navajo, sits in a 500-foot alcove and looks out over a narrow canyon with stands of scrub oak, aspen, and pine trees. When summer showers send thin waterfalls over the cliff from the slickrock mesa above, not a drop of water touches the ancient fragile dwellings. Betatakin was planned and developed as an entire unit, then occupied by a single group of people in 1268 and only lived in for a short time. Centuries later, Navajos moved into this country, but they stayed away from the old Anasazi ruins, which they considered haunted. Consequently, when John Wetherill and Byron Cummings explored here in 1907, they found a huge assortment of artifacts and well-preserved buildings. In 1982, researchers from the University of Arizona's Tree-Ring Laboratory conducted a landmark study of roof beams here, and the following year at Kiet Siel. They accomplished room-by-room reconstructions of the building sequence of the pueblos. Unlike Betatakin, Kiet Siel, founded in 1245, changed over a period of two generations as people added rooms and discontinued using others.

The hike to and from Kiet Siel requires strength and endurance for, in addition to the length, there is a 1,000-foot drop into (and later climb out of) Tsegi Canyon. It's an unforgettable experience, however, along a trail that switchbacks to the canyon bottom, traverses Navajo land, and then climbs gradually up Kiet Siel Canyon. A sensible plan is to go one day, camp overnight below the ruins, and return the following day. A ranger stationed at the site will guide you to the cliff dwelling. Be well prepared with water, food, hat, and camping gear. You will find more detailed information about going to this cliff dwelling on the monument's website. Only twenty people are allowed to go there each day.

Richard Wetherill, the Mancos rancher credited for "discovering" the Mesa Verde cliff dwellings, was the first Euro-American to record Kiet Siel. He found the ruin to contain 155 rooms and six kivas, which look out over a quiet valley.

An intermittent stream flows through a meadow and past a grove of cottonwood trees, where the campground is located. Two aspects of this site that will impress you are its size and how it appears as if its occupants left much more recently than seven centuries ago. It is so large and beautifully designed and constructed that one wonders why its inhabitants didn't stay longer. The tree-ring research also provided insight into the environmental causes of the area's abandonment and reconstructed how households were organized in the pueblo.

The monument's visitor center has archaeological exhibits, an interpretive film, picnic sites, and campgrounds. During summer months, rangers offer campfire talks on the area's history and natural environment. Tourist services can be found in the town of Kayenta.

Suggested Reading: *Houses Beneath the Rock: The Anasazi of Canyon de Chelly and Navajo National Monument*, edited by David Grant Noble, Gibbs Smith Publisher, Layton, Utah, 1986.

CANYON DE CHELLY NATIONAL MONUMENT

Canyon de Chelly National Monument is located 3 miles from Route 191 in Chinle, in northeastern Arizona. Information: (928) 674-5500; backcountry permits: (928) 674-2106; www.nps.gov/cach/index.htm. No fee, but contributions welcome.

———

Millions of years ago, meandering streams wore channels through the petrified sand dunes to form the stunningly beautiful landscapes of Canyon de Chelly and Canyon del Muerto. A large watershed drains into the canyons from the Chuska Mountains and Defiance Plateau, eventually emptying into the San Juan River in southeastern Utah. Although usually a trickle, it can rise to a torrent. Alcoves in the canyons' cliffs hold Native American dwellings—hunter-gatherers, Basket-makers, and Puebloans—and the cliff surfaces served as "canvases" for pecked and painted images. Today, this national monument is a major draw for visitors from this country and around the world. It is also the home of Navajo families. The park is managed collaboratively by the National Park Service and the Navajo Nation; the word "Chelly," in fact, is a Spanish corruption of the Navajo *tsegi*, meaning "canyon." The main archaeological sites you will see on a visit to these scenic canyons are cliff dwellings and rock-art panels.

Archaeological research has shown that the earliest people present in the canyons were Archaic hunter-gatherers. Following them, after around 200 BC, Basketmakers moved here. Their numbers were modest and they lived in pithouse settlements in rock shelters. Centuries later, their culture evolved in the ancestral Pueblo or Anasazi way of life.

The Puebloans increased in numbers, partly due to immigration, and preferred aboveground masonry construction. The first phase of construction of Antelope House, along the river in lower Canyon del Muerto, was in late Basketmaker

White House.

times but building continued in the 800s, 1000s, and 1200s. What is visible today is mostly from the last building period. Although much of the village was swept away by floods, it once had between eighty and ninety rooms. In this time, rainfall was abundant and crops thrived in both the canyons and uplands. Resulting population growth motivated residents of Antelope House and Mummy Cave, further up the canyon, to build additions to both these long-occupied pueblos. Construction began on White House (which includes a Chacoan component), Battle Cove, and Ledge Ruin after around 1100 when new settlements also were founded on the plateau outside the canyon.

In the mid- to late thirteenth century, as on Mesa Verde (p. 82) and in the Tsegi Canyon system (p. 146), there occurred a building boom in the shelter of cliff alcoves. This type of housing, in addition to being well protected from the elements, had defensive advantages and left valuable land on the canyon floor open for planting.

Environmental problems compounded by food and water shortages and civil strife brought Pueblo life in these canyons to an end in the late 1200s. People in the entire Four Corners region, suffering from malnutrition, a diminished birth rate, and conflict, emigrated. Although after 1300 some Hopis visited and lived in Canyon de Chelly on a seasonal basis, the canyons were not inhabited again to any substantial degree until the early or mid-eighteenth century and the arrival of Navajos. Except for their years of internment at Fort Sumner (1863 to 1868), Navajos have lived here and in the surrounding region since then. You will see their homes and farms in the canyons, on the rims, and in the town of Chinle. Please respect their property rights and privacy.

During the Spanish Colonial and Mexican periods, Canyon de Chelly was a Navajo stronghold and was repeatedly invaded by mounted militias. On one such occasion, in 1805, soldiers led by Lt. Antonio Narbona attacked a large group of Indians who had taken refuge in a rock shelter, killing 115 people, including women and children. The site has been known since as Massacre Cave.

Navajo cliff painting of a Spanish cavalcade, Canyon del Muerto.

Sixty-one years after Narbona, another military officer led troops into Canyon de Chelly; this time, it was an American. Col. Kit Carson's mandate was to subdue the Navajos and take them as prisoners to a military post 300 miles away in eastern New Mexico. Their trek there, during which many perished, is known as the Long Walk. Carson accomplished the task by torching the Indians' homes, destroying food stores, confiscating livestock, and cutting down orchards. In 1868, after negotiating a treaty with the United States, the Navajos returned to their homeland. The first written accounts of Canyon de Chelly's ruins were made by American military surveyors after the Mexican War.

In the twentieth century, many archaeologists conducted research here, most prolifically Earl Morris, who is also remembered for his work at Aztec Ruins (p. 126). The artifacts he collected are in the collections of the American Museum of Natural History in New York City. The canyons' rock art also has been extensively surveyed and reported on.

Several options are available to visitors here. At a minimum, you can drive along the south and north canyon rims, stopping at viewpoints and ruins overlooks. At the White House Overlook, there is a trail (2.5 miles round-trip) to this iconic ruin and cliff dwelling. The trail, which is the only one in the monument you can hike on your own, has a 500-foot descent and ascent, so plan about two hours' hiking time. When you reach White House, be sure to note the pictographs on the cliff face.

Tour companies offer half- and full-day guided group tours up Canyon de Chelly and Canyon del Muerto, stopping at rock-art panels and ruins. With a hired personal guide, you can also go in your own four-wheel-drive vehicle and see sites at your leisure not included in the group tours. Horseback riding trips can also be arranged. At the visitor center, check to see if a ranger-guided hike is being offered during your stay. Remember, when you meet Navajo people in the monument, introduce yourself and ask permission before taking photographs.

The town of Chinle has restaurants, motels, and other travel services. In the busy summer and fall seasons, it is best to make lodging reservations well in advance.

Suggested Reading: *Canyon de Chelly: Its People and Rock Art*, by Campbell Grant, University of Arizona Press, Tucson, 1978. *Canyon de Chelly National Monument*, by Scott Thybony, Western National Parks Association, Tucson, Arizona, 1997.

HOMOL'OVI STATE PARK

Homol'ovi State Park is 3 miles northeast of Winslow, Arizona. From Interstate 40, take exit 257 and follow Arizona 87 north for a little more than a mile to the park's entrance. Information: (928) 289-4106; azstateparks.com/Parks/HORU/index.html. Entrance fee.

———————

North of Winslow, Arizona, lies the reservation of the Hopi Indians, some of whose oral traditions tell of their history living in the Homol'ovi villages. Their predecessors, the Motisinom (pre-agricultural people) and Hisat'sinom (ancestral Pueblo farmers) lived in the Southwest for millennia or, as they express it, "since time immemorial." After their emergence into this world, the Hopi ancestors moved around the Four Corners region, staying in particular locations for a period of time. Some of these places now are set aside as protected parks and monuments. Homol'ovi is believed to be the final gathering place of some clans before they continued on to the Hopi Mesas, where they live today. The word *Homol'ovi* translates loosely as "place of the buttes"; you can see the buttes from the park.

Archaeologists of Arizona State University's Homol'ovi Research Project found more than three hundred sites in and around the park, including the remains of eight communities that were occupied between around 1250 and 1400 CE. To the Hopi, they are sacred ancestral homes, whereas to archaeologists, they represent a rich source of information about the past. Investigations of the sites have been a collaboration between the tribe, the university, and Homol'ovi State Park.

Jesse Walter Fewkes, an anthropologist from the Smithsonian Institution, conducted the first excavations here in 1896. When he talked to Hopi consultants about their connection to these sites, he learned that certain Hopi clans had once lived in the Homol'ovi villages and there were stories passed down about them. Nearly a century later, archaeologists and students from Arizona State began doing research in the park, a general aim being to reconstruct the cultural history of

Reconstruction of Homol'ovi II. Courtesy of Doug Gann and the Homol'ovi Research Program, Arizona State Museum.

the pueblos. The project, which is ongoing, has resulted in a series of published volumes on the prehistory of the Homol'ovi area.

As E. Charles Adams and his colleagues reconstruct Homol'ovi's past, the Hisat'sinom first lived here, probably on a seasonal basis, beginning around 600 CE. During this time, which was wetter than normal, they resided in small pit-house hamlets and dry-farmed sand-dune areas. Later, when the weather turned drier, they moved away, probably to the Hopi Mesas. Two centuries later, drawn by Homol'ovi's relatively reliable water supply and good farming and hunting potential, some of their descendants came back to renew life along the Little Colorado River.

After 1250, Homol'ovi's population grew markedly. This was a period of much movement and migration of Four Corners people. The Homol'ovi folk initially built a series of hamlets on the east side of the river, then two pueblos, Homol'ovi III and IV, on the west side. Around 1300, the residents of these two villages moved across the river. At the same time, small hamlets were coming together to form much larger villages, such as Homol'ovi I and II, with more than a thousand rooms each.

The people farmed the river's floodplain as well as the dunes, valleys, and upland areas. Corn, of course, was the staple, but they also raised a variety of beans, squashes and gourds, and lots of cotton, which they bartered with neighbors for pottery, obsidian, and other goods. Although deer and antelope were a source of protein, rabbits were more important. They probably killed these animals in organized hunting drives much as the Hopi and other groups did in historic times and probably the Motisinom long before. The Homol'ovi people imported much of their pottery (a distinctive coal-fired yellow ware) from the Hopi villages, especially the town of Awat'ovi, 50 miles to the north.

As the population grew, society became more centrally organized, especially in the way it controlled land use. This is reflected in the arrangement of pueblos around a central plaza, where people worked and held communal religious ceremonies. After 1325, the iconography of pottery decorations and rock art shows the appearance of the kachina religion, which the Hopi and other Pueblo people still follow today. At their peak, the Homol'ovi villages reached a total population of around 2,500 people. Eventually, living here became less viable and Homol'ovi society no longer thrived as it had. By the early 1400s, the pueblos were deserted. The next settlers of the area were Mormons in the late nineteenth century.

It goes without saying that the Southwest's ancient farming communities were extremely sensitive to even minor shifts in climatic and environmental conditions. As archaeologists reconstruct the settlements and abandonments of the Homol'ovi villages, one key factor was having just the right amount of water from the Little Colorado River, a nearly perennial stream. Too much flow and floodplain farming was curtailed; too little, and agriculture declined. When the river experienced major flooding, uprooted trees and branches carried downstream and deposited along the banks were the main source of wood for the Homol'ovi communities.

The Homol'ovi people traded widely. Cotton was their main export, but also the abundant natural resources in their riverine environment—plants, bird feathers, and turtles, for example—which were highly marketable to folks living in dry upland regions.

Homol'ovi State Park was created in 1986. It has a visitor center with museum and shop, an interpretive program, and a campground. One highlight is its interesting interactive computer program where you can learn about the archaeological research that has taken place. Trails lead to three of the park's major sites, Homol'ovi II being the largest. An important function of the park is to protect these sites from looting, which has been a huge problem in the past. Although pot hunting used to be a common pastime, such activity is prohibited by state and federal laws (see p. xviii). Looting ruins robs us all of a portion of our heritage and causes special injury to Native Americans.

You will find abundant travel resources in nearby Winslow, including the historic former Fred Harvey hotel, La Posada. The Rock Art Ranch, a private enterprise located between Winslow and Holbrook, offers tours of petroglyphs on its property to the public by prior arrangement and for a fee. To make a reservation, call (928) 386-5047 or (928) 288-3260. If you are headed west, don't miss the opportunity to see Walnut Canyon National Monument (p. 166), which is five minutes off I-40.

Suggested Reading: *Homol'ovi: A Cultural Crossroads*, by William H. Walker, Arizona Archaeological Society, Homol'ovi Chapter, Winslow, Arizona, 1996.

ANASAZI STATE PARK MUSEUM

Anasazi State Park is located in Boulder, a small town along Highway 12 in south-central Utah. Information: (425) 335-7308; stateparks.utah.gov/park/anasazi-state -park-museum. Admission fee.

———————

The southern slopes of the Aquarius Plateau is a region blessed by fertile soils, good sources of water, plentiful game, abundant wood for fuel and construction, and other resources needed to sustain human settlement. At an elevation of 6,700 feet, the area also has a comfortable year-round climate. It is not surprising, therefore, that ancestral Pueblo people moved here and settled in the late 1000s.

At Anasazi State Park, you will find a museum and the remains of a prehistoric village known as the Coombs site. When archaeologists conducted research here in the late 1950s, they surveyed, mapped, and partially excavated the site. Their work was part of a much larger archaeological mitigation program preceding the building of Glen Canyon Dam on the Colorado River. The Coombs site itself wasn't threatened by the rising water in Lake Powell, 45 miles distant, but the research here was deemed advisable in order to acquire a better understanding of the prehistory of the region to be inundated, where there were few village sites.

Reconstruction of the Coombs Village, circa 1100 CE. Courtesy of the University of Utah Press. Drawing by George A. King, published in *The Coombs Site* by Robert H. Lister.

The village was situated on the western border of the ancestral Pueblo, or Anasazi, world. Its residents irrigated fields along local streams, hunted game ranging from bighorn sheep and mule deer to rabbits and rodents, and foraged for many edible wild plants and seeds. Especially interesting is that archaeologists view it as a cultural crossroads where settlers of the Kayenta branch of Puebloans interacted with their nearby Fremont (p. 183) and Virgin River neighbors. Influences of all three cultural groups were found to be present.

Coombs contained nearly a hundred aboveground rooms and ten pithouses and thrived for about three generations, between around 1160 and 1235. Apparently, a conflagration engulfed the pueblo, possibly causing its abandonment. Fires in pueblos were not uncommon, often accidental but sometimes intentional during times of conflict. The cause of this one is not known. Where the Coombs inhabitants went remains unclear, although it is speculated that they moved south and east to the San Juan River. For seven centuries, their houses, soon to be buried under blowing dust and dirt, lay undisturbed.

You can visit this site and museum in half an hour or so. A self-guided interpretive trail leads through the ruins, whose main feature is an L-shaped block of rooms covered by a canopy. It has been left as it was when excavated. As you walk around, you will also see a partially restored pithouse and there is a suite of reconstructed pueblo rooms you can enter. The museum has interesting displays of artifacts from the site.

The park has a picnic area and you can camp and hike at Calf Creek, which is south of Escalante along Highway 12. Boulder has a restaurant, gas station, and general store. This is a region of extraordinary scenic beauty, an asset that was officially recognized in 1998 when President Bill Clinton dedicated Grand Staircase-Escalante National Monument. The monument contains almost two million acres of pristine wilderness marked by stunning geologic features.

Suggested Reading: *The Coombs Site*, 3 vols., by Robert H. Lister, University of Utah Press, Salt Lake City, 1959–1961.

PETRIFIED FOREST NATIONAL PARK

The north entrance to this park is at exit 311 along Interstate 40, 25 miles east of Holbrook, Arizona. The south entrance is along US 180, 18 miles southeast of Holbrook. Information: (928) 524-3567; www.nps.gov/pefo/index.htm. Fee area.

The great majority of visitors to this unusual park come to see its extraordinary collection of petrified wood, which is visible along the road and trails, ranging from chips and chunks to stumps and entire tree trunks. They tell a story from two hundred million years ago when this now desert landscape was a vast forested floodplain inhabited by crocodiles, dinosaurs, and many other life forms.

But Petrified Forest boasts other attractions, too. One is stunning scenery, most notably the Painted Desert where, especially in early-morning and late-afternoon light, you will see a variety of unexpected and subtle earth colors.

Puerco Pueblo.

Another is archaeology: for thousands of years Native Americans have known this landscape. The first to come made temporary camps as they quarried stone, collected plants, and hunted game. After knowledge of agriculture spread throughout the Southwest, some Basketmaker people made their homes—shallow slab-lined pithouses with dome-like roofs made of sticks, brush, and mud supported by poles—in the uplands. After around 900, Puebloan people, often called Anasazi, built villages and planted crops along watercourses. In some places, they built simple water-control systems to divert rainfall to their gardens. They also hunted; rabbits and pronghorns were a favorite prey. Archaeologists have recorded more than six hundred sites in the park, from potsherd and lithic scatters to dense petroglyph panels and villages.

One village, along Mainline Road, is the partially excavated Puerco Ruin, which overlooks the nearby Rio Puerco, a tributary of the Little Colorado River. This single-story, hundred-room pueblo, occupied between 1250 and 1380, was used for living, storage, and religious functions. In addition to farming and hunting, its inhabitants quarried the petrified wood (agate) to fashion tools and weapons, which they certainly traded with neighbors. The site has been described as a lithic manufacturing center.

Close to the pueblo you will find a fascinating collection of petroglyph panels, and about a mile down the road, you'll come to another known as "Newspaper Rock," not to be confused with a site of the same name in Utah (p. 117). Among its many glyphs, thought to date to between around 1000 and 1350, are human-like figures, animals, birds, lizards, and various nonrepresentational designs. The park contains an abundance of distinctive petroglyph sites made in the Pueblo II and Pueblo III periods in a style referred to as the Winslow tradition; to see them, obtain more information and a backcountry hiking permit at the visitor center. A third easily accessible site, in the south end of the park, is Agate House. Reconstructed in 1935, this small prehistoric house is made of chunks of petrified wood.

It was a post–Mexican War exploratory expedition of the U.S. Army that first reported Petrified Forest in 1851. After the railroad came through in the 1880s, tourists, souvenir hunters, and gem collectors began to arrive. The conservationist John Muir came here in 1905–1906 with his ailing daughter, hoping the dry air would cure her, and he became interested in the area's Indian history and natural resources. He actually made the first archaeological excavation at the Puerco Ruin. However, what particularly concerned him was the environmental impact of a nearby stamp mill that was crushing petrified logs to manufacture abrasives. Muir took the case to President Theodore Roosevelt, who proclaimed Petrified Forest a national monument.

A 28-mile road leads through the park along which are opportunities to take walks into the landscape. At its south end is a museum where you can learn more

Petroglyphs near Puerco Pueblo.

about the area's geology and history. Backcountry permits are available here, too. Plan on several hours to see the park's main archaeological sites and scenic views and take a couple of trail walks. Holbrook has travel services and Winslow boasts La Posada, a restored Harvey House along the railroad. Also in Winslow is Homol'ovi State Park (p. 150).

Suggested Reading: *Tapamveni: The Rock Art Galleries of Petrified Forest and Beyond*, by Patricia McCreery and Ekkehart Malotki, Petrified Forest Museum Association, Petrified Forest, Arizona, 1994.

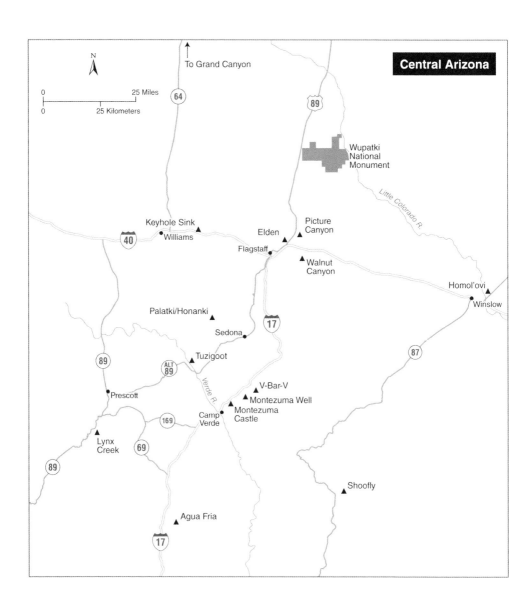

The Sinagua

Determining what name to give a pre-contact indigenous culture is difficult. For more than a century, archaeologists have been referring to the people who lived around present-day Flagstaff, Arizona, and in the Verde Valley as the Sinagua, whom they divided into northern and southern groups. The word comes from early Spanish explorers having called the local mountains the *Sierra Sin Agua*, the "mountains without water." The Hopi, some of whose clans came from this region, call their ancestors Hisat'sinom; however, this Hopi word refers to ancestral Southwestern farming peoples in general and is not limited to those living around present-day Flagstaff and in the Verde Valley.

For thousands of years, as in other parts of the Southwest and in North America, people living in or passing through the Sinagua region were mobile hunters and gatherers. Then, in the late 600s, some began planting crops in the fertile alluvial soils of basins along the flanks of the San Francisco Peaks, where pinyon pines and junipers interface with the higher ponderosa forest. By 900 CE, these Sinagua folk, who lived in rustic pithouses, were trading with Kayenta settlements to the north and Hohokam communities to the south. Another Sinagua group farmed the fertile mesas along the Mogollon Rim. They used stones as garden mulch to moderate soil temperatures and prolong the growing season, and also exchanged goods with the Hohokam, who apparently taught them the fundamentals of irrigation technology and introduced them to the ball court.

Travelers approaching Flagstaff today from the north or east will notice a series of cinder cones. They are part of the 1,800-square-mile San Francisco volcanic field, which was formed between six million and 900 years ago. Sunset Crater, now a national monument, erupted between 1050 and 1100 CE, spreading ash and black cinders in varying depths over a wide area, in some cases burying Sinagua

Imported pottery excavated at Elden Pueblo.

dwellings. The eruptions, which were preceded by earth tremblers, sent fountains of fire and clouds of smoke so high in the air that Indians hundreds of miles away witnessed the event. No doubt this was a terrifying and destructive natural occurrence, which may have lasted for several decades. Interestingly, environmental researchers have found that the moisture-retaining effect of the cinder blanket, when between one and three inches deep, benefits agriculture. This explains why, after the traumatic eruptive period, farmers began moving to these areas. Some were local Sinagua folk, but ceramic evidence shows that people moved here from surrounding areas: Kayenta, Mogollon, Cohonino, and possibly Hohokam.

After around 1150, the northern Sinagua reached their highest cultural expression (Elden Phase), which is apparent in technological achievements such as monumental architecture, more complex social organization, and population growth. Large villages such as Elden Pueblo (p. 163) and Ridge Ruins were founded and Sinagua Indians spread into the Wupatki and Walnut Canyon (p. 166) areas and as far away as the Mogollon Rim.

Developments to the south parallel those of the Flagstaff area. The southern Sinagua—some researchers theorized they migrated down from the north— settled the Verde Valley by around 700 CE. This well-watered region along the Verde River and its tributaries lies 4,000 feet lower in elevation than Flagstaff and offered an ideal climate for foraging, farming, and comfortable living. Small settlements eventually consolidated to form large pueblos like Tuzigoot (p. 178).

For reasons that remain unclear to archaeologists, the northern Sinagua left their homelands between 1250 and the early 1300s. Diminished rainfall, crop failures, and resulting conflicts likely were important factors motivating the emigration. Some traveled southeast to establish settlements such as Nuvakwewtaqa on Anderson Mesa and others went to the Verde Valley. A century or so later, the southern Sinagua packed up and left their homeland and also headed to Anderson Mesa.

At this point, Sinagua culture begins to blend with that of the Hopi Indians, who view some Flagstaff, Verde Valley, and Anderson Mesa sites as ancestral. The Hopi have passed down stories about their history in these places: Sunset Crater is the abode of the wind god, Yaponcha; the Katsinas, their supernatural friends, make their home in the San Francisco Peaks; and the moisture-laden clouds, which rise over those mountains in summer and drift over the Hopi mesas to drop rain, embody the spirits of their ancestors.

Suggested Reading: *Hisat'sinom: Ancient Peoples in a Land without Water*, edited by Christian E. Downum, School for Advanced Research Press, Santa Fe, New Mexico, 2012.

WUPATKI NATIONAL MONUMENT

From Flagstaff, take US 89 north for 12 miles and turn right at the sign for Sunset Crater Volcano and Wupatki national monuments. The visitor center is 21 miles from this junction. Information: (928) 526-1157; www.nps.gov/wupa/index.htm. Entrance fee.

———————

Wupatki National Monument encompasses a vast and desolate landscape where the ruins of numerous pueblos and other sites are to be found. Seasonal temperatures here can plummet to zero and rise above 110 degrees. Life forms must be hardy indeed to survive such extremes, and it seems unlikely that this desert once sustained a sizable human population.

The presence of a large Clovis-period camp not far from Wupatki and Archaic tool-manufacturing sites along the gravel terraces of the nearby Little Colorado River prove that people have been here, at least off and on, for a dozen millennia. Farming around Flagstaff and Wupatki, surprisingly, began to be practiced around 400 CE, about two thousand years after places in southern Arizona. Perhaps hunting and gathering was too productive to give up in favor of the more precarious agricultural way of life.

What captures visitors' attention in this monument, however, are the highly visible stone pueblos of Wupatki, Wukoki, Citadel, and Lomaki, which stand relatively intact since their occupants left them some seven centuries ago. In the late eleventh century, nearby Sunset Crater erupted, spreading cinders and ash across the landscape. Researchers Mark D. Elson and Michael H. Ort have concluded that cinder and ash deposits of more than four inches would have collapsed the roofs of Sinagua houses and deeper deposits close to the volcano would have buried dwellings. Archaeologists, therefore, find it hard to estimate the pre-eruption population.

The eruptions, however, brought benefits as well as fear and devastation. Where not too deep, the cinders acted as mulch, helping to retain precious moisture and extending the growing season, which improved farming conditions. The effects shown in the archaeological record for settlement density increased in the early 1100s. In addition, there was more rainfall, which further attracted settlers to the area.

Who the occupants of Wupatki, Wukoki, and the other pueblos were and where they came from is a topic that researchers have long pondered. Some clues lie in the pottery styles found at individual sites, and other hints can be seen in the style of architecture and other artifacts. Certainly, local people moved to the newly enhanced farming areas, but inhabitants of surrounding regions probably immigrated here as well. Archaeologists often find it hard to determine if artifacts of a certain style found at a given site were imported through exchange or made by immigrants. Whatever the origins of the Wupatki inhabitants, they are commonly referred to now as "Sinagua." The Hopi, some of whose clans came from the Wupatki-Flagstaff area, call them Hisat'sinom, a word that refers generally to the pre-Hopi farming peoples who lived in the Four Corners region.

Wukoki, a Sinagua pueblo in Wupatki National Monument.

In the Wupatki area, between around 1150 and 1250, Sinagua culture reached a peak, society grew more complex and sophisticated, and trade expanded. At Wupatki Pueblo alone, there is a Hohokam-style ball court and excavators found copper bells from Mexico. Evidence of social hierarchy was demonstrated when, at a nearby pueblo site, archaeologists dug up the grave of the so-called Magician; it contained more than six hundred elaborate and unusual funerary objects.

The very existence of crumbled dwellings gives rise to the questions: why and when did the people leave and where did they go? The answers, if they are known, usually are neither simple nor clear-cut. It seems that in the late 1200s, due to a shift in weather patterns unfavorable to farming, people began to concentrate in a few defensible sites. Then, by 1300, they were leaving, many founding settlements southeast of present-day Flagstaff and in the Verde Valley. Homol'ovi (p. 150) is believed to have been established by Sinagua descendants; they lived there before relocating to the Hopi Mesas. Modern-day Americans often relocate for economic reasons, and in the prehistoric Southwest, it was no different.

The Wupatki visitor center offers exhibits on the region's cultural history and should be your starting point before going on to see the ruins. Ask there about the possibility of seeing rock art in the monument. Although picnic sites are available, blustery winds, heat, or cold often discourage sitting around outdoors. A visit to nearby Sunset Crater will nicely complement your experience at Wupatki, as will touring Walnut Canyon National Monument (p. 166). Flagstaff offers many travel services as well as the outstanding Museum of Northern Arizona with its archaeological and ethnographic collections.

Suggested Reading: *Wupatki National Monument*, by Susan Lamb, Western National Parks Association, Tucson, Arizona, 1995.

SITES IN FLAGSTAFF, ARIZONA

Elden Pueblo

Elden Pueblo Archaeological Site is located on the west side of US 89 North, 1.8 miles north of this highway's interchange with Interstate 40 and just south of its junction with Townsend-Winona Road, in Flagstaff, Arizona. Information: (928) 526-0866.

Elden Pueblo is a sixty-five-room, two-story, northern Sinagua pueblo among ponderosa pines on the outskirts of Flagstaff. People settled here around 1070 CE; however, the community really flourished during what is known as the Elden Phase (1150 to 1275) when many people in the region were moving from farmsteads and hamlets to form larger villages. During this time, it became an active trade center. When environmental conditions deteriorated in the mid-1200s, the pueblo's population swelled briefly but then everyone left and the site became vacant around 1275.

Elden Pueblo.

The builders of this village used rocks eroding from the base of nearby Mount Elden for construction material. As a community, they were well situated: building stone and wood were close at hand as was a spring, and not far away were open areas with arable soil. In addition, the region offered good hunting for elk, deer, antelope, mountain bighorn sheep, bear, turkey, and small game.

When you visit Elden Pueblo, pick up a printed trail guide and follow the short, easy trail leading around the site. A highlight of the tour is the large excavated community room, built in 1250, with its seating bench around all four sides. Archaeologists think it was a gathering place for social and ceremonial activities, and it suggests how important Elden was as a political and religious center. This interpretation is reinforced by Hopi oral traditions. The Hopi believe that some of their societies and clans originated here and in other nearby pueblos. Their name for the site, or the area, is *Pasiwyi*.

Along the trail you will also pass excavated and unexcavated rooms and a boulder with grinding slicks. Pithouses and cemeteries have been found outside the main pueblo, as has a "prepared outside activity surface." This unusual feature around the north, west, and south sides of the pueblo has plastered surfaces and storage and roasting pits.

Mary-Russell Colton came upon Elden Pueblo in 1916 while out horseback riding. She and her husband, Dr. Harold S. Colton, surveyed the area for archaeological sites. They also founded the still-thriving Museum of Northern Arizona in Flagstaff, which is a must-see when you are in Flagstaff, especially for its excellent archaeological and cultural exhibits. In the summer of 1926, Jesse W. Fewkes conducted excavations at Elden Pueblo with John Peabody Harrington (later to become a noted linguist) as his assistant and a crew of a dozen men. Theirs were the first archaeological excavations to take place in the Flagstaff area. They dug up 35 rooms, more than 150 burials, and some 2,500 artifacts. To the consternation of local citizens, Fewkes sent the material to the Smithsonian Institution in Washington, D.C. Despite all the work Fewkes did, his scientific documentation (notes, photographs, maps, reports) of the findings was minimal. Small-scale investigations of a more professional nature took place here in the 1960s and 1970s.

In recent decades, under the guidance of archaeologist Peter J. Pilles Jr., research has continued at Elden Pueblo through programs of public archaeology. Organized groups of students—from schoolchildren to senior citizens—come to the site to learn about the past by participating in the archaeological process. Coconino National Forest, which administers the site, has played an active role in this Elden Pueblo Project.

Picture Canyon

The Picture Canyon trailhead is on El Paso Flagstaff Road. From Routes 180 and 40 Business, go about 2 miles east on Route 66 to El Paso Flagstaff Road. Very soon you will pass the Wildcat Hill Wastewater Treatment Facility on the right. The parking area is a short distance beyond. From the Walnut Canyon exit on Interstate 40, drive west on Route 66 to El Paso Flagstaff Road.

Less than 2 miles east of Elden Pueblo is an archaeologically significant nature preserve known as Picture Canyon. Here, an interpretive trail follows along the east canyon rim, crosses the Rio de Flag, and returns on the other side. The canyon is in the course of the river but, except after heavy rains, its water flow comes mostly from the nearby Wildcat Hill Water Treatment Facility.

On the canyon's cliffs and boulders, you will be able to spot a series of rock-art panels containing hundreds of images. (Bring binoculars for best viewing.) Some you'll be able to see close-up. They are of the Sinagua culture and were made, very likely, by the inhabitants of Elden Pueblo and other nearby sites.

Picture Canyon was researched by Harold S. Colton and has been known for a long time. However, the Rio de Flag was diverted into a channel and the canyon became cluttered with trash. In recent years, the Friends of the Rio de Flag and the Picture Canyon Working Group have restored the area to its former beauty and developed trails. Most important, the city of Flagstaff purchased the land. Now the canyon is on the National Register of Historic Sites.

While in this area, you will find visits to nearby Wupatki (p. 161) and Walnut Canyon national monuments of much interest.

WALNUT CANYON NATIONAL MONUMENT

Walnut Canyon National Monument has its own exit (204) off Interstate 40, 7 miles east of Flagstaff, Arizona. Information: (928) 526-1157; www.nps.gov/waca. Entrance fee.

————————

Walnut Canyon is imbued with a magical quiet and peaceful atmosphere; archaeology aside, it is worth experiencing just for its beauty and ambiance. Deeply cut through layers of limestone laid down millions of years ago on sea beds, it contains cliffs with scores of shallow caves under ledges. It was here that Sinagua people made their homes in the 1100s and 1200s.

The monument offers two hiking opportunities and has a visitor center with exhibits. The Rim Trail, a flat twenty-five-minute walk, begins at the parking lot, passes pueblo ruins and a pithouse, and continues to canyon overlooks. A mile-long trail, which has spectacular views, leads past several cliff houses and many more can be seen across the canyon. It has a drop/climb of 185 feet and demands considerable effort, especially at the monument's 7,000-foot elevation. Be sure to bring a camera and binoculars.

Before the building of upstream dams, water flowed seasonally in the canyon, making it an attractive environment for human use and habitation. Archaic hunter-gatherers came here as they pursued their seasonal rounds, leaving a few clues to their presence for later archaeologists to find. But it was between around 1125 and 1225 that the canyon really hummed with human activity. Some Sinagua families made their homes in the cliffs, others in pueblos on the rims, where they farmed, hunted, and collected pine nuts and other plant foods. They clustered their homes near several unusual large stone rooms constructed on peninsulas at bends in the canyon. Most researchers used to view these structures as forts, or possibly housing for visiting traders from Hohokam country to the south; now, however, they are more often interpreted as ceremonial buildings.

Those who chose to live in the cliffs built small, cozy, extended-family dwellings scattered within earshot of each other. The deep, winding canyon contains numerous microenvironments with a diversity of plant life. Add to this an abundance of mule deer, wild turkeys, and other animals and it is easy to see why the Sinagua liked this place. In the mid-1200s, however, they left. It is thought that many went south to the Verde Valley while others drifted eastward toward present-day Winslow and the Hopi country. Why did they go? Warfare may have been a reason. Possibly, too, valuable resources such as wood, soil fertility, and game became overexploited and the Sinagua saw advantages to moving on.

After the building of the railroad in the 1880s, European American settlers began coming to the Flagstaff area in large numbers and recreational outings to

Cliff dwelling along the trail in Walnut Canyon.

Walnut Canyon became a popular pastime. So did pot hunting and looting. To facilitate digging in the inner rooms of the cliff dwellings, they sometimes used dynamite. Consequently, many of the ancient houses were damaged and their contents vanished.

When civic leaders in Flagstaff finally realized the city was losing a valuable tourist attraction, they took measures to safeguard the ruins. In 1915, President Woodrow Wilson set aside Walnut Canyon as a national monument. Even so, it took another two decades before adequate supervision of the archaeological sites was implemented. By that time, Walnut Canyon's cliff dwellings had been so devastated that one archaeologist referred to the place as "a monument to vandalism." This history has made it difficult for archaeologists to reconstruct the canyon's past. On the positive side, Depression-era programs like the Civilian Conservation Corps contributed to stabilizing walls, improving trails, and assigning guides to visitor groups.

Pot hunters and looters, happily, left the rim sites virtually untouched, and they have proven to be a valuable source of cultural information. The first scientific person to survey sites in Walnut Canyon, in 1912, was Dr. Harold S. Colton, a professor of zoology at the University of Pennsylvania. In 1926, he moved to Flagstaff with his family and founded the Museum of Northern Arizona. He soon was joined by Lynden Hargrave, and together they conducted professional excavations in the canyon. Archaeological research has continued sporadically over the decades, and in the 1980s, a complete monument survey recorded 242 sites ranging from small artifact scatters to multiroom pueblos.

As a jumping-off place for the Grand Canyon, Flagstaff has an abundance of travel services. Elden Pueblo (p. 163), Wupatki National Monument (p. 161), and the Museum of Northern Arizona are all nearby and interesting to see. You may also wish to take a drive through scenic Oak Creek Canyon to Sedona.

Suggested Reading: *Walnut Canyon National Monument,* by Scott Thybony, Western National Parks Association, Tucson, Arizona, 1996.

SEDONA AREA SITES

The region around Sedona and Oak Creek boasts iconic views of Arizona's landscape, and one way to savor this Red Rock Country is to explore in your car. Another is to take advantage of the extensive network of hiking trails. Still another is to visit ruins and rock-art sites. In some cases, you will need a Red Rock Pass, which is sold at various locations. For information: (928) 203-2900; www.redrockcountry .org/passes-and-permits/index.shtml. A visit to the Red Rock Visitor Contact Center at 8375 State Road 179 is also helpful.

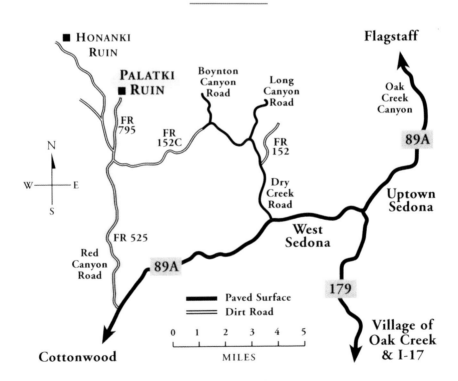

Map showing roads to Palatki and Honanki near Sedona, Arizona.

While in the Verde Valley, visits to Tuzigoot and Montezuma Castle (pp. 178 and 175) are highly recommended, as is going to the historic (now touristic) mining town of Jerome. Travel services are available in Sedona, Cottonwood, and Clarkdale.

Suggested Reading: "The Pueblo III Period along the Mogollon Rim: The Honanki, Elden, and Turkey Hill Phases of the Sinagua," by Peter J. Pilles Jr., in *The Prehistoric Pueblo World: A.D. 1150–1350*, edited by Michael A. Adler, University of Arizona Press, Tucson, 1996.

Palatki Heritage Site

Palatki is half an hour's drive west of Sedona, Arizona. From Sedona, drive 7 miles west on Arizona 89A and turn north on Forest Road 525. After about 5 miles, where the road forks, bear right to Palatki, which is another mile and a half. An alternate route is by way of Dry Creek Road and Forest Road 152C. There is good signage. For information and to make a reservation, call (928) 282-3854. Admission by Red Rock Pass, which can be purchased at the visitor center.

———————

Over the past half century or so, growth and development in the Verde Valley has threatened many fragile archaeological sites. Local and national organizations dedicated to cultural preservation have been active in saving them, including the Palatki, Honanki, and V-Bar-V Heritage sites. Palatki has a small parking lot and limited volunteers, which makes it advisable to call ahead for a time-specific reservation.

Southern Sinagua Indians lived in the Verde Valley region from around 650 to 1400 CE, followed by Apache and Yavapai Indians, some of whom still live nearby. In the late 1800s, the archaeologist Jesse Walter Fewkes of the Smithsonian Institution became immersed in studying Hopi culture and history. This led to his exploring the Verde Valley, where some Hopi clans traced their lineage. He documented and photographed Palatki and Honanki and gave them their Hopi names, which mean "red house" and "bear house," respectively.

From the visitor center, a short, easy trail, though not wheelchair friendly, leads to a pair of cliff dwellings in a box canyon. The first one has impressively high stone walls made of red sandstone blocks. Some room walls are rounded, an unusual characteristic that helped give them strength and durability. A white shield-like pictograph, visible high on the cliff face above the dwelling, is thought to be a clan symbol of the former residents. From this site, you can look west along the cliff to a second complex of masonry rooms that were built when the number of residents increased. This extension is too deteriorated to allow close access. Palatki is thought to have been built in the early twelfth century and was occupied for about 150 years.

Another trail takes you along a cliff where you can observe several pictograph panels. By special arrangement, you can have a guide lead you to a series

Palatki cliff dwelling.

Pictographs at Palatki Heritage Site.

of alcoves farther along the cliff containing examples from Archaic, Sinagua, Apache, and Yavapai rock art. The images range from very ancient abstract designs to more recent pictures of animals and even horseback riders. Also along the extended trail is a large gray mound where Indians roasted hearts of agave, an edible desert plant.

Honanki Heritage Site
Honanki also is reached via Forest Road 525; however, after 5 miles bear left where the road forks and continue 4 miles. This is a rough road requiring high-clearance vehicles. Ask about road conditions at Palatki. Admission by Red Rock Pass.

An easy ten-minute path winds along the base of a butte and past the remains of rooms and a cliff dwelling that were occupied by Sinagua Indians between around 1100 and 1300. The sixty-room cliff dwelling is relatively well preserved despite the long effects of weathering and some vandalism. In his 1896 report, Fewkes sounded frustrated at not being able to collect more of Honanki's abundant artifacts, writing, "I can readily predict a rich harvest for anyone who may attempt systematic work in this virgin field." His remark reflects his archaeological times, when the emphasis was more on collecting artifacts for museums than conducting methodical scientific research. From his findings, Fewkes deduced that Apaches and Yavapai later camped in Honanki rooms. There are many examples of Sinagua and Yavapai rock art here, too.

At one point during its occupation, a fire in the east wing of Honanki destroyed many rooms. The residents reused the stones to rebuild. Honanki is the "type site" for the Honanki Phase (1150–1300) of the southern Sinagua cultural sequence. It is also one of the largest cliff dwellings in the region.

V-Bar-V Heritage Site

This large rock-art site is located 3 miles south of the intersection of Arizona 179 and Interstate 17, which is 12 miles south of Sedona. Admission by Red Rock Pass, which can be purchased there and is good for Palatki and Honanki. Hours: 9:30 a.m. to 3:00 p.m., Friday through Monday. Information: (928) 203-2900.

———————

It was of great benefit to the public when, in 1994, the Coconino National Forest was able to acquire an extraordinary rock-art site, which had long been owned and protected by the V-Bar-V Ranch. Today, it is administered in cooperation with the Verde Valley Archaeological Society and the Friends of the Forest.

The site consists of several panels of petroglyphs that include anthropomorphic figures, animals, birds, snakes, and abstract or geometric designs. The glyphs are densely packed, frequently touching each other or linked by wandering lines. This interconnectivity suggests that the individual elements may contribute to an intended meaning of the whole, as if stories were being told. Another interesting characteristic is the presence of many small cupoles (cup-like pockets) pecked into the bodies of anthropomorphic and animal figures, often in vital areas such as the chest. Do they reflect attempts to obtain power from the figures?

The introduction to this section of the book mentions two Sinagua branches, and it was the members of the southern one who made these petroglyphs. The Verde Valley has much more rock art, but most of it is on private property. Nearby, along Beaver Creek, is a Sinagua residential site, and it may well have been people from there who made the petroglyphs in the panel. On the other hand, an old trail along Beaver Creek would have seen heavy traffic by local and regional travelers in times past and from this trail, the petroglyphs were visible.

Scholars who have studied these petroglyphs classify them as the Beaver Creek Rock Art Style and date them to between 1150 and 1400 CE. They also think the images were made at roughly the same time. This contrasts to sites like Newspaper Rock (p. 117) whose glyphs were made by several cultural groups over many centuries. Why they were made and what they meant to their makers is something that scholars today cannot decipher. Most attempts are speculative. If any people have insights into these questions, it might be the Hopi, some of whose clans descend from the Sinagua. Even so, such information usually is in the sacred realm and kept private.

A portion of the petroglyph panel at the V-Bar-V Heritage Site.

The V-Bar-V petroglyphs are very accessible. An easy half-mile trail leads from the parking area and visitor center to the site where you can view the glyphs close-up. The hillside along this trail is covered with farming terraces; however, they are hidden by vegetation. Site docents offer information (and sometimes subjective interpretations) about the site.

As an adjunct to visiting the V-Bar-V Heritage Site, you may wish to go on a short way to Sacred Mountain. To get there, continue past the V-Bar-V turnoff for half a mile to a parking area. From there you will see a white-capped hill, which is Sacred Mountain. By the parking area you will see a ranch road. Follow it about 300 yards to a gate. (Close it behind you.) On the other side of the gate, follow a rough trail to the right along a fence. Shortly, you will pass through a turnstile from where the path circles up the side and to the top of Sacred Mountain, from where you'll enjoy a stunning 360-degree view of the surrounding countryside. The round-trip hiking time is about 45 minutes and the hike is easier than it looks.

At the southeast base of the mesa is an unexcavated Hohokam-style ball court; you'll have to study the terrain carefully to make it out. Archaeologists from the University of Arizona conducted a survey of the area and found evidence of farming below the mesa. At the top of Sacred Mountain you will find not only a beautiful view but also the ruins of a Sinagua pueblo. Its rooms, built of stone, are mostly collapsed, and the site is overgrown with bushes

Sacred Mountain.

and grasses. The Coconino National Forest manages this site and it is open to public visitation, but cultural information about it is not offered along the trail or easily available elsewhere. However, it fits into what David R. Wilcox and colleagues have dubbed the "Central Arizona Tradition," which extends from the foothills north of Phoenix to the Mogollon Rim and from the Big Sandy drainage on the west to the Mazatzal Mountains on the east. Within this region, they theorize, a "Verde Confederacy" provided mutual assistance in both subsistence and war. The defensively sited pueblo on Sacred Mountain seems to fit their model.

Other interesting sites in this vicinity are Montezuma Castle, Montezuma Well (p. 177), and Tuzigoot National Monument (p. 178). The Verde Valley Archaeological Center in Camp Verde also makes an interesting stop. Travel services are available in Sedona and Camp Verde and the Beaver Creek Campground is less than half a mile away.

MONTEZUMA CASTLE NATIONAL MONUMENT

Montezuma Castle

To reach Montezuma Castle, follow Interstate 17 to exit 289, drive east for half a mile, then turn left on Castle Road. Information: (928) 567-3322; www.nps.gov/moca/index.htm. Entrance fee.

———————

Visually, Montezuma Castle is all we expect in a cliff dwelling and has become an iconic image of the ancient American Southwest. In 1906, following passage of the Antiquities Act, President Theodore Roosevelt, recognizing the site's "ethnological value and scientific interest," made it a national monument. Because of its fragility, the castle may no longer be entered. A paved pathway about a quarter of a mile long takes you from the visitor center to an excellent viewpoint, continues on to Castle A, and loops back along Beaver Creek. It is an easy, pleasant walk in the shade of sycamore trees. Do not expect to be alone; the monument accommodates hundreds of tourists each day.

The famous cliff dwelling is dramatically and impregnably situated on the ledges of a 150-foot limestone cliff overlooking Beaver Creek in the lush Verde Valley. Its twenty well-preserved rooms reach up to five stories. They were built of limestone blocks laid in mortar and roofed by sycamore timbers overlaid by poles, sticks, grass, and several inches of mud. The exterior ones, amazingly, are nearly flush with the cliff face and form a concave arc that conforms to the surrounding cave. The slope below is partially covered with a deep fill containing household trash, graves, and the remains of older house structures.

To reach their domicile, the Sinagua used two access routes. One, from the valley floor, required ladders, and the other, from the side of the cliff, joined it partway up. A small smoke-blackened room at the junction is thought to have

been a sentry post. The rooms themselves are compact and have small doorways. This design made hostile entry most difficult and helped to conserve heat. The pueblo was high above the cold air that settles on the valley floor, and its southern orientation made for passive solar heating in winter.

Castle A, situated a hundred yards away at ground level, also attained five stories. Together, the two buildings housed a considerable number of people, who raised corn, beans, squash, and cotton in nearby irrigated fields and participated in widespread trade. Excavations turned up plant remains, such as seeds, nuts, and agave, which indicate that the Sinagua here also foraged for food.

Sycamore wood does not produce datable tree rings, and firm dates for Montezuma Castle are elusive. However, it seems the Sinagua began building these pueblos in the early 1100s and left the Verde Valley in the early 1400s. Why they left is uncertain, but they probably went north to live in the vicinity of today's Hopi villages. Some Hopi clans, indeed, have oral traditions about having once lived in the Verde Valley.

In the 1880s, before archaeology became a scientific discipline, many tourists and collectors, especially from nearby Fort Verde, climbed up into the cliff dwelling and stripped it of its well-preserved contents. Castle A, fortunately, was less impacted by looting and was the subject of systematic excavations in the 1930s. This large building, archaeologists discovered, collapsed in a conflagration while it was being inhabited. Excavators found many burials here, one of which held a stunning array of jewelry. The deceased person, a woman in her thirties, apparently had special status in the community.

Montezuma Well

From I-17, take exit 293 (4 miles north of the Montezuma Castle exit) and drive 4 miles through McGuireville and Rimrock to the entrance. Information: (926) 567-3322; www.nps.gov/moca/montezuma-well.htm.

———————

Sunk into a hill 6 miles north of Montezuma Castle is one of the most unusual geologic spots in the Southwest. Known as Montezuma Well, it is a limestone sink, 470 feet in diameter, formed millions of years ago by a spring. Ducks swim on the serene surface of this small, round lake and coots poke along its reedy shores. Muskrats, turtles, and other animal life sometimes can be spotted as well. Carbon-dioxide-infused water flows into the lake at a rate of a million and a half gallons per day. It is little wonder that this was a popular place for the Hohokam and Sinagua Indians to live.

A short trail leads up to the rim of the hill, where you will have a view of the lake and some cliff dwellings. You can continue down to the water's edge, passing some habitations in caves along the way; walk along the rim where you'll come to more ruins; and go down the back side to see where the overflow water flows from

Montezuma Castle.

Montezuma Well.

the lake to form a travertine-lined creek. At 76 degrees, the water has created its own lushly vegetated environment.

The first Hohokam settlers came here in the seventh century CE. The Sinagua came later and stayed until the 1400s. Being farmers, they used the sinkhole's outflow to irrigate their fields. Population around the lake peaked around 1300 when, it seems, everyone drew together for security.

Along the road to Montezuma Well, you will pass the roofed-over remains of a Hohokam pithouse, one of the few in the Southwest that have been preserved. Its walls and roof, of course, decomposed long ago, but you will see the floor features and a scale model of how it looked when in use.

Restaurant and travel accommodations are available in Camp Verde and near most other interstate exits. To complement seeing this national monument, you will enjoy visits to Tuzigoot, located in Clarkdale, and the V-Bar-V Ranch petroglyph site (p. 172), which also is nearby.

Suggested Reading: *Ruins along the River*, by Carle Hodge, Western National Parks Association, Tucson, Arizona, 1986.

TUZIGOOT NATIONAL MONUMENT

Tuzigoot National Monument is along US 89A between Cottonwood and Clarkdale, Arizona. It is 52 miles south of Flagstaff and 90 miles north of Phoenix. Information: (928) 634-5564; www.nps.gov/tuzi/index.htm. Admission fee.

Across the varied landscapes of the American Southwest, travelers are often struck by how suddenly lush environments of river valleys morph to arid terrain only a short distance away. A case in point is the Verde Valley. Its river, fed by Oak Creek, Beaver Creek, and other tributaries, has produced a fertile green swath with abundant wildlife and moderate climate in which people have thrived, with some gaps, from ten thousand years ago to the present.

The pueblo of Tuzigoot—an Apache word meaning "crooked water" because of a nearby crescent-shaped body of water—sits atop a ridge to enjoy a wide view over the middle Verde Valley. About a millennium ago, a group of southern Sinagua people migrated here from the north and constructed a small cluster of houses; in the 1200s and again in the 1300s, they built additions until the village attained some ninety rooms of limestone and sandstone blocks. The building spurts reflect the coming together of small settlements in the area.

Tuzigoot is situated along a travel corridor midway between the higher plateau pueblos of the northern Sinagua, near present-day Flagstaff, and Hohokam communities around Phoenix. Its inhabitants, consequently, enjoyed a lively trade of pottery, shell, minerals, and agricultural products. Cultural intermingling always accompanies trading relations, and in the Verde Valley peoples of dissimilar traditions and skills came together and learned from each other. Some have called the valley a cultural melting pot. The Hohokam (p. 45), who had settled the upper valley before the Sinagua arrived, became neighbors of Tuzigoot Pueblo around 1100 and must have shared their expertise both in the crafting of fine jewelry and irrigation agriculture.

The southern Sinagua, including those living in Tuzigoot, left the Verde Valley around 1400 CE. Archaeological evidence, as well as some Hopi clan narratives, tells us that Verde Valley residents migrated north and east to Anderson Mesa, Chavez Pass, and the Hopi Mesas. Some probably settled along the Little Colorado River near present-day Winslow. It's possible others stayed put, later to become absorbed among the late-arriving Yavapai Indians.

The first European to describe the Rio Verde was the Spanish explorer Antonio de Espejo, whose perambulations in 1583 took him on an extensive journey through the American Southwest. In northern Arizona, he recruited Hopi guides to lead him along the Palatkwapi Trail to the Verde Valley, where he was shown quarries that Native Americans had long used. Centuries later, one of these would develop into the famous copper-mining town of Jerome. The monument's land indeed once belonged to the United Verde Copper Company.

Tuzigoot has an interesting archaeological history. In 1892, it and other sites in the middle Verde Valley—about fifty have been recorded—were scientifically surveyed by Cosmos Mindeleff of the Bureau of American Ethnology, who fortunately made note of irrigation systems that later were demolished by modern development. Soon afterward, a colleague, Jesse Walter Fewkes, conducted more research, trying to link the prehistoric residents of the valley to the Hopi Indians. In 1933–1934, Tuzigoot was the subject of intensive excavations led by

two University of Arizona graduate students: Louis R. Caywood and Edward H. Spicer. This was a Depression-era project funded by the Federal Emergency Relief Administration and provided work for as many as forty-eight laborers, who, under supervision, dug out the entire pueblo. The artifacts were cleaned in a nearby school building before being sent to a museum. This type of methodology, typical of its era, left much potentially valuable data about Tuzigoot's cultural history unrecorded. Moreover, no parts of the site remained undisturbed for future study.

The monument's visitor center dates to the 1930s and has a fine, recently renovated museum for which you should allocate plenty of time. The ruins trail is only a quarter of a mile long and can be done relatively quickly. There are picnic tables and camping is available at nearby Dead Horse Ranch State Park. As this is a populated area, there are many nearby travel services. Several public archaeological sites are only a short drive away, and the town of Jerome makes an interesting and scenic excursion.

Suggested Reading: *Tuzigoot National Monument*, by Rose Houk, Western National Parks Association, Tucson, Arizona, 1995.

Tuzigoot ruins looking over the Verde Valley.

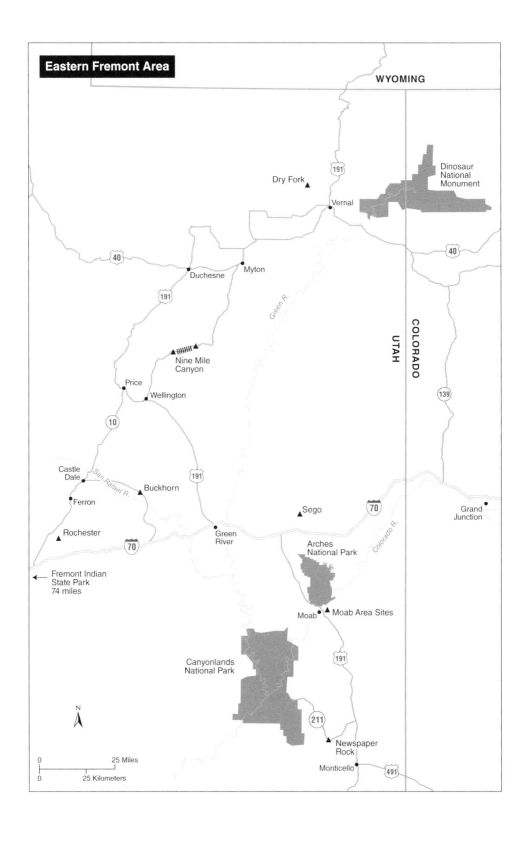

Eastern Fremont Area

WYOMING

Dinosaur
National
Monument

191

Dry Fork ▲

Vernal

40

40

Myton

Duchesne

191

Green R.

COLORADO

UTAH

Nine Mile
Canyon

139

Price

Wellington

10

Castle
Dale

San Rafael R.

Buckhorn

191

Sego ▲

70

Grand
Junction

Ferron

Rochester ▲

70

Green
River

Arches
National Park

Colorado R.

Fremont Indian
State Park
74 miles

Moab ● ▲ Moab Area Sites

Canyonlands
National Park

191

N

211

Newspaper
Rock

0   25 Miles

Monticello

491

0   25 Kilometers

The Fremont

Among the various peoples who inhabited the Southwest in ancient times, the Fremont have perhaps most puzzled archaeologists. They were first archaeologically found and defined in 1931 by Noel Morss, a Harvard graduate student, who was investigating sites along the Fremont River in Utah. Since then, scholars have debated the origins, characteristics, fate, and even existence of the Fremont as a culture distinct and separate from the ancestral Pueblos, or Anasazi. Archaeologists define cultural groups by the material objects they find at sites. After carefully studying the material evidence—houses, pottery, stone tools, and skeletons and sometimes perishables like cloth and food—they attempt to describe a given culture and reconstruct how it developed and how its members behaved.

The Fremont would have been amused by the confusion of researchers about their identity for, no doubt, they knew exactly who they were, how they were organized, what they believed in, and why they did what they did.

A common archaeological trait found throughout the Fremont region—there is general agreement on this point—is a thin-walled, plain gray pottery, variations of which have been found at sites throughout most of Utah, the eastern part of Nevada, and the western edge of Colorado. On a topographical map, the Fremont culture area lies in the eastern Great Basin and western Colorado Plateau, which roughly coincides with the present state of Utah.

The Fremont produced other distinctive artifacts besides plain gray pots though they are rarely found at the same site. One was a style of basketry (one-rod-and-bundle) that differs from that made by Puebloan and Numic peoples, who were neighbors. Other distinctive artifacts are a certain style of moccasins and remarkable clay figurines, which have been found in caves. The figurines resemble the anthropomorphic figures in Fremont rock art: they have similar body types and wear elaborate headdresses, fine jewelry, and well-designed clothes.

Fremont petroglyphs, Dry Fork Canyon.

Most Fremont residential sites consist of a few pithouses, but during the peak of their culture in the eleventh century, they built aboveground adobe and stone-masonry pueblos similar to those of their Pueblo neighbors to the south. Some are large villages and a few have been excavated. Other types of sites are seasonal camps, farmsteads, and rock-art panels. Many habitations lie under modern towns or were plowed under in the process of recent farming.

Beginning around 500 CE, when conditions allowed, the Fremont cultivated corn. Some researchers have viewed them as less affluent and sophisticated country cousins of the Puebloans, who migrated up from the south. Indeed, some Fremont rock art resembles that seen along the San Juan River. A reasonable reconstruction of Fremont origins is that indigenous Desert Archaic folk were joined by Basketmaker pioneers and their cultures intermingled. Farming in and around the Great Basin is marginal and the Fremont had to be adaptive—farming when possible, foraging and hunting when necessary, and probably always doing some of both.

What happened to the Fremont also has been a subject of speculation and de-bate with several scenarios having been proposed. The culture reached its great-est extent around 1050. Depending on the area, the archaeological record shows Fremont sites diminishing after around 1150 or 1200 and being gone by 1350.

Possibly, people returned to a nomadic life of hunting and gathering and became archaeologically less visible. Interestingly, their disappearance coincides to some extent with the arrival of Numic-speaking groups—Utes, Paiutes, and Shoshones. Did the Fremont become absorbed by them? Did the Numa push them out? To answer these questions will require much more research.

Most Fremont villages and hamlets are visually subtle or submerged beneath modern development and unlikely to be developed into public parks or monuments. The exception is rock-art sites, of which there are many, and they are truly impressive. When you stand before these sometimes large human-like figures with their individualized faces, you cannot help but feel the presence of those who made them centuries ago. This book includes a sampling of accessible, well-monitored rock-art sites; there are many other others that, even if legally open to the public, are hard to find, not well protected, and vulnerable to vandalism. If you wish to see them, consult a local expert or museum.

MOAB ROCK-ART SITES

In and near the town of Moab, in southeastern Utah, are four easily accessible public rock-art sites in the Fremont tradition. Anthropologists subdivide the Fremont into four cultural branches, and the Moab sites fall into the Southern San Rafael, as do San Rafael Swell sites south of Interstate 70. These Fremont Indians lived just north of the ancestral Pueblo region between around 500 and 1300 CE. Archaeological sites, including petroglyphs, reflect the influence of their southern neighbors; Puebloan migrants, indeed, may have made some of the petroglyphs.

———————————

Start at the Moab Information Center at Center and Main Streets where you can obtain information about the rock-art sites and pick up copies of the brochure *Moab Area Rock Art Auto Tour* and the booklet *Moab Rock Art*. Moab is a major regional center of recreational activities such as hiking, bicycling, river rafting, flying, and scenic drives.

The most impressive rock-art site in this general area is at Sego Canyon (p. 15).

Suggested Reading: *Moab Rock Art*, by Janet Lowe, Canyonlands Natural History Association, Moab, Utah, 2001. *Petroglyphs and Pictographs of Utah*, volume 1, by Kenneth B. Castleton, Utah Museum of Natural History, Salt Lake City, 1984.

Golf Course Petroglyphs

Along US 191, 4 miles south of the corner of Main and Center Streets, turn east on Spanish Trail Road. At the roundabout, proceed on Westwater Drive. There is a pull-out at the petroglyphs half a mile down the road on the left. The panel, which has several components, includes an impressive Fremont-style anthropomorph, bighorn sheep and other animals, and abstract markings.

———————————

Petroglyphs of bighorn sheep and deer or elk, Golf Course site in Moab.

Kane Creek Site

From Main Street in downtown Moab, turn west on Kane Creek Drive and go 0.8 miles to its intersection with 500 West. Keep to the left (still Kane Creek Drive) and continue just over 2 miles to Moon Flower Canyon. You'll find petroglyphs—Archaic and Fremont—on the cliff here, some in poor condition. Another panel is located 1.2 miles farther along the road on the left. Drive another 1.7 miles and you will come to a pull-out above a large boulder with an interesting collection of petroglyphs. Most notable is one that appears to show a woman giving birth.

———————

Potash Road Petroglyphs

The Potash Road Petroglyphs are located along the north side of Utah 279, 9 miles west of Moab. Follow US 191 for 4 miles north of town, turn west on 279, and continue 5.5 miles where road signs mark a series of petroglyph panels. You will see rows of triangle-shaped human figures holding hands and possibly dancing. Some wear horned headdresses and carry spears and shields. The panels include a variety of animals and nonrepresentational designs. Some figures may have been made by Ute Indians after the Fremont had gone.

———————

Courthouse Wash Rock Art

To find this site, drive 4 miles north of Moab on US 191, crossing the Colorado River and Courthouse Wash, to a parking lot on the right side of the highway. From here,

A rock art panel along Kane Creek. Note the birthing scene, centipedes, sandal prints, and large human figure with necklace and headdress.

a footpath leads a half mile back across a bridge over the wash. The pictographs and petroglyphs are along the base of the cliffs. You will find faint but impressive paintings of humanlike figures in the Barrier Canyon style. The head of one resembles an upended horseshoe; another has pointed horns or ears. There are also animals, birds, abstract elements, and large white shields. This site made national headlines in 1980 when it was heavily and systematically vandalized. Although restoration efforts were made, the pictographs were permanently damaged.

DINOSAUR NATIONAL MONUMENT

Dinosaur National Monument straddles the border of northeastern Utah and northwestern Colorado. From Vernal, Utah, follow US 40 east for 12 miles to Jensen, then drive 7 miles north on Utah 149 to the monument entrance leading to the dinosaur quarry museum. Another visitor center is in Dinosaur, Colorado. Information: (435) 781-7700; www.nps.gov/dino/index.htm. Entrance fee.

Most people are drawn to this monument by the extraordinary collection of in situ dinosaur fossils and associated exhibits in the quarry museum. Others come for the thrill of rafting on the Yampa and Green rivers, both renowned for their beauty and whitewater. But the park has still another appeal—archaeology—and this section briefly introduces some of the sites you can see by car, foot, or boat.

Hunter-gatherers roamed the mesas, canyons, and river drainages thousands of years ago, finding shelter in caves and rock shelters. They were followed by Fremont people who, after around 200 CE and especially after 650, farmed corn, beans, and squash while continuing to hunt and forage in the manner of their predecessors. The most visible evidence of their presence is at rock-art sites. After the Fremont, Ute Indians moved into the region, making their camps in some of the same places as their predecessors. Today, the Utes live nearby on the Uintah-Ouray reservation around the town of Duchesne.

Swelter Shelter

Swelter Shelter, a shallow rock overhang with petroglyphs, is located a mile east of the entrance to the visitor center and quarry. A short, level path leads to it from a parking area along the road.

————————————

In 1964–1965, an archaeological team conducted excavations in the floor of this small alcove and uncovered five prehistoric occupation levels. They found McKean and Lake Mojave spear points at the fourth level, dating them to between 7000 and 4000 BCE. Another floor level existed below that but had no identifiable material. The shelter was used again between 3000 and 1500 BCE and again between 1500 BCE and 100 CE. It was the later Fremont who pecked the now faint images on the back wall. They include human figures, deer, and other animals, as well as various patterns.

The researchers uncovered two hearths and collected other stone tools, including blades, scrapers, manos, a drill, and a hammer stone. The crew worked in the south-facing shelter in summer: thus, its name. If that wasn't bad enough, they all came down with coccidioidomycosis (valley fever) from spores in the soil.

The park service has installed interpretive signs along the trail. Plan about twenty minutes to see the site.

Cub Creek Petroglyphs

About 9 miles beyond Swelter Shelter, there is a panel of petroglyphs along the road. A mile beyond this site you'll come to the historic Josie Morris Cabin. These glyphs, in the Classic Vernal Fremont style, date to around 1000 CE and are similar to those in Swelter Shelter. From here, walk a hundred yards farther along the road and you will be able to spot two large petroglyphs of lizards on a rock high up the slope to the left. Binoculars will help see them. The size and subject matter of these glyphs are highly unusual.

————————————

McKee Springs Petroglyphs

Petroglyphs at McKee Springs in Dinosaur National Monument.

This extensive rock-art collection is along the Island Park Road. From Main Street in Vernal, go north on Vernal Avenue, then east on 500 North. After about 3 miles, turn right on County Road 1420. (The turn is signed Buckskin Hill Complex South.) Drive 8 miles and turn left on Brush Creek Road. Go 5 miles and turn right on Island Park Road. At around 10 miles you'll easily see a petroglyph panel with human-like figures and a buffalo on the right side of the road. A very short distance farther on, you'll come to parking pullouts and a trail leading to a series of outstanding Fremont petroglyph panels along the edge of a mesa on the left.

Jones Creek Rock Art

The Jones Creek Trail passes by a series of rock paintings and petroglyphs. If you are boating, the trail begins at Jones Creek campground along the Green River. It is about a 2-mile hike. The upper end of the trail starts at the Jones Hole fish hatchery. From Vernal, take 500 North (the scenic Diamond Mountain Road) and drive 40 miles to the hatchery and trailhead. It is a beautiful 1.25-mile hike along the stream to two side-trail loops to view the rock art.

———————

Deluge Shelter is located at the south end of the pictographs—it was excavated in 1966 and 1967. Shallow alcoves like this one served as a dry camp for transient hunters. Archaeologists found fifteen levels of cultural material buried in 10 feet of floor deposits. The lowest level showed a 5000–4000 BCE occupation. The Fremont, who painted the pictures on the cliff, used it in the tenth century CE, and other Indians, probably Utes, came here after 1300. The mound in front of the alcove is back-dirt from the excavations. Excavated artifacts included stone beads and pipes; bone awls, pendants, and gaming pieces; antler flakes; and pottery.

The pictographs, painted in reddish-brown pigments, show human and animal figures and abstract patterns, one of which resembles a long fishing or hunting net. The Utes, and probably the Fremont, were expert fishers. Several figures appear to be carrying burden baskets on their backs. As this rock art is extremely fragile, be sure not to touch it. The Park Service maintains a campground about half a mile below the rock-art panels. You can obtain reservations and permits at the Dinosaur Quarry. From the campground, another trail leads up Ely Creek to a waterfall.

Pictographs near Deluge Shelter along Jones Creek.

Archaeological Sites along the Yampa River

A float trip down the Yampa and Green rivers offers opportunities to see still other archaeological sites in the park. Commercial rafting companies in Vernal run multiday raft trips during spring runoff season. Pick one with experienced local river guides. The best-known site is Mantle's Cave, located up a short trail at mile 37 in Castle Park. The cave is a huge, vaulted, north-facing alcove that was systematically excavated (after being repeatedly looted) in 1940. It contained four dozen storage chambers, ranging from lined and lidded bell-shaped cists to masonry granaries to large slab-lined pits. They held a wealth of material, which is archived in the Museum of Natural History, University of Colorado, Boulder. (To view items on the Internet, go to: cumuseum.colorado.edu/research/anthropology/collections/mantles-cave.)

In one cache, investigators found a deer-scalp headdress with attached ears that had quill ribs to make them stand rigid. The most remarkable find, however, was a ceremonial headdress made of 370 flicker feathers and a white ermine headband. It resembles headdresses shown in Fremont rock art. It was radiocarbon dated to 1250 CE.

Two petroglyph panels can be found in Echo Park near the confluence of the Yampa and Green rivers. From the Echo Park boat landing, walk up the road a few hundred yards to a short trail branching off to the right. It leads to a panel of glyphs that seem to reflect Basketmaker influence from the south. Farther up the road is Whispering Cave, a pleasantly cool place to escape the sun's heat. Continue on and you will arrive at another foot trail on the right leading past a cliff face with many large-scale anthropomorphic figures in the Fremont style with headdresses and necklaces.

The town of Vernal offers a wide selection of motels, restaurants, and stores, as well as river outfitters. The Utah Field House of Natural History is certainly worth a visit, and for a beautiful view of the confluence of the Yampa and Green rivers, drive to Harpers Corner.

DRY FORK CANYON PETROGLYPHS

The Dry Fork Canyon petroglyphs, on the McConkie Ranch, are 10 miles north of Vernal, Utah. From Main Street in Vernal, drive north on 500 West, then west on Utah 121, then turn right on 3500 West (Dry Fork Canyon Road). After 6.8 miles, you will see a sign for the Indian Petroglyphs and McConkie Ranch on the right. From there it is a short distance to the parking area. Information: (800) 837-6258. Donation requested.

———————

It is rare for private land owners to allow public access to their property, especially when they own an attraction such as this outstanding collection of petroglyphs. However, the owner of the McConkie Ranch generously has been doing this for years. How long this will continue is a question so it is best to call the Vernal Chamber of Commerce for current information about the site's status.

These petroglyphs are among the best of Fremont petroglyphic art and are the "type site" for the Classic Vernal Style, which is centered in northeastern Utah's Uinta Basin. The rock art here has been well known—among anthropologists, at least—since Albert B. Reagan surveyed them in the 1930s for Harvard's Peabody Museum. (You will see the letter "P" with a number next to many of the glyphs—a long-since discontinued method of cataloging.)

From the parking lot, two trails lead up and along a slope to the petroglyphs. The left-hand one goes to a series of large human-like figures. It is well marked though rough in places and takes about fifteen minutes one-way. A second trail leading to the right goes a short distance to more glyphs. A third trail across the road traverses a meadow and leads through pinyon and juniper trees past many petroglyphs along the base of a cliff. It terminates at the "Three Kings" panel (in fact, there are six large figures), which is high up on a promontory. To best see them bring binoculars.

The anthropomorphic figures have broad shoulders and rectangular or bucket-like heads on tapered torsos. They are shown front-on and have individualized faces with slit or dot eyes, some with tear streaks. Many wear elaborate headgear and earbobs and around their necks hang necklaces of beads or pendants. The ornamental detail in their stylized costumes, executed with stone tools, shows fine technique and skill. In her book *The Rock Art of Utah*, Polly Schaafsma writes that these artists were "highly concerned with decorative effects and the elements of design, which in most instances take on a geometric quality." These figures have similarities to the Barrier-Canyon Style anthropomorphs of Canyonlands (p. 17) and to clay figurines found in caves in the region.

Societies like the Fremont, which emerged from a hunter-gatherer tradition, placed responsibility for healing rituals and religious activities in the hands of specialized practitioners or shamans. These individuals had ways to induce out-of-body journeys to contact supernatural powers. Some of the imagery at the Dry Fork Canyon site is often interpreted in terms of shamanic rites. At this site, however, you will also see signs of conflict—robust figures carrying shields and holding what look like severed heads. Other less potent and mystical pictures depict animals, birds, and abstract designs.

There are picnic tables by the parking area and a hut with information about the place and notes of appreciation left by prior visitors. Nearby Dinosaur National Monument (p. 187) and Nine Mile Canyon (p. 194) have more rock-art sites. The Harpers Corner Trail offers a spectacular view over the confluence of the Yampa and Green rivers. Vernal has a natural history museum with good exhibits for children. Vernal has many travel services.

Suggested Reading: *The Rock Art of Utah*, by Polly Schaafsma, University of Utah Press, Salt Lake City, 1994.

Petroglyph of Fremont anthropomorph along the Three Kings Trail.

NINE MILE CANYON

From the south, the road to Nine Mile Canyon (Soldiers Creek Road) starts along Highway 6/191, 7 miles south of Price, Utah. From the north along Highway 40/191, take County Road 33 1 mile west of Myton. A sign here indicates Nine Mile Canyon. After 1 mile, bear right and proceed 30 miles. Information: (435) 637-3009; (800) 842-0789; www.blm.gov/ut/st/en/fo/price/recreation/9mile.html.

———————————

Nine Mile Canyon has been called the longest art gallery in the world. Almost 50 miles long (not 9) from the headwaters to Green River, it has hundreds of rock-art panels, some accessible by short trails and others visible with binoculars. You should plan a full day here to explore sites along the road in the central part of the canyon. To find the rock art, obtain a canyon guidebook or use the widely distributed *Exploring Nine Mile Canyon* brochure, which indicates the locations of some public sites. Respect private property. A map also can be downloaded from the Internet. There are road pull-offs near many panels. To find a personal guide, consult the Castle County Regional Information Center at (800) 817-9949; www.castlecountry.com or www.ninemilecanyoncoalition.org.

Here are a few notable sites: First Site (milepost 26.2); Granary View (38.8); Daddy Canyon Complex (43.8); Big Buffalo (45.7); and the Great Hunt panel (45.9). This is the most famous panel in the canyon. There are also a series of panels along the cliff just east of the intersection of Nine Mile Road and Harmony Canyon Road. And the well-known Sandhill Crane Site is one tenth of a mile west of milepost 36.

The Great Hunt Panel (milepost 45.9).

In addition to rock art, the prehistoric sites in Nine Mile Canyon include residential pithouses, masonry structures and granaries, stone alignments, and cairns. Most are Fremont (p. 183), dating to between 900 and 1300 CE, and are in the "Northern San Rafael" style, which differs from that seen in Dry Fork Canyon (p. 191) and Dinosaur National Monument (p. 187) to the northeast.

In the course of their hunting and gathering rounds, Paleo and Archaic Indians must also have been here, but, to date, the archaeological evidence found of their presence is minimal. After the Fremont Indians left, Utes arrived; their presence is evident in petroglyphs and paintings showing horses and riders.

In the nineteenth century, Euro-American trappers, freighters, soldiers, and prospectors began traveling through Nine Mile Canyon and eventually cattlemen settled here. Today, much of the land along the road is private property and some property owners do not welcome trespassers. When looking for rock art, therefore, it is important to respect property rights, which sometimes means viewing petroglyph panels from the roadside.

Predictably, the draw to living here was Nine Mile Creek and the presence of land suitable for farming—and later, grazing. Also, the canyon's riparian habitat provided natural food resources and attracted birds and animals. In addition, the nearby uplands of the Tavaputs Plateau offered wood, an essential resource for building and heating homes.

The first Euro-American to explore this region was John Wesley Powell after the Civil War. In the late nineteenth and early twentieth centuries, after a number of avocational and professional archaeologists explored and reconnoitered the canyon, its archaeological wealth came to be known, especially the rock art. In recent decades, archaeologists and students have conducted more thorough and methodical inventories but excavation has been limited. Investigators have located Fremont settlements near the canyon bottom and at a variety of other sites hundreds of feet above on terraces, ridges, and pinnacles. Some of these sites, high up and far from water and farmlands, appear very defensive and not lived in for extended periods. It has been suggested that they were places of temporary refuge used during times of danger.

Nine Mile Canyon is located in an area that contains a treasure of another sort; the energy industry has been exploiting oil and gas resources on the surrounding West Tavaputs Plateau. Happily, Nine Mile Canyon Road now is paved and dust raised by traffic is no longer damaging the rock art.

Nine Mile Canyon is in a remote area without facilities. Be sure to bring water and have a full tank of gas. You will find a picnic site at milepost 27.2. Nine Mile Ranch (as of this writing) has campsites, cabins, Dutch oven dinners, and guided tours. Call (435) 637-2572 or go to www.ninemilecanyon.com. It is near milepost 22.

Suggested Reading: *Nine Mile Canyon: The Archaeological History of an American Treasure*, by Jerry D. Spangler, University of Utah Press, Salt Lake City, 2013. *Horned Snakes and Axle Grease: A Roadside Guide to the Archaeology, History, and Rock Art of Nine Mile Canyon*, by Jerry D. Spangler and Donna K. Spangler, Uinta Publishing, Salt Lake City, Utah, 2003.

The "Balloon Man" panel, just under a mile east of the intersection of Argyle Canyon and Nine Mile Canyon roads.

FREMONT INDIAN STATE PARK

Fremont Indian State Park is in Sevier in central Utah, 21 miles south of Richfield. From Interstate 70, take exit 17 and follow signs to the park entrance along West Clear Creek Canyon Road. Information: (435) 527-4631; stateparks.utah.gov/park/fremont-indian-state-park-and-museum. Admission fee.

———————

In the early 1980s, when the western segment of Interstate 70 was about to be constructed, archaeologists from Brigham Young University surveyed the highway easement and made note of artifacts showing the presence of an ancient settlement. Since the site was soon to be destroyed, they excavated it in its entirety and found that it was a Fremont village of considerable size. They excavated nearly forty pithouses and half that many surface structures (mostly food storage rooms) as well as numerous activity areas. Since the typical Fremont settlement was thought to consist of only a few pithouses, the Five Finger Ridge project became scientifically important and added much to existing knowledge of Fremont culture. Today, many fine examples of the site's unearthed artifacts can be seen in Fremont Indian State Park's museum.

The archaeologists believe the village existed between about 1000 and 1350 and in the late 1200s reached a population of some sixty to a hundred people. Each family, they learned, lived in a single pithouse, used its roof as a place to work, and had a storage room close by. Although corn was a staple in their diet, they also consumed a variety of wild plants, such as cattail, and hunted cottontail rabbits and other game. They were part of a larger dispersed community along a 4-mile stretch of Clear Creek Canyon.

What Fremont Indian State Park is well known for, at least among the public, is the abundance of rock art it contains and conserves—thousands of petroglyphs and pictographs in hundreds of panels. Although most of them were made by the Fremont, some are Numic and others may be Archaic. You can see many of the panels along the park's numerous hiking trails for which the visitor center will provide a map. The quarter-mile wheelchair-accessible pathway behind the visitor center has numerous glyphs along it, and other short trails with rock art can be accessed along the frontage road. Some longer, more difficult trails require special permission to hike.

As you explore the rock-art sites, you'll note plenty of abstract designs, bighorn sheep, and anthropomorphs. These are common motifs throughout the Great Basin and Colorado Plateau, suggesting an ideographic tradition that was widespread geographically and had time depth as well. The triangular-shaped bodies of the anthopomorphs show a Fremont link but also suggest earlier origins. The Numic rock art was created by Paiute and Ute Indians, who were mobile hunter-gatherers. Although they did not live here, they used this resource area and

Petroglyphs near the visitor center and museum.

traveled the Paiute Trail through Clear Creek Canyon in late prehistoric and early historic times. One unusual Numic panel shows a two-story house with chimneys and two smoke-belching railroad trains. The longer train has many wheels and about eight cars with windows. It also has three human figures standing on its roof. According to the report referenced below, the panel was made in part by Hunkupp, a Ute Indian from Kanosh, Utah, who was illustrating his journey to the East Coast.

This state park has two campgrounds and a picnic ground. Also, the Paiute ATV Trail runs through the park, for which there are parking areas. Overnight accommodations and travel services are available in Richfield.

Suggested Reading: *Rock Art of Clear Creek Canyon in Central Utah*, by Shane A. Baker and Scott E. Billet, Museum of Peoples and Culture, Price, Utah, 1999.

PAROWAN GAP

In the town of Parowan, Utah, which is north of Cedar City, turn west off Main Street onto 400 North. Continue 10.5 miles to Parowan Gap. Information: (435) 865-2401; parowan.org/index.php/heritage/parowangap.html.

———————

Parowan Gap, the site of an extensive collection of rock art, is located in a lonely sector of southwestern Utah in the eastern edge of the Escalante Desert. The Gap is a 600-foot-deep canyon that cuts through an uplift known as the Red Hills. The river that wore down a passage through the ridge is long gone, replaced today by a road. Rock art should be seen in the context of the landscape in which it was created. "The Parowan Gap in southwestern Utah is a stark example of a place of power and significance," anthropologist Steven R. Simms wrote in *Traces of Fremont: Society and Rock Art in Ancient Utah*. While the Gap is itself an attraction, it is best known for many hundreds of petroglyphs that Native Americans made on boulders. Euro-American pioneers and explorers became aware of this trove of pictures in the mid-nineteenth century. Paiute Indians living in the region, of course, knew them well already.

Archaeologists have studied the rock art of this area less than in other parts of the Southwest, and as a result, detailed and authoritative information in the literature about the cultural context of Parowan Gap is meager. However, there is general agreement that some of the iconography is a western expression of the Fremont culture (p. 183). This is evident in anthropomorphic figures with trapezoidal bodies and horns. The site has both representational and abstract markings—lines and clusters of dots, rakes, curving lines—suggestive of the Western Archaic Style, which long predates the Fremont. Other motifs in these petroglyphs have been ascribed to Shoshonean origin and ancestral to the Southern Paiutes. Some glyphs are superimposed over others.

One study of Parowan Gap, by V. Garth Norman, asserts that some of the petroglyphs record movements of the sun and moon and, in concert with topographical features, the site forms an astronomical observatory. He details his theory in *The Parowan Gap: Nature's Perfect Observatory*. It makes sense that several cultural groups pecked and chiseled these images and did so over many centuries for the Gap has long served as a route for migrants, traders, and other travelers. It still does today and modern graffiti is present, as well.

The Zipper Glyph rock art panel along the Parowan Gap road.

When you drive through the Gap, you will come to a turnoff with an interpretive kiosk put up by the Bureau of Land Management. From there, continue on foot and you will almost immediately begin to see rock art, including a dense collection of designs known as the Zipper Glyph panel. It includes a large V-shaped line with hatch marks along it and a round bulb at the bottom. Continue walking to the west end of the canyon. In some places, you'll see informal trails up the talus slope where people have walked to see higher-up panels.

Travel services are available in the towns of Parowan and Cedar City.

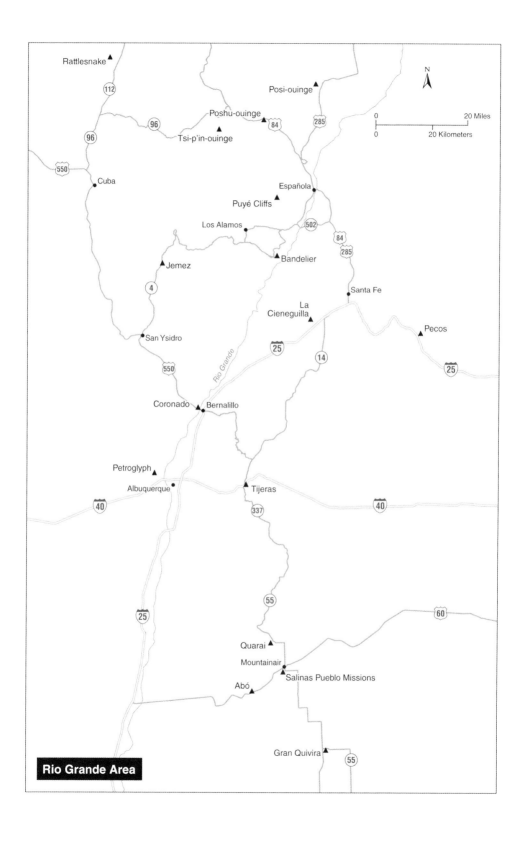

Rattlesnake ▲

112

Posi-ouinge ▲

285

96

Poshu-ouinge ▲

96

84

Tsi-p'in-ouinge ▲

550

Cuba ●

Española ●

Puyé Cliffs ▲

Los Alamos ●

502

84

285

Jemez ▲

Bandelier ▲

4

Santa Fe ●

La Cieneguilla ▲

Pecos ▲

25

San Ysidro ●

550

Rio Grande

25

14

Coronado ▲ ● Bernalillo

Petroglyph ▲

Albuquerque ●

Tijeras ▲

40

40

337

25

55

60

Quarai ▲

Mountainair ●

Abó ▲

Salinas Pueblo Missions ▲

Gran Quivira ▲

55

N

0   20 Miles

0   20 Kilometers

Rio Grande Area

The Greater
Rio Grande Region

In the sixteenth century, two cultural traditions in the American Southwest—Native American and European—became inextricably entwined.

When ancestral Pueblo people left the Four Corners region in the late 1200s, places like Mesa Verde, Grand Gulch, and Canyon de Chelly were left vacant. Many of them—refugees, if you will—migrated to new areas, including the Rio Grande Valley and surrounding region. As the newcomers moved in, putting pressure on existing local communities, new villages were founded. Poshu-ouinge (p. 211), for example, appeared in the lower Chama River Valley; Tyuonyi Pueblo was constructed in what is now Bandelier National Monument (p. 205); and the pueblo of Kuaua (p. 223) was founded north of present-day Albuquerque. Farming communities of various sizes, whose members spoke half a dozen different tongues, thrived along the Rio Grande corridor from the foothills of the Rockies to what is now the border with Mexico.

The other tradition came from Spain via Mexico. In 1540, a Spanish army with mounted knights in glittering armor approached the Zuni pueblo of Hawikuh in central-western New Mexico. On a summer afternoon, the two cultures came face to face, conflict erupted, and the Pueblo world was catapulted into a new era. The effects of the contact between Spaniard and Indian were immediate, and even after four and a half centuries, they remain a subject of controversy.

Diseases from Europe, such as influenza and smallpox, devastated the health of indigenous America. Untold numbers of Natives perished. In the Southwest, Roman Catholic missionaries introduced a new religion, Christianity, to peoples who had long held their own traditions of religious faith and practice. Contrasting value systems became apparent as well. The Europeans sought material wealth and ownership of territory and tried to impose their religion and language—all strange concepts to the Native Americans, who did not "own" land or hoard gold.

A cavate along the trail on Tsankawi Mesa, Bandelier National Monument.

Along with the Spaniards came domestic animals: horses, cattle, and sheep, for example. Their presence affected the economy and way of life as well as the environment and methods of warfare. In the arid environments of the region, people, whatever their backgrounds, gravitated to water and, as you would expect, this valuable resource was most available along streams and in river valleys. It logically came about, therefore, that many Spanish settlements grew near Indian pueblos. In some instances, Spanish settlers moved right into Pueblo villages, welcome or not, to obtain shelter, food, and protection. Franciscan missionaries always took up residence among the Indians, who were obliged to provide the labor to build churches and mission buildings. This amounted to a huge expenditure of time and energy, which they often could ill afford. Over the centuries, the two disparate groups intermingled, sometimes in a spirit of cooperation, sometimes in an atmosphere of coercion and conflict.

Steeped as New Mexico history is in complex cultural and human relationships, it holds much fascination. The differences in Indian and Spanish perspectives and customs, combined with the stresses inherent in trying to survive in a challenging environment, often evoked extreme responses in human behavior. The most dramatic and historically significant manifestation of this was the Pueblo Revolt in 1680, sometimes called the First American Revolution. During this upheaval, Franciscan priests were killed, churches burned, colonists driven into exile, and independence regained by the Pueblo Indians, at least for a decade or so.

To learn about these events, you can turn to a wealth of historical literature. But there is another way: get in your car and go to some of the places where history happened. Enter an ancient cave dwelling, place your hand on the walls of a crumbling or restored mission church, or examine mythic figures pecked on a cliff face, and the past comes alive.

BANDELIER NATIONAL MONUMENT

Bandelier National Monument, near Los Alamos, New Mexico, is located 46 miles from Santa Fe. From Santa Fe, take NM 285/84 north. At Pojoaque, merge onto NM 502 toward Los Alamos, then turn on NM 4 to White Rock and Bandelier. At one mile, on the left, you will pass the parking area for the Tsankawi unit of Bandelier. The monument entrance is 12 miles beyond White Rock. During the busy season, buses shuttle visitors from White Rock to the monument. Information: (505) 672-3861, ext. 517; www.nps.gov/band/index.htm. Entrance fee.

———————

Centuries-old Puebloan ruins, cave dwellings, and rock art all can be explored in this park, which is situated on the Pajarito Plateau on the west side of the Rio Grande in northern New Mexico. The plateau stretches across the east flank of the volcanic Jemez Mountains. This area contains many archaeological sites ancestral to the Tewa- and Keres-speaking Pueblo Indians who today live in villages along the Rio Grande.

Although Pueblo Indians had been living and farming in the Rio Grande Valley since around 500 CE, the Pajarito Plateau was uninhabited until influxes of ancestral Pueblo people began settling it between around 1150 and 1250. Immigrants from Chaco Canyon (p. 121) and the central San Juan Basin may have accounted for much of this settlement directly or indirectly by pressuring existing Rio Grande Valley communities to move to the Pajarito uplands. Then, in the late 1200s, according to some scholars, more immigrants arrived from the Mesa Verde region to the northwest.

Eventually, too many people were competing for limited natural resources with the result that residents of small pueblos aggregated to form large villages. Tshirege, Otowi, and Puyé outside the park boundaries are some examples, as are Tyuonyi and Tsankawi within the monument. Tyuonyi is a circular pueblo on the floor of Frijoles Canyon near the monument's visitor center. It was excavated between 1910 and 1912 by School of American Archaeology students under the direction of Edgar Lee Hewett. Although some minor excavations were conducted in Tsankawi Pueblo, it looks pristine and appears as overgrown rubble mounds containing collapsed blocks of rooms. It has an estimated three hundred rooms surrounding a spacious central plaza. Large villages like Tyuonyi and Tsankawi had a more centralized sociopolitical order that is reflected in their having a single plaza used as a public space.

The people who once lived on the Pajarito Plateau, in Frijoles Canyon, and on Tsankawi Mesa were farmers who also gathered seeds and fruits and a variety of native edible plants and hunted in the game-rich Jemez Mountains. They also probably fished in the river and streams, though there is scant evidence of this activity in the archaeological record. Success, of course, depended on the region's variable weather conditions. The plateau's higher elevation provided more rain and snowfall than the valley but had a shorter growing season. Pajarito folk also participated in a wide-ranging trade network. Trails leading across the plateau and up and down the canyons bear testimony to the importance of this activity. (You will walk along one of these ancient trails on the walk to Tsankawi Pueblo.) The inhabitants of the Bandelier area left in the 1500s, probably due to drought, and relocated to the Rio Grande Valley where their descendants still live.

On your visit, stop first at the visitor center and its museum. From there, follow the Main Loop Trail, which is 1.2 miles. The first section, which is accessible to wheelchairs and strollers, goes past Big Kiva to the ruins of Tyuonyi Pueblo. It then climbs up and down stairs on the north talus slope past a series of cave dwellings (called cavates) cut into the relatively soft volcanic tuff. Some of them you can enter by ladder. The cavates, built between the mid-1200s and early 1500s, served as dwellings and storage rooms and for special purposes such as ceremonies. The trail continues to Long House, built along a sheer cliff that is incised with petroglyphs of birds, animals, faces, spirals, and other designs. Inhabitants made the high-up ones by standing on the upper-story roofs of their houses. You will then cross Frijoles Creek, where the trail divides. One branch goes half a mile farther to Alcove House while the other loops back to the visitor center. National Park Service staff at the information counter will advise you about longer hiking options.

The Tsankawi Unit offers a loop trail about a mile and a half long. Part of it follows an ancient Indian pathway worn and cut in the rock; it leads to the pueblo mounds on top of the mesa. Beyond that, you descend a ladder to a trail along the south edge of the mesa, where there are more cavates. There is a spectacular view from here over the Rio Grande Valley toward the Sangre de Cristo Mountains.

The monument is named for Adolph F. Bandelier (1840–1914), an archaeologist, historian, and archivist who explored Frijoles Canyon in 1880, describing it in his journal as "the grandest thing I ever saw."

Facilities in the monument include a campground, picnic area along Frijoles Creek, bookshop, café, and gift shop. A nearby attraction is the scenic Valles Caldera, which offers hiking, hunting, and fishing. Also close by are the Puyé Cliffs Dwellings (p. 208), an archaeological park owned and managed by Santa Clara Pueblo. The Bradbury Museum in Los Alamos offers hands-on exhibits relating to current scientific research and the Manhattan Project.

Suggested Reading: *The Peopling of Bandelier: New Insights from the Archaeology of the Pajarito Plateau*, edited by Robert P. Powers, School for Advanced Research Press, Santa Fe, New Mexico, 2005. Also, *The Delight Makers*, by Adolph F. Bandelier, Harcourt, Brace, Jovanovich, New York, 1971.

Tyuonyi Pueblo in Frijoles Canyon.

PUYÉ CLIFF DWELLINGS

The Puyé Cliffs ruins are located on the Santa Clara Indian Reservation south of Española, New Mexico. From Española, take NM 30 south 5 miles to the Welcome Center in the Valero gas station at the corner of NM 5 (Santa Clara Canyon Road). From Santa Fe, follow US 285/84 north to Pojoaque, then take NM 502 and turn north on NM 30. The park is open daily but it is advisable to confirm this beforehand. Information and to make advance tour reservations: (888) 320-5008; www .puyecliffs.com. Tour fees.

———————

Puyé (pronounced *poo-yay*) Cliff Dwellings is an archaeological park on the northern Pajarito Plateau owned and managed by Santa Clara Pueblo. Santa Clara guides lead tours to the cliff dwellings and mesa-top village. Visitors also may see the 1920s-era Harvey House, which serves as a visitor center, exhibit space, and gift shop. Tour tickets can be purchased online or at the Welcome Center.

Puyé is one of several large Classic-period (1300–1525) pueblos on the Pajarito Plateau. According to the noted linguist J. P. Harrington, the Tewa name means "where the rabbits assemble." The ruins of two other large villages, Tyonyi and Tsankawi, are in Frijoles Canyon and on Tsankawi Mesa, respectively, in Bandelier National Monument (p. 205). Archaeological research shows that farming began to be practiced in the northern Rio Grande Valley sometime after 400 or 500 CE, and by around 850 settled villages had appeared on the landscape. People moved up on the Pajarito Plateau about three centuries later, establishing Puyé in the mid-1200s. Santa Clara Indians see the village's founding as having occurred earlier, in the 900s. It thrived until the late 1500s, when its inhabitants moved down to where Santa Clara Pueblo is today.

The guided tour along Puyé Cliffs passes by a series of cavates—deep openings excavated into the soft volcanic tuff by the Indians to form rooms. The lower level of these dwellings and storage rooms runs for a mile along the cliff. Steps lead to an upper level as well. As you go, you'll see numerous petroglyphs that were carved and pecked in the cliff surface by the ancient residents. This volcanic rock was deposited more than a million years ago during explosive volcanic eruptions in the Jemez Mountains. Huge amounts of ash and rock formed the Pajarito Plateau on the east flank of the mountains. In the mid-twelfth century, Pueblo Indians began inhabiting the plateau, building farmsteads, then hamlets, and eventually villages reaching the size of Puyé.

The mesa-top tour goes to the extensive remains of Puyé Pueblo. Its size and layout—roomblocks surrounding a central plaza—are indicative of population growth and a need for centralized social organization. A portion of the site was excavated in 1907 by Edgar Lee Hewett, founder of the Museum of New Mexico and School for Advanced Research in Santa Fe. Two years later, Sylvanus G. Morley, one of his students, who later became a leading figure in American

Remains of a habitation, Puyé Cliffs.

archaeology, conducted excavations in the South House of the site. In that era, archaeologists focused more on opening up sites and collecting artifacts than on conducting disciplined research. Detailed scientific reports on the Puyé excavations, unfortunately, are lacking.

Bonuses on this tour are the spectacular view from the top of the mesa over the Rio Grande Valley and toward the Jemez Mountains and the opportunity to climb down a ladder into a reconstructed kiva, a round underground room. You will feel as if you are stepping into the past.

In conjunction with touring Puyé Cliff Dwellings, you may wish to walk around Santa Clara Pueblo and visit some of its arts and crafts shops. Its artisans are particularly noted for their pottery making. Also plan to visit nearby Bandelier National Monument. The Santuario de Chimayo, only a short drive away, is a beautiful example of Spanish-Colonial ecclesiastical architecture. The town of Española has an abundance of restaurants, lodging, and other travel services.

CHAMA VALLEY SITES

This section introduces three ancestral Tewa Pueblo sites in the Chama Valley north of Santa Fe, New Mexico. Archaeologically speaking, Poshu-ouinge, Posi-ouinge, and Tsi-p'in-ouinge (all Tewa-language names) have similar histories.

The Chama River Valley and its tributaries contain the remains of a dozen pueblos ancestral to the Tewa Pueblo Indians who today live in villages along the northern Rio Grande between Española and Santa Fe. Archaeologists generally agree that when Puebloan people depopulated the Four Corners region in the late 1200s, some migrated south and east to the Rio Grande Valley. The Chama River would have been a natural travel corridor, as it was in historic times and still is today. At the same time, Native people were leaving Gallina pueblos (see Rattlesnake Ridge section, p. 237). As the population of the existing Tewa communities swelled, some groups split off to found villages along the lower Chama River.

Within a couple of generations, these new settlements became thriving villages whose residents farmed, hunted in the nearby Jemez Mountains, and took advantage of the rich riparian environment of the Chama River and the streams flowing into it. Near most of the ancient pueblo sites can be found the remains of centuries-old agricultural fields, often referred to as "grid gardens." They are recognizable today (especially in aerial photographs) by the lines of river cobbles that bordered garden plots. The farmers also spread gravel on top of the tilled ground. The stones slowed erosion and collected warmth in the daytime, which radiated into the earth at night, moderating soil temperatures and extending the growing season, which at 7,000-feet elevation was barely long enough to produce a corn crop. The mulch also helped retain soil moisture, which was critical in the dry climate. These gardening methods even allowed farmers to grow cotton.

Life in the lower Chama River Valley carried on until around 1500 when people moved back to the Rio Grande Valley. Most of these pueblos were uninhabited in 1540–1541 when the Spanish explorer Francisco Vásquez de Coronado arrived in the region.

Poshu-ouinge

Poshu-ouinge is located along US 84, 2.5 miles south of Abiquiu, New Mexico, and 16 miles north of Española. The parking area, where the trail begins, is just off the west side of the highway. Information: (575) 758-8851 (Taos Field Office, Bureau of Land Management).

———————

In the Tewa language, *Poshu* means "muddy river" and *ouinge* means "village." This pueblo was founded around 1400 CE. The availability of water from the Chama River and from nearby springs attracted settlers, as did the presence of arable land along the river's banks and lower terraces. Also, there was good hunting in the Jemez Mountains. From their homes, Poshu-ouinge residents could look across the valley and see two sister pueblos.

Adolph F. Bandelier, the noted anthropologist-explorer for whom the nearby national monument is named, visited Poshu-ouinge in 1885, but not until 1919 were formal excavations conducted at the site. At that time, J. A. Jeançon dug 137 rooms and produced a report consisting mainly of an inventory of unearthed artifacts. It lists many stone tools, such as polishing stones for floors, andirons, mortars, and arrow-shaft polishers. Bone implements included awls, tanning tools, breastplates, turkey calls, flutes, spatulas, and knives. He and his crew also unearthed ceramic pipes, dishes and vessels, spindle whorls, pot lids, and gaming pieces (Indian gaming did not begin with casinos). Among ceremonial items found were fetishes, ceramic cloud blowers, and lightning stones. The last are

Artist's reconstruction of Poshu-ouinge along the Chama River. Painting © and courtesy of Mary Beath.

small, smooth, white quartzite pebbles that produce a faint flickering light that resembles distant lightning when rubbed briskly together in the dark.

Poshu-ouinge had about seven hundred ground-floor rooms surrounding two huge plazas, in one of which a large kiva depression is clearly visible. The pueblo also had second-story rooms and possibly a few above those. The construction, of adobe mud mixed with river stones, was not the best with the result that soon after everyone left, the walls melted to low mounds. The late Tewa Pueblo anthropologist Alphonso Ortiz told me that his people, from Ohkay Owingeh (San Juan Pueblo) have stories passed down over the generations about their ancestors living in this village.

A well-marked trail leads up the river terrace, skirts along the edge of the ruins, and continues up to a bench and ramada overlooking the site. If you continue to the top of the hill, you will have an even better view over the Chama Valley. There you'll also find a circle of stones, believed to be an ancient shrine. You should allow yourself forty-five minutes to an hour or so to do the full hike. Please stay on the trail and do not collect any artifacts.

The nearby historic village of Abiquiu has a gas station, general store, and inn with a restaurant. Georgia O'Keeffe lived here and arrangements to join a tour of her home and studio can be made at www.okeeffemuseum.org/her-houses.html.

Posi-ouinge

Twenty-five miles from Poshu (12 as the crow flies), on a ridge overlooking the community of Ojo Caliente, lies the ancestral Tewa pueblo of Posi-ouinge. From Española, take US 84-285 north for about 7 miles and turn right on US 285. Continue 16 miles to Ojo Caliente River and follow signs to Ojo Caliente Hot Springs and Spa. The trailhead is just beyond the main building. Information: (575) 758-8851.

Posi-ouinge (Greenness Village) also was built on a river terrace from where its residents enjoyed a lovely view over the Ojo Caliente, a tributary of the Chama. From their elevated position they could see anyone coming into their territory. At least three other pueblo sites from the same general time period are located in this valley, and some researchers estimate that the population of the lower Chama River region in the 1400s may have exceeded that of today.

The pueblo is made up of some five plazas embraced by two- and three-story apartment blocks. The ground-floor rooms alone are estimated to number a thousand. Systematic archaeological excavations have never been done here, but surveys and analysis of pottery designs lead researchers to think the site dates to between around 1300 and 1500 CE, and probably reached its maximum size in the late fifteenth century.

When you follow the path over the house mounds and across one of the plazas, you will realize how large this compact village was, its many residents living in close quarters with one another. As a community it had a strong political structure

Reconstruction of Posi-ouinge along the Ojo Caliente River. Courtesy of
Dennis Holloway, architect.

providing for an orderly, harmonious society. Residents reached the second and
third stories of their houses by ladder and entered their living quarters through
rooftop hatchways. If they felt threatened by intruders or came under attack, they
could withdraw the ladders to impede entry. Bottom-level back rooms were best
suited for food storage while upper and exterior rooms were more comfortable
to live in. However, in good weather, people spent much of their time on their
rooftops where they fashioned tools and household utensils and processed food
and did many other daily chores. The plazas, too, were used as work areas and as
places in which to conduct ceremonies and dances. Turkeys were raised for food
and feathers, and archaeologists sometimes find their pens and nests around the
edges of plazas.

The village of Ojo Caliente has several restaurants and a gas station and the spa
has overnight accommodations. While visiting Posi-ouinge, it is enjoyable to take
advantage of the resort with its mineral hot springs.

Tsi-p'in-ouinge

Tsi-p'in-ouinge is situated atop a 7,400-foot mesa overlooking Abiquiu Reservoir,
north of Abiquiu town. To visit this site, you must obtain a permit (free) from the
Coyote Ranger District, Santa Fe National Forest, HC-78, Box 1, Coyote, New Mexico
87012. (505) 638-5526; www.fs.usda.gov/recarea/santafe/recarea/?recid=75518.
With your permit, you will be given directions to the site and a trail guide.

Ruins of Tsi-p'in-ouinge.

Tsi-p'in-ouinge is perched on a high peninsular mesa with a view across to Pedernal Mountain. *Pedernal*, in Spanish, means "flint" and the site's Tewa name translates to Village at Flaking Stone Mountain. The mountain indeed has a chert quarry from which, for thousands of years, Native Americans obtained stone for fashioning tools and weapons. It was often painted by Georgia O'Keeffe.

Some may find getting to this site a challenge for it involves driving on a rough back road and then hiking a steep trail at over 7,000-feet elevation. A high-clearance, four-wheel-drive vehicle is recommended. If you make the effort, however, and have about six hours for the round-trip from the highway, the experience is most rewarding.

This was once a large active village whose apartment blocks and plazas were built along the edge of the mesa's cliff. Today, what you will find here are rubble-covered mounds, some standing room walls, and plazas and kivas. You will be impressed by how, using stone hammers and chisels and stone axes, the people excavated several kivas in the volcanic-tuff bedrock. The building blocks used to construct the houses were also shaped of tuff, which is a relatively soft workable stone. One especially large kiva may have been a community gathering place. The trail guide points out other features, such as a path worn in the bedrock and a place where the villagers quarried building stone. The pueblo's inhabitants dug caves in the cliff face below the rim of the mesa and built masonry rooms in front of them.

Tsi-p'in-ouinge was occupied between about 1300 and 1400–1450, with major building having taken place between 1312 and 1325. The presence of Santa Fe Black-on-white pottery suggests that some people may have been living here even earlier. Stone metates and manos found on the site's surface tell us that the inhabitants were grinding corn—their fields were in the valley below—and the presence of animal bones shows they were consuming deer, elk, rabbits, and squirrels, all of which were available to hunters in the vicinity. Axes, mauls, hoes, and arrow-shaft straighteners point to the many other daily activities the inhabitants engaged in to make their livelihood.

The main archaeological work here has consisted of survey and mapping. J. A. Jeançon, however, did some testing in 1923 and in 1937; Frank Hibben, of the University of New Mexico, reported that some of the cavates were filled with trash from the pueblo above and contained burials. This suggests that people lived in them prior to building the pueblo and the cavates later became places to put refuse. Archaeologists have also found a reservoir on the mesa top, defensive walls at the north and south ends of the pueblo, a few petroglyphs, a circular stone shrine, and a possible equinoctial sun-sighting station. Unfortunately, as has happened at so many ancestral sites in the Southwest, looters have dug holes there and carried off artifacts. The site is important to Indians from the Tewa pueblos in the Rio Grande Valley and has much still to tell archaeological researchers. Please treat it appropriately.

When you go to Tsi-p'in-ouinge, wear sturdy shoes and bring water and a snack. In wet weather, parts of the trail will be slippery and the access road may even be impassable. You will find some travel services along Highway 96 and more in Abiquiu.

Suggested Reading: *Valley of Shining Stone: The Story of Abiquiu*, by Leslie Poling-Kempes, University of Arizona Press, Tucson, 1997.

LA CIENEGUILLA PETROGLYPHS

In Santa Fe, New Mexico, drive to the intersection of Airport Road and NM 599. From there, continue 3.5 miles west on Airport Road (County Road 56). You will see the La Cieneguilla Petroglyphs parking lot on the right.

———————

Readers who wish to view ancient rock art but are not inclined to long-distance hiking will find the La Cieneguilla petroglyphs both convenient and rewarding. More than four thousand petroglyphs, pecked centuries ago in basalt rock with hammers and chisels made of stone, are strung along the edge of a volcanic escarpment.

Petroglyph panel at the La Cieneguilla site.

From the parking area, follow the marked path about 50 yards and turn left at the fence. After about ten minutes, you will come to an informal gate in the fence leading to a trail. From here, follow white arrow markers to climb a steep trail to the base of the cliff, where the petroglyphs are to be found. Given the rough terrain, a walking stick is useful. An unimproved (at the time of this writing) trail goes to the left along the base of the cliff close to the rock-art panels. Pay close attention to the trail, which is rocky and uneven. To the south, you will be looking down on the Santa Fe River.

You will see many depictions of birds (including parrots), animals, snakes, dragonflies, plants, abstract designs, faces (or masks), anthropomorphic figures, and humpbacked flute players. Look for faces pecked on the corners of rocks to give them three-dimensionality and faces that have natural holes for eyes. Images that are scored with a sharp edge probably were made later in time.

Although some of the rock art along this escarpment is earlier, most of it dates to the Rio Grande Classic, or Pueblo IV, period (1325–1600 CE), a time when most Pueblo Indians of the region lived in large villages built around a single central plaza. The ruins of one of these villages lie below the petroglyphs. La Cieneguilla Pueblo was inhabited from the early 1300s to the 1680 Pueblo Revolt, which scholars believe to be the time frame of the rock art.

There are places along the trail where you can climb to the top of the escarpment, an old lava flow, and gain stunning views in all directions. If you walk west along the edge, you will come to openings in the cliff leading back down to places where there are more petroglyph panels. In the valley below, look for a small white rectangular building, the San Antonio de Cieneguilla Chapel—it was built in 1820. La Cieneguilla Pueblo, which has 30 roomblocks and approximately 1,000 rooms, lies under and around the chapel as well as across the road. Some of the land is private property, some is owned by the Bureau of Land Management, and none of the site is open to public access.

Allow at least an hour to see a good sampling of the rock art, more time for further exploring. Please take great care not to cause any damage to the petroglyphs.

Other interesting archaeological sites in the area are Pecos National Historical Park and Bandelier National Monument (p. 205). Also recommended are the Museum of Indian Arts and Culture and New Mexico History Museum in Santa Fe.

PECOS NATIONAL HISTORICAL PARK

Pecos National Historical Park is located off Interstate 25 approximately 25 miles east of Santa Fe, New Mexico. Travelers driving north on I-25 should take the Glorieta-Pecos exit (299) to NM 50 and proceed 8 miles through the village of Pecos to the monument. If you are traveling south on I-25, take the Rowe exit (307) and continue 4 miles north to the park. Information: (505) 757-7241; www.nps.gov/peco/index.htm. Entrance fee.

The remains of Pecos Pueblo sit on a hill in the wide, fertile Pecos Valley. Nearby, the Pecos River flows out of the Sangre de Cristo Mountains and continues on its long journey through New Mexico to join the Rio Grande in Texas. High mesas border the valley to the south and to the west lies Glorieta Pass, a gateway to the Rio Grande Valley and the site of a Civil War battle. From the ruins, the valley descends gradually eastward, to open on the southern Great Plains.

A highlight of this park is its museum with its collections of ancient and historical artifacts. A twenty-minute film shown regularly in the visitor center and narrated by Greer Garson makes a good introduction to seeing the ruins. Using a trail guide, follow the path behind the visitor center to the old pueblo and the mission and *convento*. You'll be struck by the monumental scale of Pecos's eighteenth-century church, which overlies the even larger earlier church. To see everything, plan at least an hour and a half here.

Geography, beyond providing the Pecos Indians a beautiful and varied environment, played an important part in the life and economy of the pueblo. Close by were fertile farmlands, reliable springs, and fuel wood. Beyond, the high country offered game and timber. Also, the materials for making tools, weapons, pottery, and basketry were close at hand. But what gave the Pecos people a special advantage was their strategic location between the agricultural Puebloan communities of the Rio Grande and the nomadic hunting tribes of the plains. The resulting thriving trade much benefited the Pecos Indians. Even so, there was sometimes a price to pay when Comanches, Apaches, and Caddoans raided their village after the summer harvest.

Settlement of the Pecos Valley goes back to the ninth century CE when migrants from the Rio Grande Valley formed pithouse settlements here. For several centuries, their numbers slowly increased until, after 1200, the population really burgeoned. Pecos Pueblo itself was founded around 1300 and eventually grew to nearly seven hundred rooms built in multilevel community houses around a central quadrangle. The village's commanding situation and fortress-like design allowed its inhabitants to defend themselves effectively against outside attack.

At its peak, the population of Pecos reached some fifteen hundred people. Less than fifty years after Columbus landed in the New World, they were paid a visit by the conquistador Vásquez de Coronado, who was on a treasure-seeking expedition in what is now New Mexico. Mistrustful of the Spaniards, the Pecos Indians enticed Coronado to follow his dream out onto the vast windswept plains to the east, where they hoped he would lose his way.

Coronado eventually returned to Mexico empty-handed; however, his expedition was followed in 1590 by another, led by Castaño de Sosa. This group of adventurers, reinforced by Mexican Indians, stormed and occupied the pueblo, whose residents took refuge in the hills. Castaño reported that Pecos had four-story-high apartment blocks, which the inhabitants reached by ladders. He noted that the men wore cotton blankets under a buffalo robe, and the women were dressed "with a blanket drawn in a knot at the shoulder and a sash the width of a palm at the waist." Over this garb they wore colorful blankets or turkey-feather robes.

Spanish Franciscans established a mission at Pecos in 1618 and built, with Indian labor, a massive adobe church and convento complete with living quarters for the priests, a carpenter shop, weaving rooms, tannery, stable, and school. They introduced wheat, orchards, metal tools, animal husbandry, and Christianity, but suppressed the Indians' own religious practices.

The Pecos Indians destroyed the original mission in their 1680 revolt against Spanish rule, but it was rebuilt in the early eighteenth century. Epidemics hit the Indians hard during this century, and to make matters worse, they were repeatedly attacked by Plains tribes. By the latter part of the century, the pueblo's once proud warrior force had been so reduced that the Indians depended on the Spanish colonists for defense. By 1838, less than twenty souls remained here, and these last occupants trekked 80 miles northwest to live at Jemez Pueblo.

In 1999, the descendants of the Pecos Indians at Jemez Pueblo received back a large collection of their ancestors' skeletons and grave goods, which had been excavated in the 1920s by archaeologist Alfred Vincent Kidder and his crew and subsequently stored in institutions in the east. It was the largest return of artifacts from a single site under the Native American Graves Protection and Repatriation Act.

The eighteenth-century mission church at Pecos Pueblo.

A. V. Kidder was a leading archaeologist of his generation whose initial reputation was made for his methodical multidisciplinary research at Pecos Pueblo. In the summer of 1927, he invited his colleagues to come to Pecos to view his diggings and discuss common archaeological issues and problems. The Pecos Conference, which takes place each year in the Southwest, is a continuation of that meeting. Kidder's work at Pecos is now recognized as a landmark in the development of North American archaeology.

The park now includes a large portion of the Forked Lightning Ranch, which formerly belonged to Greer Garson and Buddy Fogelson, whose generosity helped build the visitor center and museum. It also encompasses the Civil War battlefield in Glorieta Pass. Tours of these places can be arranged by reservation.

The park has a pleasant picnic area, and Pecos village has restaurants, a general store, and a gas station. Camping and fishing can be found up the Pecos River Canyon above the village. From Santa Fe, a trip to Pecos National Historical Park makes a pleasant and interesting half-day excursion.

Suggested Reading: *Kiva, Cross, and Crown: The Pecos Indians and New Mexico, 1540–1840*, by John L. Kessell, University of New Mexico Press, Albuquerque, 1987.

PETROGLYPH NATIONAL MONUMENT

The entrance to Petroglyph National Monument's headquarters, along Albuquerque's West Mesa, is at the junction of Unser Boulevard and Western Trail. To reach the monument from I-40, take the Unser Blvd. exit north; from I-25, exit at Paseo del Norte and follow signs. Directions to the park's three sections and their petroglyph-viewing trails can be obtained at the visitor center. Information: (505) 899-0205; www.nps.gov/petr/index.htm.

––––––––––––––––

Indian rock art—petroglyphs and paintings on stone (pictographs)—can be found throughout the Americas and in many parts of the world; however, the Southwest, with its abundant exposed sandstone cliffs and basalt boulders, contains an especially rich collection. Petroglyph National Monument is the only unit of the National Park Service devoted solely to preserving and interpreting this form of expression and making it available for the public to see. The petroglyphs, numbering some twenty thousand, are concentrated in three separate areas of the park, all within easy driving distance of each other. Hiking time on the various trails ranges from a few minutes to a couple of hours.

Most of the rock art appears on basalt boulders that have tumbled off the 17-mile escarpment of West Mesa. This geological formation is the eastern edge of a lava flow that erupted from a fissure three miles to the west some 110,000 years ago: a recent event in geologic time scales. From higher points along the monument's trails, a series of volcanoes are visible on the western horizon. On the human scale, the oldest glyphs were pecked into the patina of the rocks by

Petroglyph figures, Boca Negra Canyon.

hunter-gatherers at least two millennia ago during the Archaic period. Often they are abstract in design: circles, dots, and squiggly or curvilinear lines. Some can be seen in the vicinity of the volcanoes on the west side of the monument.

Scholars think most of the rock art here dates to between around 1300 and the late 1600s CE. The earlier date was when many Puebloan people were migrating to the Rio Grande Valley from the Four Corners region. Spanish domination and the imposition of European cultural values beginning in the seventeenth century and disruptions caused by the Pueblo-Spanish wars between 1680 and 1696 seem to have had a negative effect on the making of rock art by the Indians. Most of the images you will see in the park are characteristic of what anthropologists refer to as the Rio Grande Style. These forms also are reflected in kiva mural painting and pottery designs from the same time.

Anthropologists, sometimes in consultation with Native American elders, have made efforts not only to describe and date rock art, but also to interpret the meaning of the imagery. Although the latter exercise can be quite speculative, some of it is well grounded in research. As you walk the trails, you will come to signs that help put the petroglyphs in historical and cultural context. You'll notice quite a few "faces," or masks, which probably relate to the Pueblo katsina religion

Petroglyph, Rinconada Canyon.

that is thought to have come into the Southwest in the 1300s. Star imagery, mountain lions, and shields possibly are war imagery whereas bears and badgers suggest the presence of medicine societies.

Spanish and Mexican inhabitants, often sheepherders, sometimes etched Christian crosses among the old glyphs to cancel the evil influence of the pagan symbols.

The region surrounding Petroglyph National Monument, which Vásquez de Coronado called the Province of Tiguex, has many Puebloan habitation sites dating from the Pueblo IV (1300–1700 CE) period. Two examples that are open to the public are Kuaua Pueblo in Coronado State Monument and Tijeras Pueblo (p. 228). Today's Tiwa Pueblo Indians of nearby Sandia and Isleta pueblos are descendants of the people who made the rock art in the park and consider many images to be sacred. With this in mind and for reasons of conservation, please be respectful and refrain from touching them.

A major threat to archaeological sites is urban growth and development and you can certainly witness this around this park. Protecting this rock-art collection has been a priority and challenge to preservationists and still is as the city of Albuquerque expands and new subdivisions and highways are built.

The three units of the monument are Boca Negra Canyon (several miles north of the visitor center off Unser Boulevard); Rinconada Canyon (a short distance south on Unser); and Piedras Marcadas (off Paseo Del Norte to the northeast). Staff at the visitor center will advise you which trails best suit your available time and physical ability. While in the area, you will also enjoy visits to the Maxwell Museum of Anthropology and the Indian Pueblo Cultural Center.

Suggested Reading: *Indian Rock Art of the Southwest*, by Polly Schaafsma, University of New Mexico Press, Albuquerque, 1980. *Petroglyph National Monument*, by Susan Lamb, Western National Parks Association, Tucson, Arizona, 2005.

CORONADO HISTORIC SITE

Coronado Historic Site is located off US 550 in Bernalillo, New Mexico. From Albuquerque, drive 16 miles north on Interstate 25 to exit 242. Then go 1.7 miles west on US 550 to Kuaua Road, which is the entrance to the site. Information: 505-867-5351; www.nmmonuments.org/coronado. Hours: 8:30 a.m. to 5:00 p.m., Wednesday through Monday. Admission fee.

Tiwa-speaking Pueblo Indians founded the village known as Kuaua along the west bank of the Rio Grande around 1300 CE. At this time, many Pueblo inhabitants of the Four Corners region were relocating to the Rio Grande Valley, boosting its population. The remains of Kuaua are contained in a park managed by the Museum of New Mexico. An interpretive trail leads through the ruins. The visitor center, which was designed by noted architect John Gaw Meem, has exhibits of Indian and Spanish artifacts.

The adobe wall stubs in Kuaua Pueblo.

During the centuries that Kuaua thrived as a community, its residents planted gardens along the margins of the river and hunted a variety of animals and migrating waterfowl that were attracted to this waterway. The Sandia Mountains provided many other useful resources.

Kuaua is a proto-historic site, meaning that it was lived in both before and after the arrival of Europeans. In the summer of 1540, a detachment of Vásquez de Coronado's army explored the Rio Grande Valley and later that year Coronado led his full expeditionary force—three hundred soldiers and many Mexican Indian allies and servants as well as hundreds of horses and mules—to the nearby pueblo of Alcanfor to spend the winter months. They must have visited Kuaua but did not camp here. Coronado's chronicler, Pedro de Castaneda, recorded his observations of Indians doing house construction.

> They all work together to build the villages, the women being engaged in making the mixture and the walls, while the men bring the wood and put it in place. They have no lime but they make a mixture of ashes, coals, and dirt which is almost as good as mortar, for when the house is to have four stories, they do not make the walls more than half a yard thick.

The Spaniards counted a dozen pueblos along the river between Kuaua and Isleta and called the area the Province of Tiguex. During that winter, they commandeered food and clothing from the Indians, allegedly molested a Pueblo woman, and set up an adversarial relationship with the Indians. In retaliation, Pueblo warriors drove off and killed some forty of their horses. Later, when open warfare broke out, Coronado's troops overwhelmed two Tiwa villages, destroying one entirely and killing many of its inhabitants.

Today, there are two distinct groups of Tiwa Pueblo Indians: those living in the northern pueblos of Picuris and Taos, and those in the south, who reside in the villages of Sandia and Isleta. They speak different Tiwa dialects. Kuaua Pueblo was active until the late 1500s when its occupants drifted away. Archaeological research has not shed light on why but population reduction caused by the introduction of epidemic diseases may have been a factor.

The Kuauans built up courses of adobe for their house walls, allowing each to stiffen before laying on another. Today, the wall remains are made of much-eroded adobe bricks, the result of partial reconstruction in the 1940s. Archaeological excavations at Kuaua took place in the 1930s under the direction of Edgar Lee Hewett and the sponsorship of the Museum of New Mexico, the University of New Mexico, and the School of American Research. In addition to conducting scientific research, Hewett wanted to promote New Mexico's history in preparation for the four-hundredth anniversary celebration of Coronado's *entrada* in 1540. With the latter in mind, he had his crews partially rebuild the pueblo's walls, even making them appear eroded by time.

The highlight of the archaeological investigations was the discovery of a square kiva, a subterranean room, which contained seventeen layers of painted murals. Each layer was painstakingly removed, and the kiva restored including copies of some of the murals. Entering the kiva is a tour feature and fifteen original kiva mural paintings are on display in the visitor center.

Near the archaeological park is a picnic area overlooking the Rio Grande. Other nearby sites of interest are Jemez State Monument and Petroglyph National Monument (p. 220).

Suggested Reading: *Coronado: Knight of Pueblo and Plains*, by Herbert E. Bolton, University of New Mexico Press, Albuquerque, 2015. *The Latest Word from 1540: People, Places, and Portrayals of the Coronado Expedition*, edited by Richard Flint and Shirley Cushing Flint, University of New Mexico Press, Albuquerque, 2011.

JEMEZ HISTORIC SITE

Jemez Historic Site is located along New Mexico 4 in Jemez Springs, New Mexico, 45 miles from Albuquerque and 87 miles from Santa Fe. From Interstate 25 at Bernalillo, take US 550 west to San Ysidro, then follow NM 4 for 18 miles to the site. On the way, you will go through Jemez Pueblo. Information: (575) 829-3530; www.nmhistoric sites.org/jemez. Admission fee.

At Jemez Historic Site, you will experience a place where indigenous people came in close contact with colonists and missionaries from Spain. The park includes the remains of an ancient Jemez village and a massively built stone church. An interpretive trail leads from the visitor center along the highway through the Indian and Spanish ruins.

Jemez Pueblo (*Walatowa* in the native Towa language) sits along the Jemez River on the west flanks of the Jemez Mountains. Some Jemez oral traditions say that their ancestors migrated to their present area from the upper San Juan River country to the north. Archaeologists tend to agree with this, though some also look to Gallina sites, such as Rattlesnake Ridge (p. 237), as an area of origin. The migration probably occurred in the late thirteenth century.

When Spanish conquistadores first ventured into the Jemez Mountains in 1541, they found these Pueblo people living in seven major villages as well as some small hamlets and farmsteads. The remains of one of these villages, Giusewa (pronounced *gee-say-wah*), can be seen at Jemez Historic Site. Other sections of the site, which extend beneath Highway 4 all the way to the river, were razed by development.

The other pueblos the Spaniards observed were strung along the valley floor or perched atop nearby steep-sided mesas. Most were at some distance from each other. Their inhabitants were farmers, who raised corn as their main staple

San José de los Jemez church.

and beans and squash. They collected edible and medicinal plants in the valley's riparian habitats and hunted game in the surrounding mountains. Although their settlements and farmlands were concentrated on the mesas and in the river valleys, the Jemez used a much wider territory for hunting and gathering and for religious functions. This distinction between *settlement* and *use areas* would become, in the twentieth century, a key issue in tribal land claims. Today, the people still farm on a small scale but many more make their living in other ways.

Fifty-eight years after the initial Spanish explorations, Don Juan de Oñate led a large colonizing expedition into New Mexico and established his headquarters at Ohkay Owingeh (formerly called San Juan Pueblo) along the Rio Grande near present-day Española. Very soon, he sent a Franciscan missionary, Friar Alonzo de Lugo, to the land of the Jemez to promote Christianity and gain converts. This priest initially established a *visita* at Giusewa using Indian labor. In 1621, the Franciscan Fray Jerónimo de Zárate Salmerón directed construction of the massive San José Church and mission.

Since the Jemez people had a religion of their own, many were unreceptive to conversion to another. The missionaries' efforts also were hindered by having to visit numerous distantly scattered communities. For this reason, and to more effectively control the population, it became Spanish policy in the mid-seventeenth century to bring together small Pueblo settlements into a consolidated village. The newcomers from Europe had little appreciation for the spiritual traditions and religious practices of the Pueblo Indians, which were as old as Christianity. At this time, the Jemez people, whose population was diminishing from disease epidemics, were forced to consolidate, first in three villages, including Giusewa, and ultimately in the single pueblo of Walatowa.

In the seventeenth century, relations between the Spanish authorities and Pueblo Indians grew increasingly problematic and sometimes sank into violence that included the execution of Jemez people. In 1675, a religious leader was accused of witchcraft and hanged in the Santa Fe plaza along with other Pueblo leaders. Five years later, a general revolt erupted during which the Pueblos destroyed churches, killed priests and settlers throughout New Mexico, and drove the colony into exile. One of the martyred Franciscans was the missionary at San José de los Jemez at Giusewa.

During the period of Spanish reconquest (1692 to 1696), the Jemez Indians continued to resist, sometimes taking refuge in remote places high on the mesas. In July 1694, Diego de Vargas, the newly appointed governor of New Mexico, successfully attacked Astialakwa, which sat on a high, narrow, steep-sided mesa overlooking the Jemez River. This site is only a few miles down the river valley from Jemez Historic Site. Eighty-four Indians died in that conflict, several reportedly flung themselves off the cliffs, 361 were taken prisoner, and others took refuge among the Navajos. At this time, Vargas also recovered the body of the priest at Giusewa, who had been slain fourteen years before, finding his corpse still pierced by arrows.

Archaeologists have conducted excavations at Giusewa and San José mission on several occasions. From a scientific viewpoint, some of the research was far from exemplary, field notes having been lost and the results of investigations not published. As a result, uncertainties exist regarding many details of the site's historic sequence. Evidence suggests a founding time for the pueblo of between 1300 and 1450. One exciting discovery was a series of frescoes on the walls of the church nave. They included colorful fleur-de-lis and other floral patterns as well as Indian motifs. Also found were remnants of windows made of selenite, a translucent form of gypsum.

The Museum of New Mexico administers Jemez Historic Site in consultation with Jemez Pueblo. When you arrive at the visitor center and museum, pick up a printed trail guide and plan on forty-five minutes to an hour or more to see the site. You will first walk by brush-covered mounds of Giusewa Pueblo. The trail loops around a plaza and past an excavated kiva, which you can usually enter by ladder. You will then see the stabilized walls of excavated stone-masonry rooms. These may be the remains of a civil administrative building.

Most impressive are the remains of San José Church with its 6-foot-thick stone walls. Originally constructed in 1621, it burned two years later and then was rebuilt. As you enter the nave, imagine the space with its roof, stations of the cross, colorful wall paintings, and decorated altar. Add to this a congregation of Indians, singing, and muted sunlight streaming in the windows. The tall bell tower behind the altar was erected on an elevated platform of bedrock in the hill behind. After experiencing the church, continue on to the *convento* with its inner court and many structures that include priests' living quarters, kitchens, storage rooms, classrooms, workshops, stables, and corral. Notice, too, how beautiful the setting of this mission is along Oak Canyon Creek with scenic cliffs as a backdrop. An hour at this site is a most pleasant way to experience and learn about New Mexico history.

Some Jemez Pueblo plaza dances that are open to the public are on January 6, August 2, November 12, and December 12. The Pueblo also has a museum and gift shop along Highway 4. In Jemez Springs you will find places to eat and stay overnight. Driving north on NM 4, you will pass the Valles Caldera National Preserve and Bandelier National Monument (p. 205), one of the Southwest's premier archaeological parks.

Suggested Reading: *Nee Hemish: A History of Jemez Pueblo*, by Joe S. Sando, Clear Light Publishing, Santa Fe, New Mexico, 2008. *Pueblo at the Hot Springs: Archaeology and History of Giusewa Pueblo and San José de los Jémez Mission*, by Michael L. Elliott, forthcoming.

TIJERAS PUEBLO

Tijeras Pueblo is in Tijeras, New Mexico, 10 miles east of Albuquerque. From Albuquerque, take I-40 east to the Tijeras exit (175) and follow NM 337 south for half a mile. The site is behind the U.S. Forest Service station on the east side of the road. From the north, follow NM 14 south to Tijeras.

———————————

Tijeras Pueblo is one of two relatively large fourteenth-century villages in Tijeras Canyon, the other being San Antonio. Its inhabitants located it at the intersection of important north-south and east-west travel routes. To the north were contemporaneous pueblos at Paa-ko, several villages in and near present-day Santa Fe, and others in the Galisteo Basin; and to the south were the Salinas pueblos (p. 231). On the other axis, Tijeras Canyon connected the pueblos in the Rio Grande Valley and tribes of the Southern Plains. The Tijeras people benefited from trade in all directions. The actual site of Tijeras Pueblo, however, was selected because of a nearby seep and creek.

Tijeras Canyon began seeing human settlement, probably seasonal, around 700 CE, and two pithouses found during excavations certainly predate the pueblo. After a couple of centuries, Puebloan people began living in the area more permanently, in farmsteads and small hamlets, and the population gradually increased. Then, around 1300, the settlements in the canyon began to concentrate into considerably larger villages: Tijeras and San Antonio pueblos and Paa-ko.

Numerous excavations have taken place at Tijeras Pueblo over past decades. The most notable research, however, between 1971 and 1976, involved students of the University of New Mexico's summer field schools under the tutelage and direction first of W. James Judge and then Linda S. Cordell. They brought in specialists in stone tools, pottery, bone, botany, and dendrochronology. It was learned that the pueblo's construction began in 1313, and during the first half of the fourteenth century, it consisted of about two hundred rooms, most of which were in house blocks loosely arranged around a plaza and kiva. The building materials consisted of sun-dried adobe, stone, and wood.

In addition to its location along travel routes, Tijeras benefited from the presence of streams and seeps nearby—essential resources for a community this large. There was also good hunting for both large and small game in and around the canyon and, at least initially, plenty of wood used for heating fuel and construction. At an elevation of over 6,000 feet, however, growing crops would have been challenged by a short growing season and the tendency of cold air to drain into canyons. Archaeologists have not yet found their fields.

Around 1360, due probably to water and food shortages, about half the inhabitants appear to have left with the result that many rooms fell into disrepair and even disintegrated to ground level. Later, when conditions improved, the pueblo revived and new room blocks were built on top of the old ones on the ridge. The end came in the mid-1400s when Tijeras's residents moved away. There's evidence that for a while some returned to camp at the site, perhaps while tending nearby cornfields. The depopulation of the pueblo coincides with a marked decrease in precipitation; however, population centers such as Tijeras need many

A model of Tijeras Pueblo.

natural resources besides water—wild game, wood, and fertile soil, to cite several examples—and these may have become depleted from overuse. Southern Tiwa-speaking people from Sandia and Isleta pueblos, as well as Zunis, occasionally visit the site: they have a collective memory of its being part of their history.

Today, a ⅓-mile trail winds through the site. Along it are signs conveying the pueblo's history and the archaeology that has taken place. The path leads up a hillside, over the pueblo's mounds, and past an unexcavated roomblock and a large, circular, much-eroded underground structure, or "kiva." Off the trail, you will spot sources of white and red clay; however, ongoing research indicates that the higher-quality clays used by Tijeras potters were imported. You will eventually come to the visitor center, operated by the Friends of Tijeras Pueblo, where you'll find cultural exhibits, photographs, and learning stations for children that address archaeology, pottery, food, shelter, stone tools, and clothing.

A visit to Tijeras Pueblo could be combined with Petroglyph National Monument (p. 220) on the west side of Albuquerque and the Maxwell Museum of Anthropology in Albuquerque. Somewhat more distant are the pueblos and missions of Abó, Quarai, and Gran Quivira.

Suggested Reading: *Tijeras Canyon: Analyses of the Past*, edited by Linda S. Cordell, The Maxwell Museum of Anthropology and the University of New Mexico Press, Albuquerque, 1980.

SALINAS PUEBLO MISSIONS NATIONAL MONUMENT

The headquarters of this monument is at the corner of Broadway and Ripley Streets in Mountainair, in central New Mexico. From Albuquerque, take I-40 east to exit 175 and follow State Highway 337 south through the villages of Torreon and Manzano to Mountainair. From the south on I-25, follow US 60 east to Mountainair. The three sites in the monument—Abó, Quarai, and Gran Quivira—are all located near Mountainair. Information: 505-847-2585; www.nps.gov/sapu/index.htm.

———————

In the mystery that envelopes everything connected with these ruins—as to when, and why, and by whom they were erected; and how, and when, and why, abandoned—there is much food for very interesting speculation.

—Major James Henry Carleton, U.S. Army, at Abó, December 17, 1853

The Salinas pueblos are "proto-historic," meaning that they were occupied both before and after the arrival of Europeans in New Mexico in 1540. This has made them of particular interest because archaeological research can throw light on the impact Europeans had on these Native communities. The name "Salinas" reflects nearby salt flats and shallow ephemeral saline lakes from which the Indians and later Spaniards collected salt. In the time of the last Ice Age, nomadic hunter-gatherers camped along the margins of these brackish bodies of water to hunt mammoths and other Pleistocene animals, and investigators have found the remains of their campsites.

It wasn't until after around 600 or 700 CE that this area began to see its first permanent human settlements. Their inhabitants, thought to be largely of Mogollon (p. 21) stock, lived in pithouse hamlets and made an unpainted reddish-brown style of pottery. When you visit the monument's sites, however, what you will see are the remains of ancestral Pueblo occupation, which began in the late 1200s and came to an end in the early 1670s.

Coronado bypassed this area in 1540–1541, but in 1598 Juan de Oñate led a colonizing expedition into New Mexico with a large force of mounted troops. Three decades later, acting under the authority of both the pope in Rome and the king in Spain, Franciscan missionaries arrived among the Salinas pueblos, usually accompanied by a few soldiers. Their objective was to convert the Indians and instruct them in the ways of European culture. In the monument, the remains of three churches and a *convento* built with Indian labor bear testimony to their faith and power.

The missionary enterprise among the Salinas pueblos—there were nine—was fraught with difficulties. Beyond the challenges of promoting European religious and cultural values to Pueblo Indians, drought, famine, and disease struck the region and some villages rebelled. What was more, Apaches from the Plains attacked, and a serious conflict arose between the missionaries and the civil authorities based in Santa Fe. All came to an end in the 1670s when the Pueblo

Ceramic vessel in the Gran Quivira visitor center.

Indians and Spanish priests and ranchers, unable to survive any longer, withdrew to communities in the Rio Grande Valley. The Salinas region then lay deserted for a long time before finally being resettled; however, even today the population is sparse and the economy struggling.

This is a wide, dry landscape sprinkled with cholla cacti and stunted juniper trees on the flatlands. Wooded hills and forested mountains provided game, timbers, and other natural resources. You should plan a full day to walk around Quarai, Abó, and Gran Quivira and see the main visitor center. You'll learn about the relationship between two very disparate cultures and how, in the end, both survived and found ways to accommodate each other.

At the time of this writing, Mountainair had a restaurant and motel. Each ruins site has its own visitor center, trail guide, and picnic area.

Suggested Reading: *Salinas Pueblo Missions: Abó, Quarai & Gran Quivira*, by Dan Murphy, Western National Parks Association, Tucson, Arizona, 1993.

Gran Quivira

Gran Quivira is 25 miles south of Mountainair on New Mexico 55. Information: (505) 847-2770.

———————

Exposed to winds and scarce in rainfall, the site of Gran Quivira seems an unlikely place for a large village. Its inhabitants were Tompiro-speaking Pueblo Indians who had fields in nearby low areas, which they watered from hand-dug wells, and carried on a lively trade with buffalo-hunting tribes in the southern Plains to the east. It was one of these tribes, the Jumanas, who gave this pueblo its Spanish name, Las Humanas. Why it later became known as Gran Quivira is uncertain. Its Indian name was Cueloce.

Numerous archaeologists have surveyed and excavated here over time, each adding incrementally to our knowledge of the history and makeup of the community. Particularly informative studies were done in the early 1950s by Gordon Vivian and the mid-1960s by Alden C. Hayes. One curious bit of evidence they uncovered points to an influx of people here from the Zuni area in the 1540s. These newcomers, who cremated their dead and made Zuni-style pottery, apparently came here to start a new life after Vásquez de Coronado attacked and occupied Hawikuh (p. 245) in 1540.

Ruins of Las Humanas Pueblo looking toward San Buenaventura mission.

Pueblo settlement began here around 1300 CE with the building of a circular formation of rooms similar to Tyuonyi in Bandelier National Monument (p. 205). Later generations built over this site and expanded the village. The first missionary to Las Humanas, in 1629, was Francisco Letrado, who rented and renovated a small block of rooms (in Mound 7) and began proselytizing. He soon recruited a local workforce and began construction of the smaller church you will see along the trail. Letrado stayed only a short time before transferring to Hawikuh, where he was killed after calling the people to mass during one of their own religious festivals.

Construction of Las Humanas's second and larger church, San Buenaventura, was begun by Father Diego de Santander late in the pueblo's occupation and never completed or used for worship. Even so, its limestone walls, now stabilized by the National Park Service, are impressive to see. It was foolhardy to attempt the construction of a large church and convento at a time when water and food were in very short supply. What happened to this community was heartbreaking. In 1668, more than four hundred Las Humanas people died of starvation. The priests had to secure diminishing food supplies in a windowless storage room. Three years later, Apaches attacked, killing eleven residents and taking thirty away as captives. This tragic event is the last mention of the pueblo in Spanish documents.

Along the interpretive trail you will pass by an area where the Indians raised beans and squash on the north side of the pueblo. Here archaeologists have found large quantities of bones of rabbits, deer, pronghorns, and even bison. There is a visible water catchment basin, too, along the trail; the Indians captured runoff from their roofs in basins, shallow pits, and cisterns. Gran Quivira's visitor center has a fine display of ceramics, stone tools, a bone whistle and flute, and other items.

Quarai

Quarai is in Punta de Agua, 8 miles north of Mountainair, a mile off New Mexico 55.

———————

In contrast to Gran Quivira, the pueblo mounds and church ruins at Quarai are nestled in a small valley in the shade of cottonwoods. The church, Nuestra Señora de la Purísima Concepción de Cuarac, a massive edifice built of red sandstone, still dominates its pastoral environs. Just to the west and south of its walls you will see the cactus-covered mounds of the pueblo known as Acolocu. Tiwa-speaking Pueblo Indians from the Rio Grande Valley founded this village and two others to the north, Chilili and Tajique, around 1300 CE. They were drawn here by the presence of water, good farmland, and plenty of building stone. The area also was favorable for hunting and collecting native plants and herbs.

When Fray Alonzo de Benevides was appointed custodian of New Mexico in 1626, he brought twelve new priests with him from Mexico. One of them, Fray Juan Gutiérrez de la Chica, he assigned to establish a mission at Quarai. The church, with foundations 7 feet deep and 6 feet wide and walls 5 feet in thickness and 40 feet high, was an ambitious structure. As at all other New Mexico missions, the construction, which took five years to accomplish, was done by Indian workers.

Nuestra Señora de la Purísima Concepción de Cuarac mission.

When Fray Juan came to Quarai, the Indians here already had a history with New Mexico's Spanish occupiers. In 1601, three years after Governor Juan de Oñate brought colonists to the territory, Indians at Abó killed two Spanish soldiers. Oñate dispatched his nephew, Vicente de Zaldivar, to "inflict such punishment on the Indians as seemed appropriate." When the troops passed by Acolocu, warriors from Abó joined the locals in an ambush but were forced to retreat into the pueblo. After a six-day siege, they gave up; it was a Spanish victory, though thirty soldiers had died in battle. By the time Fray Juan arrived, all parties were at peace again.

It is often forgotten that the Inquisition came to New Mexico and for awhile its seat was Quarai. Individuals were investigated and punished for such offenses as gossip, heresy, blasphemy, witchcraft, use of love potions, and disrespect to the clergy. In one of Quarai's cases, a trader, Bernardo Gruber, was accused of superstition. The unfortunate man languished in jail for more than two years without ever going to trial. His possessions were appropriated, his stock died, and his own health began to fail. Finally, with the help of an Indian ally, he escaped and fled south only to perish from thirst in the desert. That desert is still known as the Jornada del Muerto, the "journey of the dead man."

Quarai's history is marked by stress and conflict. The local *encomendero* (the civilian landowner who collected tribute from the Indians in return for "protection") exploited the Natives and the priests were strict with them. In the mid-1600s, drought brought more suffering, and by 1678, two years before the Pueblo Revolt, this community was just a memory.

Early archaeological investigations in Acolocu were poorly reported and most excavation has occurred in the mission complex, along with wall stabilization. When you visit Quarai, pick up a trail guide and follow the pathway past the mounds of Acolocu to the church and convento. As the trail continues further, you will find a pleasant place to rest and picnic. The nearest travel services are in Mountainair.

Abó

The ruins of Abó are 9 miles west of Mountainair on US 60 and 1 mile north on New Mexico 513. Information: (505) 847-2400.

––––––––––––––

The spring at Abó was the lifeblood of this community. It nourished aboriginal gardens, later quenched the thirst of Spanish conquistadors and priests, and still later fed the boilers of railroad steam engines. Today, it serves the needs of a small Hispanic community.

A few yards north of the spring lie the unexcavated mounds of a large Tompiro village and, adjacent to it, the ruins of the mission of San Gregorio de Abó. Like Gran Quivira and Quarai, this church was the product of the fervent missionary enterprise organized by the Franciscans in the seventeenth century. Strategically situated between the salt lagoons east of Mountainair and the Rio Grande Valley, and in an area of good pinyon harvests, Abó was a reasonably well-off community. It was reportedly from the sale of nuts, in fact, that the missionaries were able to afford the purchase of a church organ in 1661.

The salt beds of Salinas were an important commodity that drew Indians from a wide area and were treated as neutral ground where conflicts and hostilities were set aside. Local folks, of course, were best positioned to profit from salt trading. When excavating Gran Quivira, archaeologists found a large chunk of salt in a storage room, apparently awaiting transport to a distant market. The Spaniards, too, needed salt both for domestic use and to process silver ore in their mines in Mexico. They exported large quantities of it to Parral, along with Apache captives to work as slaves in the mining operations.

The Abó mission only functioned for about fifty years. During this time, relations between the Pueblo Indians and the Spaniards fluctuated from warfare to cooperation and cordiality, a familiar pattern in New Mexico.

When Adolph F. Bandelier came to Abó in the 1880s, local residents told him they remembered seeing pueblo walls standing three stories high. Today, the interpretive trail winds through the mounds and across the arroyo to even older pueblo ruins that may date to the 1100s. Archaeologist Joseph H. Toulouse Jr. excavated the church and convento in the 1930s. He did not find parts of the old church organ, but he did locate a kiva in the west patio that was contemporaneous with the church. Architectural historian James Ivey thinks the friars themselves may have built the kiva there, believing that the pueblo's leaders would feel more comfortable receiving Christian instruction in a traditional Pueblo-style space than in a church.

Toulouse uncovered the remains of turkey pens within the mission compound and recovered Old World watermelon and mission grape seeds. Originally, such seeds would have been brought up from Mexico on the triennial supply caravan to the missions. Grape growing here preceded that of the California missions by more than a century.

Abó also has some impressive rock-art sites, which can be seen by special arrangement on a ranger-led tour.

Suggested Reading: *The Mission of San Gregorio de Abó,* by Joseph H. Toulouse Jr., Monograph No.13, School of American Research, Santa Fe, New Mexico, 1949.

RATTLESNAKE RIDGE RUINS

Rattlesnake Ridge Ruins are in quite a remote area north of Cuba, New Mexico. From Cuba, take US 550 west for 4 miles and turn north on NM 96. After 13 miles, turn left on Highway 112. Go 18 miles and turn left on Forest Road 390. After two tenths of a mile, turn right on a rough dirt road. The site's parking area is one eighth of a mile. A quarter-mile trail leads to the ruins. From the east (Española), follow

US 84 north, then 96 west to the 112 turnoff. Information: (575) 638-5526; www
.cubanm.org/rattlesnakeridgetrip.html.

———————

The occupants of the Rattlesnake Ridge site were Puebloans, part of what
archaeologists refer to as the Gallina (*guy-ee-na*) Phase. From the late 1000s to
about 1275 CE, they lived in the Llaves Valley west of the Jemez Mountains. Gallina sites can be found between Lindrith, Cuba, State Highway 96, and Gallina in
northwestern New Mexico.

Rattlesnake Ridge is the largest documented Gallina site, extending about half
a mile along a ridge. It consists of nine small and two middle-size residential
houses, storage rooms, two or three towers and pit houses, and a reservoir system.
One prominent feature you will come to along the trail is a large excavated tower
with massive stone walls. Its upper section collapsed to form a mound while the
lower level is sunk deep in the ground. Surrounding the tower on three sides are
the remains of houses, some of which have been excavated. Nearby along the trail
are more pueblo-style rooms and a reservoir.

Attempts to reconstruct Southwestern prehistory have not revealed the origin
of the Gallina people, though some researchers think they came from the Gobernador region around present-day Navajo Reservoir. Around 1130, refugees from

One of the ruins at Rattlesnake Ridge.

Chaco Canyon (which was being depopulated then) may have joined them. For a while, building activity slumped only to be resumed in the early 1200s.

Gallina sites in the Llaves Valley are at high elevation along steep hillsides and river terraces, and on mesas and ridges that have stunning views over surrounding countryside. (Rattlesnake Ridge is in the latter category.) The presence of terraces, check dams, reservoirs, and recovered corn and squash testifies to the importance of farming in the Gallina economy. The game-rich Jemez Mountains provided good hunting and, like all Puebloans and those who preceded them, the Gallina folk gathered wild edible plants, nuts, and fruits as part of their diet. Their potters and tool makers produced pointed-bottomed ceramic vessels, clay elbow pipes with feet, and three-notched axes, all rather distinctive artifacts. Towers like those at Rattlesnake Ridge also are a Gallina trait.

Various archaeologists investigated Gallina sites in the 1930s, 1960s, and between 1976 and 1989. The work sometimes was poorly documented and many questions remain about this culture, one being what became of the Gallina people. Several lines of evidence indicate they got involved in warfare. In the mid- to late 1200s, defensive-looking towers appear. Numerous unburied skeletons dating to the late 1200s and found in burned houses show evidence of violent deaths. Intact household items left behind suggest they left suddenly, perhaps during conflict. Some oral traditions at Jemez Pueblo say that their ancestors came from this area. Archaeologists don't disagree with this but also think some Gallina folk moved down the Chama River Valley to join Tewa Pueblo communities.

Rattlesnake Ridge is high up in the woods. The trail divides and both branches lead to numerous separate house units and towers. You will enjoy some spectacular views over the mountains and valleys.

A word of caution: in wet conditions, both FR 390 and the access road leading to the site become slippery and rutted and it is easy to slip off the road or get stuck. Low-clearance vehicles should be careful in any weather. Rattlesnake Ridge is monitored by site stewards and rangers but is in a very sparsely populated area and there is no road signage to the site. If you see evidence of pot hunting or vandalism, please notify the Forest Service at the number above. Travel services are available in Cuba, Abiquiu, and some settlements along Highway 96.

EL MORRO NATIONAL MONUMENT

El Morro National Monument is found along New Mexico 53, 42 miles southwest of Grants and 30 miles east of Zuni, New Mexico. Information: visitor center, (505) 783-4226; headquarters, (505) 285-4641; website, www.nps.gov/elmo/index.htm.

———————

At El Morro National Monument, which has some of the best scenery in the Southwest, you will be able to explore two ancestral Pueblo village sites dating from between 1275 to 1350 and, more famously, hundreds of petroglyphs and inscriptions carved on the cliff by Indians, then Spaniards, and after 1849, Americans. The ruins are reached by the 2-mile-long Mesa Top Trail (hiking time one and a half to two hours), which ascends 200 feet to the top of the mesa. The views from the top and from A'ts'ina Pueblo are beautiful. The inscriptions are on the cliff face along a half-mile paved pathway, which is wheelchair accessible with assistance. A leisurely walk to view them takes about an hour.

Recent archaeological investigations indicate that Vásquez de Coronado stopped to camp here in late 1540 on his way from Hawikuh (p. 245) to the Rio Grande Valley. However, it was the leader of a later Spanish expedition, Juan de Oñate, who first inscribed a message at the base of the rock promontory, or *morro*. That was in 1605. Having settled his colonists in northern New Mexico seven years before, the conquistador was on his way back from a gold-seeking journey to the Pacific Coast. Later on, many others carved their names on the cliff—Spanish and Mexican travelers, American soldiers and freighters, and miscellaneous other people. The place had long been a camping spot for Indians, too; their much older markings on the rock wall are fainter.

Going much further back in time, Paleo and Archaic hunters-gatherers knew this region and, no doubt, were familiar with the sheltered camping place by Inscription Rock's pool. Real settlement in the area, however, did not begin until after 400 CE—archaeologists know this from having found pithouse villages down the valley from El Morro, nearer Zuni Pueblo. In the mid-1200s, some of these folk, apparently coping with dry conditions, decided to move to the higher elevations of the El Morro Valley, where more precipitation would improve farming prospects.

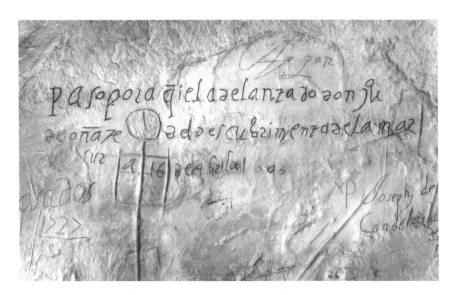

The Oñate inscription at Inscription Rock.

They established seven communities, each consisting of up to thirty separate small housing clusters with at least one situated high up to view the countryside. The area's overall population is thought to have reached several thousand. These pueblos, however, were short-lived; in the late 1200s, their inhabitants left to build larger consolidated villages, like A'ts'ina, on top of mesas. This, too, was a drought time and the planners probably had defense in mind when they scouted such locations for their homes.

A'ts'ina, a late-thirteenth-century pueblo in El Morro National Monument.

A'ts'ina was partially excavated in the mid-1950s under the direction of Richard and Nathalie Woodbury and since then more archaeological research in the park has taken place. The village's single- and double-story house blocks, containing some 875 stone-masonry rooms, surround a large square plaza. A thousand or more people lived here for three or four generations. They obtained water from natural cisterns, or *tinajas*, formed in the bedrock and from a large pool at the base of the mesa. For reasons still unclear, everyone left around 1350.

When you walk around the site, you will see a block of excavated rooms, a large kiva, and extensive house mounds covered by vegetation. The view toward Inscription Rock and over the valley cannot help but impress. After climbing the mesa, the trail skirts along the brush-covered mounds of a contemporaneous pueblo, across beautiful sedimentary rock formations, past numerous *tenajas*, and on to A'ts'ina. The elevation here is 7,200 feet, which you will notice when you climb the trail to the mesa top.

The visitor center has cultural displays and the park maintains a campground nearby. Lodgings and restaurants can be found in Grants and Zuni Pueblo. Check the monument's website for other suggestions along the highway.

Suggested Reading: *El Morro National Monument*, by Dan Murphy, Western National Parks Association, Tucson, Arizona, 2003. *Zuni, El Morro: Past & Present*, edited by David Grant Noble, School for Advanced Research Press, Santa Fe, New Mexico, 1983.

ZUNI-ACOMA TRAIL

The Zuni-Acoma Trail is a 7.5-mile trail you can hike in El Malpais National Monument near Grants, New Mexico. On the west side, the trailhead begins along New Mexico 53, 16 miles south of Interstate 40. On the east side, you access it on New Mexico 117, 15 miles south of I-40.

———————

In ancient times, a widespread network of trails linked American Indian communities in the Southwest and other regions of North America. Shells from the Pacific Coast, for example, have been found in archaeological sites in Arizona and New Mexico; traders carried high-quality flint from the Texas Panhandle to many distant communities; and macaws were brought up in cages from Mexico for their colorful feathers. It was along such trails that Indian guides led Francisco Vásquez de Coronado and his army into the Southwest in 1540. Some ancient Indian trails later became historic wagon roads and eventually modern highways.

The Zuni-Acoma Trail once linked the inhabitants of two pueblos in New Mexico: Acoma and Zuni. A segment of it, which crosses the lava flows in El Malpais National Monument, is open to intrepid hikers. The hike across it is for the physically fit and well prepared and should be done in good hiking weather.

The west end of the Zuni-Acoma Trail.

Malpais means badlands and, in this case, the landscape was formed by eruptions of nearby volcanoes, including Mount Taylor, which is visible to the north. Some of the volcanoes spewed out their lava more than a million years ago; others less than a thousand. The trail terrain is rough in some places, though traversable by foot. Spanish conquistadores found that the sharp lava injured their horses' hooves and presented a barrier to their carts and wagons.

The Acoma and Zuni Indians have myths about the origin of *el malpais*. The Acomas say the black lava was blood, which flowed from the eye sockets of the katsina KauBat after he was blinded by his sons, the Twins, to punish him for his gambling. (Despite the apparent moral of the story, Acoma Pueblo operates a casino nearby.) The Indians maintain shrines deep within the badlands and regularly visit other sacred sites here that were used by their ancestors.

Archaeological research along the trail has shown that it was in use as early as the ninth century CE by Pueblo Indians but hunter-gatherers probably used it long before then. Travelers marked the route with stone cairns and put rocks in crevices as bridges. There are other sites in the badlands: shrines, stone circles, agricultural features, petroglyphs, and even pueblos. Other interesting features in the national monument are ice caves, lava tubes, and frozen subterranean ponds. Such places were useful to the Indians to store perishable foods in summer. In one location, a cache of finely woven baskets was found. Regrettably, some sites in *el malpais* have been looted in years past and artifacts have been stolen.

You will experience beauty and adventure in hiking the unusual landscape along the Zuni-Acoma Trail. There are grassy meadows, sculpted sandstone formations, and dwarfed trees. You may see melanistic forms of wildlife, including black frogs and squirrels. However, you should be aware that there are hazards, too. To assure a safe experience, the Park Service recommends that you allow plenty of time (six to seven hours); carry enough water, especially in hot weather; wear sturdy hiking shoes and a hat; bring some food; do not go alone; tell someone of your plans; and beware of lightning storms. Be sure to keep track of the members of your party and do not wander away from the trail and become lost. Finally, of course, you will need a vehicle at your destination end of the trail. The Park Service's ranger station has trail maps.

The town of Grants has motels, restaurants, and gas stations. A nearby historically fascinating and scenic place to visit is El Morro National Monument (p. 239), which includes the famous Inscription Rock.

Suggested Reading: *El Malpais National Monument*, by Marilyn Mabery, Western National Parks Association, Tucson, Arizona, 1990.

ZUNI RESERVATION SITES

Zuni Pueblo is located on the Zuni Reservation along New Mexico 53, 35 miles south of Gallup and 64 miles west of Grants, New Mexico. Information: (505) 782-7238; www.zunitourism.com/tours.htm.

Visits to Hawikuh (*Hawikku*) and Village of the Great Kivas on the Zuni Reservation offer an opportunity to learn about two important archaeological sites under the guidance of a tribal member. Reservations need to be made well in advance by calling the Visitor Center at the number above.

When you arrive in Zuni Pueblo, stop first at the Ashiwi Awan Museum and Heritage Center. Then, on your own or with a guide, you can stroll through the old part of the pueblo, visit shops featuring Zuni-made pottery and jewelry, and have a meal at a local café. Also recommended is a guided tour of the restored Our Lady of Guadalupe Mission with its beautiful murals.

Archaeologists date the early presence of Zuni Pueblo culture to the mid-1200s. However, Village of the Great Kivas is even older, and nomadic people foraged and hunted in the region for thousands of years before then. The Zuni region (often referred to as Cibola in archaeological literature) has a very long history, which is slowly being learned, and in which the Zuni Indians (the *A:shiwi*) have their roots. Three cultural traditions inform us about this history: Zuni traditional knowledge and stories; historical documents in libraries and archives; and archaeological research.

In 1540, at the time of the Spanish *entrada* into what is now New Mexico, the Zunis were prosperous, living in six villages: Hawikuh, Matsaki, Kiakima, Kwakina, Kechipauan, and Halona. Halona is at the heart of present-day Zuni Pueblo. The other village sites remain on the landscape but, except for Hawikuh, are not open to the public. Historical documents tell about events at Zuni from first contact with Spanish *conquistadores* through the periods of Spanish and Mexican colonialism, and into the more recent eras under the United States. Much as this is an interesting and revealing story, this section will focus on two places: Hawikuh and Village of the Great Kivas.

Hawikuh

When Frederick Webb Hodge conducted archaeological investigations at Hawikuh in the early 1920s, he found that the village was inhabited as early as 1300 CE. However, he was primarily interested in the period when the Zunis and Spaniards first met and he left the earlier (deeper) layers of the site relatively untouched. In Hodge's time, backfilling an excavation was not practiced and weathering slowly reduced the exposed standing walls to rubble mounds, which is what the visitor sees today at the site.

In 1540, after hearing a report of treasure to the north, Francisco Vásquez de Coronado raised the funds to lead a Spanish expeditionary force into Pueblo lands and what is now New Mexico. In midsummer, tired and short of food, he arrived in Hawikuh where the Zunis denied him and his army access to their formidable multistory hilltop town. A battle ensued, which the Spaniards won, though not easily. Unlike Pizarro and Cortez, Coronado found no trove of gold, but rather, as his chronicler wrote, "what we needed more than gold and silver, and that was much corn, and beans, and turkeys." The conquistadores ate and

Hawikuh.

rested before sending detachments of soldiers to explore the Rio Grande Valley and other parts of the region.

Later, when the Spaniards colonized New Mexico, Franciscan priests came to Hawikuh and Halona, built churches, and preached the gospel. Having a long-established religion of their own, the Indians did not welcome the missionaries and resisted their teachings. They repeatedly burned the church, the last time being in 1680, when the Pueblo Indians throughout New Mexico rose up and overthrew Spanish domination. At this time, they also vacated Hawikuh, never to live there again.

Village of the Great Kivas

This site, near the farming village of Lower Nutria, is named for two large kivas that appear as circular depressions in front of the pueblo remains. The floor diameter of the larger, which was excavated, is 78 feet. Both appear originally to have been partially below and partially above ground level. The excavated kiva had a raised fire box, two floor vaults, and roof-support pillars made of masonry and cedar poles. In addition to the kivas, the site consists of roomblock mounds and an eighteen-room Chacoan great house whose exposed walls have Chaco-style banded masonry. Chaco Canyon is 60 miles to the northeast. Some room-blocks are of later construction.

Frank H. H. Roberts Jr., who excavated portions of the site in the 1930s, dated occupation to the eleventh and early twelfth centuries CE. However, from pottery styles, other researchers arrive at somewhat later dates: early 1100s for the great house and 1200s for a later apartment block.

After Chaco Canyon was vacated in around 1140, some outliers, including possibly this one, continued to be lived in or used in some way. The Village of the Great Kivas community may have remained active, eventually blending with the following Zuni culture. Thus, continuity from Chacoan times to the present day is likely.

The residents of this community made petroglyphs on rocks above the site, and in the early or mid-twentieth century, Zuni Indians painted spiritual figures and masks in a sheltered alcove nearby. This rock art can be viewed during a guided tour.

Zuni Pueblo has a café, market, gas station, and bed-and-breakfast inn (The Inn at Halona). More travel services are available in Gallup.

Suggested Reading: *History of Hawikuh, New Mexico: One of the So-called Cities of Cibola*, by Frederick W. Hodge, Southwest Museum, Los Angeles, California, 1937. "Village of the Great Kivas on the Zuni Reservation, New Mexico," by Frank H. H. Roberts Jr., *Bureau of American Ethnology Bulletin* 111, 1932.

Sites of Other Cultural Traditions

⊰I⊱

The chapters in this guidebook are organized according to the ancient cultures (archaeological categories) to which the sites belong—Archaic, Fremont, Hohokam, and so forth. However, there exist some stand-alone sites; that is, in a particular cultural category, they are the only examples that are open to the public. Keyhole Sink is Cohonina, for example, and Lynx Creek is in the Prescott Tradition. This final chapter of the book includes five such sections.

THE DINETAH

To enter the Dinetah, follow US 64 east from Bloomfield to Blanco, New Mexico. After crossing the San Juan River, turn right on County 4450. From there, you will need the Bureau of Land Management map/brochure *Defensive Sites of Dinetah*, which shows back roads and locations of eight archaeological sites. Another approach is to hire a professional guide. Information: (505) 564-7600; (800) 842-3127; www .blm.gov/nm/st/en/prog/recreation/farmington/dinetah_pueblitos.html.

The Dinetah is an extensive canyon-cut area northeast of Bloomfield, which Navajos regard as their ancestral homeland. Archaeological research confirms that many sites around the Largo and Gobernador river drainages date back to early Navajo presence in the Southwest.

The three types of archaeological sites that you will find of particular historical interest in the Dinetah are *pueblitos*, forked-pole hogans, and rock-art panels. Dinetah archaeological researcher Ronald H. Towner has described the first as "small stone structures built on boulders, mesa rims, and other prominent topographic features." Although most consist of only four or five rooms, some are smaller and others as large as forty rooms. Often, the remains of early-style hogans are found near the pueblitos. These dwellings, which resemble tepees in general form, were made by first leaning together three cedar poles in a tripod structure. More poles were laid against these to form a conical framework that was covered by bark and earth. The Dinetah also is noted for its stunning petroglyph and pictograph panels, some of which are easily accessible and well preserved. They, too, reflect early Navajo, as well as Pueblo, occupation of the region.

The Navajos, or Diné, are of Athapaskan origin and related to Indians of northern Canada and to the Apache. Anthropologists think their southward migration began around 1000 CE and that they arrived in the Dinetah, and probably some other areas, sometime after 1450. Because of sparse archaeological data, science-based reconstructions of early Navajo history are uncertain and have been much debated. Navajo origin stories, on the other hand, tell of a long-ago emergence into this world from a subterranean domain and contact with supernatural beings.

Navajo rock art panel in Crow Canyon in the Dinetah. Dating to the eighteenth century, it depicts a corn plant, a yei figure, and various designs including concentric circles.

Dendrochronology (tree-ring dating) shows that construction of most pueblitos took place from the early to mid-1700s. Their locations and design suggest their Navajo builders were much concerned about defense. Ute and Comanche raiding parties posed an ongoing danger to the Dinetah settlements; in addition, they were under pressure from the expanding Spanish colony in the Rio Grande Valley. Little hard evidence of actual violence and conflict, however, has been found at the few sites that archaeologists have excavated.

A pueblito in the Largo-Gobernador region.

After the Pueblo Revolt in 1680 and subsequent conflicts with Spanish military forces between 1692 and 1696, some Pueblo refugees came to the Dinetah region. One pueblito in particular, Tapacito Ruin, built in 1694, appears to be Puebloan, rather than Navajo. Pueblo Indians had other interactions with Navajos through both trade and warfare, and some Navajo clans originated through these contacts.

Since the Dinetah region had limited land suitable for farming and grazing, it eventually could not support a growing Navajo population. Consequently, in the mid-1700s, many Navajos moved to more favorable areas to the south and west. Conflicts with the Utes and Comanches provided addition motivation to move away. Today, three hundred years later, their stone houses, many precariously situated but well built, remain for us to see.

A day exploring the Dinetah can be very rewarding. You can expect to see rooms built of stone, some perched on boulders or along the edge of cliffs. The views from them over the landscape are spectacular. You will gain a sense of how threatened the Navajo occupants of these habitations must have been three hundred years ago. The rock-art panels in Crow Canyon are truly impressive as well and provide insights into Navajo ceremonialism and religious beliefs.

To make the most of visiting this area, a guided tour can be arranged through Salmon Ruins (p. 129) or the Bureau of Land Management. You should be prepared to drive miles on unpaved roads, which can be dusty or slick depending on weather conditions. A high-clearance, four-wheel-drive vehicle is recommended. On weekdays, expect to encounter truck traffic from the area's active oil and gas industry.

Suggested Reading: *Defending the Dinetah*, by Ronald H. Towner, University of Utah Press, Salt Lake City, 2003.

AGUA FRIA NATIONAL MONUMENT

Entrances to Agua Fria National Monument are located along Interstate 17, 40 miles north of central Phoenix, Arizona. The Badger Springs (256), Bloody Basin (259), and Cordes Junction exits lead into the monument. A short distance from the exits are informational kiosks with large-scale maps. Information: (623) 580-5500; www .blm.gov/az/st/en/prog/blm_special_areas/natmon/afria.html.

––––––––––––

Agua Fria was proclaimed a national monument in 2000 in large part to protect its many archaeological sites: pueblo ruins, rock-art panels, agricultural terraces, and some linear features colloquially called "racetracks." The Bureau of Land Management, which manages the 70,000-acre preserve adjacent to Tonto National Forest (which contains similar sites), has made improvements to facilitate access to four sites: Pueblo La Plata, Badger Springs, the 1891 School House, and the Tesky Homestead. The last two historic sites are accessed through the Cordes Junction entrance.

Pueblo La Plata in Agua Fria National Monument.

Perry Mesa, a 75-square-mile expanse of grassland in the eastern portion of the monument, contains a wealth of archaeological resources. Investigators have determined that between around 1250 and 1425, the people who lived here had their own particular cultural identity, which is recognizably distinct from that of the nearby Sinagua, Hohokam, and Salado. They call this identity the "Perry Mesa Tradition." The mesa and ancestral Native American group were named for a homesteader, William H. Perry.

The high, semi-desert, basalt-covered plateau is cut by a series of deep canyons and creeks, tributaries of the Agua Fria River and other streams. The roads are unpaved, rough, and rutted in places and become muddy in wet weather. Therefore, high-clearance vehicles are a necessity and four-wheel drive advisable. Save for two public toilets, there are no facilities or campgrounds. To reach archaeological sites other than those marked on the map, obtain detailed information from monument staff. Important as Agua Fria National Monument is for its ancient sites and natural history, it is a place to be explored by the well prepared.

Many archaeologists have investigated Perry Mesa in past years and looters have been active as well. Researchers have explored, surveyed, mapped, and collected samples of surface artifacts for study. The Arizona State University, Museum of Northern Arizona, and Verde Valley Archaeological Association have been especially active in these efforts, benefiting from a cadre of volunteers. In recent decades, David R. Wilcox with colleagues J. Scott Wood, Gerald Robertson

Jr., and others, have focused much attention here and recorded the remains of a series of pueblos situated around the perimeter of Perry Mesa. In the 1300s, they think, these sites were lookouts and forts designed to block invaders from accessing the mesa. During this time period warfare likely was taking place between the Perry Mesa people and Hohokam farming centers in the Phoenix Basin such as Pueblo Grande (p. 48) and Mesa Grande (p. 50). Wilcox views the Perry Mesa community as "a militarily integrated system of settlements designed for defense." Other archaeologists dispute this model and focus on understanding the agricultural techniques and social cooperation that sustained the Perry Mesa communities during what may have been favorable conditions for farming. We have here a great example of scientific research in action.

Pueblo La Plata

To reach this site, enter the park at the Bloody Basin exit off I-17. Very soon, you will come to an informational kiosk. From there drive 8.3 miles, past Horseshoe Ranch, across the Agua Fria River, past a public toilet, and up on the mesa. After you pass Road 9269C on the right, take the next left (9023). A sign indicates this is the turn to Pueblo La Plata. In about a mile, you'll come to the parking area next to a pair of circular cattle tanks in the ground. A short trail leads to the pueblo.

———————

This compact eighty-room settlement sits on a rise and has views in all directions. Built of stone blocks in wide-open country, it must have been an imposing sight in its day to anyone approaching. Today, as you walk around, be careful not to disturb the walls or sprain an ankle on the rough terrain.

Although Pueblo La Plata was not built on a steep-sided mesa or hilltop, as often was the case in the Verde Valley, its large size and compact layout suggest that its inhabitants had defense in mind. Interestingly, large quantities of potsherds found here—Winslow Orange Ware and Jeddito Yellow Ware, for example—indicate strong links between these villagers and pueblos such as Homol'ovi (p. 150) and those on the Hopi Reservation.

Badger Springs Petroglyphs

Badger Springs is accessed from exit 256 on I-17. Drive one-half mile beyond the kiosk to the parking area and trailhead. It is about a twenty-minute walk to the river and petroglyphs.

———————

Two large petroglyph panels and one small one face the Agua Fria River, which flows by. Pecked in granite, they depict some two dozen antlered animals (deer or elk) and other designs. There is an attractive place to camp along the river. Several prehistoric grinding slicks can be seen on the ground nearby as well as the

Badger Springs petroglyph panel.

remains of an arrastra, a crude drag-stone mill once used by miners to pulverize ore. This arrastra was water-powered and may have been built and used by William Perry, who mined for gold in the area.

Agua Fria National Monument was created for its rich and diverse natural environment as well as its archaeological and historic resources. If you explore it, you may be privileged to see deer, antelope, coyotes, and other wild animals, birds, and reptiles. If you are here during hunting season, be alert and wear bright clothing.

Travel services are available in Black Canyon City and Cordes Junction. Phoenix has numerous places of cultural interest to visit, including Pueblo Grande (p. 48), Sears Kay Ruin (p. 54), and the Heard Museum.

Suggested Reading: *The Archaeology of Perry Mesa and Its World*, by David R. Wilcox and James Holmlund, Bilby Research Center Occasional Papers No. 3, Northern Arizona University, Flagstaff, 2007. *Prehistoric Cultures of the Perry Mesa Region: Proceedings of the Perry Mesa Symposium*, edited by Will G. Russell and Michael J. Hoogendyk, Friends of Agua Fria National Monument, Black Canyon City, Arizona, 2012.

LYNX CREEK RUIN

Lynx Creek Ruin is on the outskirts of Prescott, Arizona. From Prescott, take Arizona 69 to Walker Road (at a traffic light by Costco) and follow it for 1.25 miles to a gravel road on the left, which takes you to a parking area on the left. A short footpath from there leads to the site. Entrance fee.

―――――――――――

Lynx Creek is a small pueblo perched on a hill with a wide view over the surrounding mountainous countryside. The site, which is managed by Prescott National Forest, is easily accessed and can be visited in an hour. It consists of a rubble- and vegetation-covered mound at the end of about a half-mile interpretive trail. There is a brochure keyed to interpretive stops along the trail, an explanatory sign at the pueblo, and a viewing platform.

Prescott National Forest built the trail and platform to encourage public visitation and promote education. These measures together with an active site-steward program also have brought about a decrease in vandalism at the site. When you approach the pueblo on the east side, you will note a grass-covered flat area; here were found the remains of small outbuildings. A radiocarbon sample from the site gave a date of 1190, and with other evidence, archaeologists think Lynx Creek was occupied between approximately 1050 and 1200 and that twenty to thirty-five people lived here.

Lynx Creek Ruin is part of the "Prescott Tradition" centered in the vicinity of the present-day city of Prescott. Archaeologists recognize it as distinct from its cultural neighbors and believe it emerged in about the third century of the common era and went through a series of developments, reflected in pottery styles

The Lynx Creek site near Prescott, Arizona.

and architecture, until about 1300. After then it is no longer visible on the landscape. The Lynx Creek folk had relations with and appear to have been influenced by their Hohokam, Sinagua, and Cohonina neighbors. Critical in understanding cultural groups in this region is the existence of the Verde River, which functioned as a trade and travel corridor along which peoples of various and distinct backgrounds intermingled.

Forest archaeologist Jim McKie estimates Lynx Creek to have had eight to ten rooms, some possibly two stories high, with more rooms close by. Sherds uncovered at the site indicate local residents were making some pottery but importing other pottery through trade with the Hohokam. One cannot help but be impressed by the large size of some of the stones used in the pueblo's walls, and the pueblo's hilltop location suggests that its builders were concerned with defense. You will see similar characteristics if you go to Sears Kay Ruin (p. 54). It reflects what some see as a pattern of off-and-on conflict in central Arizona. There is evidence at Lynx Creek suggesting that fire destroyed the pueblo, though whether natural, accidental, or intentional has not been determined. Although Lynx Creek is a stone pueblo, more common contemporaneous sites in the vicinity were pithouse hamlets surrounding a single- or double-room masonry house.

Archaeologists have carried out two studies at the Lynx Creek site. One was done by Sarah L. Horton for her 1994 master's thesis, "Excavation of Lynx Creek

Ruin: A Study of Architectural Differentiation," which is archived at Northern Arizona University. Also, Prescott National Forest staff conducted research in connection with the building of the trail.

While you are in this area, visits to Agua Fria National Monument (p. 252), the Verde Valley Archaeological Center in Camp Verde, and the Sears Kay Ruin are recommended.

KEYHOLE SINK PETROGLYPHS

Keyhole Sink is a box canyon near Parks, Arizona. From Flagstaff, drive 17 miles west on Interstate 40 to exit 178. Make a right, then left on Route 66 and continue 4 miles to the trailhead, on the right. Parking is available in the Oak Hill Snow Play Area across the road. From Williams, go east on I-40 and take exit 171. Cross over the highway and proceed 2 miles east on Route 66 to the parking area and trailhead. For information and to report vandalism, call the Williams Ranger District at (928) 635-5600.

―――――――――――

The Keyhole Sink trail, an easy three-quarter-mile walk through a quiet, serene forest, leads to a box canyon encased on three sides by sheer basalt cliffs. As Neil Weintraub, a Kaibab National Forest archaeologist, has eloquently expressed it, this is "a beautiful and peaceful place; in the late winter and early spring there is sometimes a majestic waterfall, often a pond, in the fall, golden aspen, in the summer, water snakes, singing frogs, lizards . . . and even evidence that some beavers once made it a home. There is also nothing like Keyhole Sink after a snowfall and the blue diamonds on the trees mark the trail's course for skiers." Certainly, you will find this short hiking excursion to be a very rewarding experience. In addition, there is the bonus of discovering two interesting panels of petroglyphs.

One panel, just to the left of the pool, consists of a dense cluster of images, which range from a sun symbol to animal and human figures to abstract forms. Regrettably, in 2010, vandals painted over part of it. Soon afterward, careful conservation work succeeded in removing the paint and restoring the panel to nearly its previous condition.

Farther along the cliff to the left, you will find a second panel showing a circular enclosure with an opening toward which a troop of deer are walking. An easy and probably accurate interpretation is that the scene shows deer approaching the box canyon to drink. You might imagine hunters waiting for them in blinds near the water. It is uncommon for rock-art panels to depict a simple narrative like this. This panel is faint due to water dripping over the cliff and depositing dirt on the rock face.

Keyhole Sink is located west of Arizona's San Francisco Peaks and south of the Grand Canyon. Between around 900 and 1100 CE, this was the homeland of an archaeological culture known as the Cohonina, which was first identified in 1937 by Lyndon Hargrave of the Museum of Northern Arizona in Flagstaff.

Archaeologists view the Cohonina as an enigmatic group due to the fact that relatively little is known about their origins or what happened to them. Some contend they migrated here from the west, others that they descended from indigenous hunter-gatherers. Some of the abstract-design glyphs in the first panel indeed look as if they could be from Archaic times.

The Cohonina appear to have led quite a mobile way of life, combining hunting and foraging with some degree of farming. They made a distinctive type of pottery, known as San Francisco Mountain Gray Ware, and traded with their Kayenta Pueblo neighbors to the east. Like so many pre-Hispanic Southwestern people, their first dwellings were pithouses, but later they built aboveground masonry houses. In the late 1000s, they began leaving their homeland and moving to the east, where archaeologists have found their sites in the western part of Wupatki National Monument (p. 161) and on forested mesas south of Wupatki. A few generations later, however, they are no longer visible in the archaeological record. The Hopi have strong cultural ties with sites in the Flagstaff area, and it is possible that the Cohonina merged with the Sinagua and eventually migrated eastward to the Homol'ovi pueblos (p. 150) and Hopi mesas.

There are several rewarding sites to visit in the Flagstaff area: Walnut Canyon (p. 166), Wupatki, and Elden Pueblo (p. 163). And consider going to Sunset Crater and the Museum of Northern Arizona. Plenty of travel services are to be found in Flagstaff and Williams.

The box canyon at Keyhole Sink in the Cohonina region.

GRAND CANYON NATIONAL PARK

The two main road routes to the Grand Canyon are: from the south, Arizona 64; and from the north, Arizona 67. The South Rim is 56 miles north of Interstate 40 at Williams; the North Rim is 44 miles south of Jacobs Lake. The canyon also is accessible by float trip on the Colorado River. Information: (928) 638-7888; www.nps .gov/features/grca/001/archeology/index.html.

———————

Grand Canyon is a picture window into time past. Its many layers of colorful rock formations, which rise thousands of feet from the Colorado River, represent the hours of a regressive clock whose hands move slower than the human mind can comprehend. Within this long geologic time span, the canyon's human story accounts for but seconds.

Evidence of Paleoindian presence in and around the canyon is scarce and even few Archaic camping places have been found. However, there are two other signs of the presence of hunter-gatherers in the canyon. One is rock art—petroglyphs and rock paintings—found especially in the western reaches of the canyon. The panels include both abstract and representational pictures. Of particular artistic interest are anthropomorphic figures with slim elongated bodies painted in what scholars term the Esplanade Style. Anthropologist Polly Schaafsma believes they date to between 2000 and 1 BCE.

View of Grand Canyon from the South Rim.

Archaic figurine found in a cave in Grand Canyon.

The presence of Western Archaic people here is also indicated by figurines of animals that have been found in caves and rock shelters. They were fashioned with split-twigs and grass and some are impaled with slender sticks representing spears. Archaeologist Douglas W. Schwartz, who found a cache of thirty-two such figurines in a cave in 1955, interprets them as having been made and used in rituals to encourage successful hunts. They date to about the same time period as the pictographs. Some examples are on exhibit in the Park's Tusayan Museum. After the mobile foragers, ancestral Native American peoples—Basketmaker, Pueblo, Cohonina, and Pai—lived in and around the Grand Canyon and left their marks. Still later, Havasupai, Hualapai, and Southern Paiute Indians moved into the region, today living on reservations.

Between about 1050 and the late 1100s CE, ancestral Pueblo Indians lived and farmed, according to the seasons, either down in the canyon or on the rims. By 1200, they were gone, believed to have traveled eastward to the area of the Hopi Mesas. The Hopi village of Oraibi was founded at just about this time. The Hopi believe their place of emergence in this world was a site (the *Sipaapuni*) near the confluence of the Little Colorado and Colorado rivers.

Tusayan Ruin

Located on the South Rim between Grand Canyon Village and Desert View, the Tusayan Ruin is a small, unimposing site containing a block of rooms and a kiva. In the late twelfth century, it housed as many as two dozen people. The noted archaeologist and teacher Emil W. Haury excavated it in the 1930s. The National Park Service has developed a self-guided trail through the remains of this hamlet.

Walhalla Glades Ruin

The Walhalla Glades Ruin on the North Rim (closed in winter) is 24 miles from Grand Canyon Lodge and 2 miles from Cape Royal. This pueblo sheltered ancestral Pueblo families in the warm months between around 1050 and 1150 and is one of many sites of the same time period that have been found on the surrounding Walhalla Plateau. Its residents are thought to have moved to the inner canyon in winter to escape the frigid temperatures and deep snows of the North Rim's 8,000-foot elevation. Archaeological investigations were conducted here and at other nearby sites in 1960 and 1970 by the School of American Research.

Bright Angel Pueblo

When John Wesley Powell explored Grand Canyon in 1869, he commented on and named this site along the river. Located along the Kaibab Trail near the north end of the Colorado River footbridge, the site is accessible to inner-canyon hikers. The Park Service has installed interpretive signs. Archaeologists from the School of American Research excavated this small pueblo—it probably housed one or two extended families—in 1969, and *The Bright Angel Site* was published ten years later.

About 1050, Indians built a pithouse here but, due apparently to drought, moved away ten years later. Around 1100, more people returned and constructed a pueblo, cultivated a garden, and managed to sustain themselves until about 1140. Then they left for good. A campground and Phantom Ranch are nearby, for which reservations are needed.

Mallery's Grotto

Mallery's Grotto is a rock-art site located on the left side and above the Bright Angel Trail immediately after going through the first tunnel (upper tunnel). Here researchers recorded 269 pictographs and seven petroglyphs, as well as seven historic pictographs and many examples of modern graffiti. Numerous pictographs of animals date to the Archaic period. Other images are associated with the Cohonina culture, dating from between around 700 and 1000 CE, and some historic pictographs are associated with the Havasupai.

Considerable effort is required to see some of Grand Canyon's archaeological resources. To see Bright Angel Pueblo, for example, involves between 7 and 9 miles of hiking from the South Rim and 14 miles from the North Rim. There are sites on Unkar Delta that can be seen on a raft trip through the canyon. To find many of the rock-art sites, a guide is recommended. Still, just to know that Native Americans hunted, foraged, and lived here for millennia adds a new dimension of one's appreciation of the extraordinary landscape.

Suggested Reading: *Rock Art of the Grand Canyon Region*, by Don D. Christensen, Jerry Dickey, and Steven M. Freers, Sunbelt Publications, San Diego, California, 2013.

Index

Note: Page numbers in italics refer to illustrations.